THE
AMERICAN MAGAZINE

THE
AMERICAN
MAGAZINE

By Amy Janello and Brennon Jones

Magazine Publishers of America

American Society of Magazine Editors

HARRY N. ABRAMS, INC., PUBLISHERS, NEW YORK

The assistance of the following is gratefully acknowledged:

Apple Computer, Inc.
Champion International Corporation
Communications Data Services, Inc.
Professional Photography Division of
    Eastman Kodak Company
Fraser Paper Ltd.
The Jordan Group, Inc.
MCS/Canon Business Machines, Inc.
Neodata Services, Inc.
R. R. Donnelley & Sons Company
Simmons Market Research Bureau, Inc.
Veronis, Suhler & Associates Inc.
VNU Business Information Services Inc.
World Color Press, Inc.

Produced and edited by Jones & Janello
Designed by Beth A. Crowell

Library of Congress Cataloging-in-Publication Data
The American Magazine / by Amy Janello and Brennon
Jones for the Magazine Publishers of America, MPA
[and] American Society of Magazine Editors, ASME.
            p.   cm.
    Includes index.
    ISBN 0–8109–1909–5
    1. American periodicals — History. 2. American
    periodicals — Pictorial works. I. Jones & Janello.
    II. Magazine Publishers of America. III. American
    Society of Magazine Editors.
PN4877.A46 1991
051' .09 — dc20   91–10440
                          CIP

Published in 1991 by Harry N. Abrams, Incorporated,
New York. A Times Mirror Company

Printed in Japan

CONTENTS

P R E F A C E

The book you hold in your hands celebrates 250 years of extraordinary creativity.

Ever since the days of Ben Franklin, the American magazine has fostered the exchange of ideas and nurtured exceptional editorial, artistic, and publishing talent, generation to generation. Magazines have been a major force in shaping American society, expressing our hopes and our fears, informing and molding the way we think and act at crucial points in our history. Magazines have been a most resilient medium, readily adapting to shifts in taste and fashion, stimulating new technology in printing and graphics, and weathering the gyrations of the nation's economy. In sum, the magazine is here to stay, an American original, as integral to the national mindscape as baseball, mom, and apple pie.

What makes the survival of the magazine particularly remarkable is that nobody really *needs* it in the same sense that one needs food or shelter, heat or transport. But we all need friends, and that is what a good magazine becomes. It creates a relationship with the reader, a relationship he or she looks forward to renewing each time the magazine arrives.

Indeed, there is probably no other great American enterprise in which relationships are as important and the health of the enterprise is as dependent on bonds that cannot be defined in financial terms or quantified by pollsters. The editor and the writer, the art director and the photographer or illustrator not only share ideas; they also collaborate and give them life. And when successful, this creative spirit communicates powerfully to its readers, who inevitably — and often passionately — respond. Meanwhile, the advertiser, whose investment helps most magazines to flourish, reaps benefit from this reader involvement.

Because each magazine creates a kind of extended family, the American magazine as a whole represents a community of families, in which talent is nurtured, siblings compete, and everybody talks at once.

As you read *The American Magazine*, you will encounter the fruits of all these relationships and you will feel, we hope, what we feel: great pride in the endless creativity, inventiveness, style, and wit of those in the magazine community. With this book, we invite people worldwide to join us in celebrating our 250th birthday.

Reginald K. Brack, Jr., Chairman
Donald D. Kummerfeld, President
Magazine Publishers of America

I write as a child of magazines, awestruck early by dust-devil Western serials in *The Saturday Evening Post*, gruff detective stories in the *American Magazine*, and the amazing science fiction of the old Fawcett pulps.

But my total surrender to the world of magazines came from my subscription to *Open Road for Boys* when I was nine. The story that pushed me over the edge was entitled "Lion Fuzz," the hilarious tale of a tenderfoot's introduction to the real West. I started chuckling aloud before the first jump line and continued reading with regular interruptions as I literally doubled up with spasms of laughter. Then I set the magazine carefully on a shelf in my room and returned to it eagerly whenever I felt the need to reward myself with a special treat, to be swept away again by the power of words in a magazine. Almost every reader has a "Lion Fuzz" in his or her magazine memory.

It seemed to me then that the most marvelous prospect possible was to spend my adult life writing and editing to entertain, to astound, to play with tears and laughter. I have not been disappointed.

The book that you hold is perhaps more celebration than history. Certainly it was very much a labor of love by the small group of editors and publishers fortunate enough to have been invited to work on it. We want to thank the hundreds of editors and art directors who interrupted work on their own next issues to share with us their ideas and experiences. We are grateful to readers who shared their cherished magazine collections and let us use their illustrations — from the seventy-eight-year-old New York sculptor who opened his Soho loft to us with its priceless collection of more than 10,000 mint-condition magazines, to the Methodist preacher and his wife who shipped us boxes of magazines from their Kansas farm.

We must salute also the tiny staff of Jones & Janello, veteran book producers who worked without holiday or haven since page zero. Awakened to two and a half centuries of magazine culture and energy, Amy Janello and Brennon Jones came away wide-eyed at splendors long forgotten.

Together, we have uncovered or revisited the most extraordinary gems of individual creativity and have applauded the exceptional feats and fashions of the editors who went before us. I believe that we have left modern society a richer place by restoring to circulation the great work that has gone before.

We have not attempted to record every detail. Instead, we have tried to convey a sense of the vast achievements and the artistic and literary treasures to be found in this nation's magazines.

To the hundreds of hands that touch the magazine and bring it to life — from the editor who dreams it, the art director who visualizes it, the publisher who fills it with commerce, the photographers and writers who start with blank pages, and the craftsmen who lay it onto paper — we dedicate this book.

The story of magazines is the story of America. All we can hope is that we have been faithful in representing the diversity, the creativity, and the uniqueness of the American magazine.

John Mack Carter, President
American Society of Magazine Editors

Good Housekeeping

JULY 1931

25 CENTS

JESSIE WILLCOX SMITH

Eleanor Hallowell Abbott ~ Fanny Heaslip Lea
Dixie Willson ~ Jay Gelzer ~ Elizabeth Frazer
Edison Marshall ~ Emma-Lindsay Squier ~ Montague Glass

Shaping Opinion

THE MAGAZINE AND SOCIETY

Ben Franklin's *General Magazine* (above) was the first to be conceived in the colonies, but rival Andrew Bradford brought out his *American Magazine* three days earlier. Both publications were short-lived.

Good Housekeeping (opposite), founded in 1885, still thrives. The 1931 cover illustration is by Jessie Willcox Smith, who turned out some 200 covers for the magazine.

The legislature of the State of Georgia was so outraged that it offered a reward: $5,000 to the person who could "arrest, bring to trial, and prosecute to conviction under the laws of this state" a malefactor whose actions had infuriated the populace. His crime: publishing a magazine called *The Liberator*, which called on citizens to help slaves escape from their masters.

•

The Supreme Court of the United States had rarely tackled a case so important to the structure of the American economy. After lengthy consideration, the Court issued a ruling that limited the power of American business from that day forward: It ordered the dissolution of the Standard Oil Company. The events that led to that decision had begun a decade earlier, when *McClure's Magazine* began a relentless, two-year, multi-part series on the depredations and abuses of the all-but-omnipotent oil giant.

•

It was a part of American life; you could find it in most garages, along with the other chemicals that made for greener lawns, pest-free picnics, and better living in the fifties. Then *The New Yorker* ran an essay that changed the way Americans thought about the environment: DDT did more than kill pests, "Silent Spring" revealed. It made the shells of birds' eggs so brittle that whole species were threatened. It worked its way into the water and the land and could go on poisoning the earth for generations. Under popular pressure, the federal government removed DDT from the market.

•

William Lloyd Garrison, Ida Tarbell, Rachel Carson: the abolitionist, the muckraker, and the environmentalist. American schoolchildren still learn their names, still are taught that these three courageous journalists changed society. What is sometimes forgotten in those lessons is the medium these crusaders chose to bring their message to the attention of the public: the magazine. For 250 years, American magazines have helped shape the public discourse and define the major issues of our society.

That magazines have been at the center of some of the great controversies of American life is only fitting; after all, they were born in controversy. Most experts credit Benjamin Franklin with conceiving the first magazine in the colonies, but that incorrigible polymath actually lost the race to publish first. His

Publication of "Silent Spring" by biologist Rachel Carson (above) in *The New Yorker* in 1962 jolted the nation into an awareness of the need to protect the environment.

Harper's Weekly (opposite), which unabashedly proclaimed itself a "journal of civilization," was a staunch supporter of Lincoln, shown here in a post-election portrait based on a Mathew Brady photo.

For thirty-four years, William Lloyd Garrison pressed for the abolition of slavery in *The Liberator*. It ceased publication in 1865, when slavery was outlawed by Constitutional amendment.

old commercial rival Andrew Bradford got wind of Franklin's plans and set about to best him. Bradford published *The American Magazine* in Philadelphia on February 13, 1741, three days before the first issue of Franklin's *General Magazine, and Historical Chronicle.* (A great tradition of American magazines — the missed deadline — was born at the same time; both publications bore a January cover date.) The two men squabbled publicly over bragging rights, but neither magazine lasted long enough to make an impact: Bradford was out of business in three months, Franklin in six.

The eighteenth century was no Golden Age for magazines, which came and went with breathtaking frequency. The residents of the colonies devoured tracts and pamphlets that urged revolution, but they tended to be fickle in their support of magazines. Tom Paine, the great firebrand of the Revolution, set to work as editor of *The Pennsylvania Magazine* in 1775, three months after he arrived in the colonies. His was a persuasive voice for revolution, but even he chose to publish *Common Sense* as a separate pamphlet. *The Pennsylvania Magazine* folded in 1776, but it went out in style: Its last issue contained the text of the Declaration of Independence.

They may have appeared erratically, and sometimes they vanished almost overnight, but that did not mean that magazines had no impact on society, even in Revolutionary times.

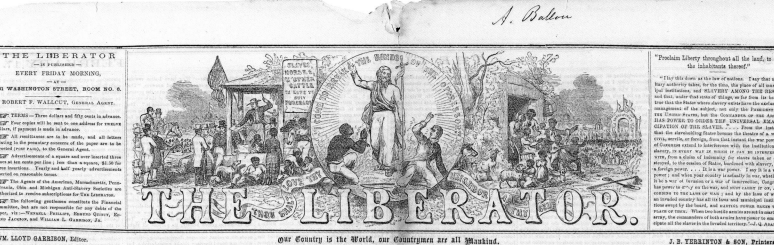

HARPER'S WEEKLY.

A
JOURNAL OF CIVILIZATION.

Vol. IV.—No. 202.]   NEW YORK, SATURDAY, NOVEMBER 10, 1860.   [Price Five Cents.

Entered according to Act of Congress, in the Year 1860, by Harper & Brothers, in the Clerk's Office of the District Court for the Southern District of New York.

HON. ABRAHAM LINCOLN, BORN IN KENTUCKY, FEBRUARY 12, 1809.—[Photographed by Brady.]

An 1850 daguerreotype of publisher William Lloyd Garrison gives little indication of his fiery personality. Editors who opposed his strong abolitionist stand thought he should be gagged.

As magazine historian James Playsted Wood has observed, "The influence of the early magazines was probably far greater than the number printed and circulated would indicate. Books and magazines were prized if only because comparatively few were available. Every page of every magazine was read carefully by many people." George Washington, who in 1788 had enough to keep him busy, still found time to write the editor of *The American Museum* to praise magazines in general: "I consider such vehicles of knowledge more happily calculated than any other, to preserve the liberty, stimulate the industry and meliorate the morals of an enlightened and free people." Recognizing the value of such upscale readership, the magazine promptly incorporated the letter into its advertising.

Magazines began to mature after the Revolution. In 1792, *Lady's Magazine* appeared, the first in a great tradition of American women's journals. Joseph Dennie's *The Port Folio* soon gained popular acceptance, publishing contributions from James Boswell, Samuel Richardson, and David Hume. Dennie was a bitter opponent of the policies of Thomas Jefferson. His idea of a great leader was his friend John Quincy Adams, a frequent contributor.

Although Dennie's anti-democratic impulse may seem dated today, his partisanship was an invigorating force for *The Port Folio*. American magazines have always been at their best when they are articulating a coherent philosophy with passion. None has been more passionate than *The Liberator*. William Lloyd Garrison borrowed some type and went to work on a hand press in Boston in 1831 to produce his first issue, with its famous declaration: "I am in earnest. I will not equivocate. I will not excuse. I will not retreat a single inch. And I will be heard." For thirty-four years, Garrison *was* heard, at first only by a small band of convinced abolitionists, at last by the nation as a whole. He turned out throngs to rally against slavery — and also riled up mobs, who sacked his presses and burned copies of his magazine.

Even for some abolitionists, Garrison's hot-tempered, uncompromising stand was hard to take. James Russell Lowell preferred to contribute his attacks on slavery to the somewhat more cerebral *Pennsylvania Freeman*, edited by John Greenleaf Whittier. The most effective assault on the institution of human bondage ever published was launched by another journal of the cause, *The National Era*, which serialized a novel by Harriet Beecher Stowe called *Uncle Tom's Cabin*. Abraham Lincoln — "half-jokingly," in historian Kenneth Lynn's

The Civil War became
a graphic reality for readers
when *Harper's Weekly* dispatched a team of reporters,
artists, and photographers
to cover the conflict.
Winslow Homer sketched
the action and then
rendered it in a woodcut.

The city council, of Georgetown have enacted
an ordinance, which imposes a heavy fine, or the
penalty of 30 days imprisonment, upon any FREE
colored person who shall subscribe for, or take out
of the post office, the Boston Liberator, a weekly
paper published by W. L. GARRISON.

Fear of the power of *The
Liberator* to mold opinion
called forth this notice,
which appeared in *The
New-England Galaxy* in
1831, the year Garrison's
anti-slavery weekly was
launched.

The February

The American Magazine

15 cts

IS THE REPUBLICAN PARTY BREAKING UP?

· THE STORY OF THE INSURGENT WEST ·

· · · BY RAY STANNARD BAKER · ·

estimation — credited *Uncle Tom's Cabin* with starting the Civil War. The war ended slavery, and it ended *The Liberator* as well.

The Civil War provided a season of growth and maturing for other magazines. *Harper's Weekly* hired a team of correspondents and photographers to cover the conflict. In the drawing rooms and libraries of the North, the war arrived in the mail every week, and for the first time in human history, people far from the front lines were able to read the descriptions and see the images of a war almost as it was happening. Secretary of War Edwin Stanton was unnerved; he thought the magazine's images, which were based on photographs, gave aid and comfort to the enemy, and ordered its publication suspended. But editor Fletcher Harper went to Washington in person and made Stanton see the truth: *Harper's Weekly* was one of the most powerful weapons in the Union's arsenal, he argued. Every week, it was strengthening the resolve and renewing the determination of the Union. Stanton lifted his ban.

Some of America's greatest literary figures formed connections with magazines even before the Civil War. Edgar Allan Poe, Ralph Waldo Emerson, Henry Wadsworth Longfellow, Walt Whitman, Henry Adams, and others became widely known through their magazine work. The prewar era also saw the flowering of women's magazines — *Godey's Lady's Book*, *Peterson's Magazine*, and *Ladies' Magazine*. They covered fashion and decorative arts and printed the popular fiction writers of the time, but they also established a tradition that women's magazines have honored to this day. Early and often, they raised the consciousness of their readers, educating

Founded in 1845, *Scientific American* (above) encouraged talented inventors and exposed fraudulent ones. In 1888, it announced Charles Sumner Tainter's invention of a "new speech recorder."

Starting in 1906, when they left *McClure's* over differences with its founder, muckrakers Lincoln Steffens, Ida Tarbell, and Ray Stannard Baker were contributors to *The American Magazine* (opposite). Inside this 1910 issue was to be found "The American Woman: Her First Declaration of Independence," by Tarbell.

"NOW, YOUNG MAN, I MAY LOOK SMALL TO YOU; BUT REMEMBER, I HAVE KNOCKED OUT BIGGER MEN, AND WITHOUT MUCH TROUBLE."

At a time when the nation was moving out in the world, this 1896 drawing from *Life* (a humor magazine that preceded the current *Life*) shows the enormity of the challenges for a young man with an education behind him.

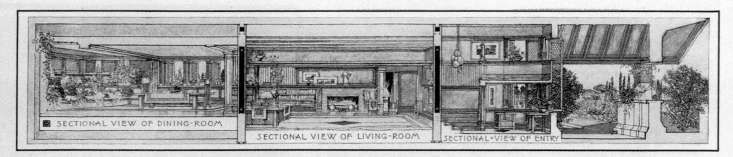

SECTIONAL VIEW OF DINING-ROOM

SECTIONAL VIEW OF LIVING-ROOM

SECTIONAL · VIEW OF ENTRY

A Small House with "Lots of Room in It"

By Frank Lloyd Wright

NINTH DESIGN IN THE JOURNAL'S NEW SERIES OF MODEL SUBURBAN HOUSES AT MODERATE COST

THE average home-maker is partial to the gable roof. This house has been designed with a thorough, somewhat new treatment of the gable with gently flaring eaves and pediments, slightly lifted at the peaks, accentuating the perspective, slightly modeling the roof surfaces and making the outlines "crisp."

The plan disregards somewhat the economical limit in compact planning to take advantage of light, air and prospect, the enjoyable things one goes to the suburbs to secure. With modern systems of heating a distinct freedom in arrangement, denied to earlier builders, is made not only possible, but may be made comfortable with modest outlay. Two large rooms, with an entry performing the function of a little, formal social office, or a waiting-room, to relieve the living-room of undesirable pressure, together with a simple arrangement of stairs and a working department, make up the scheme of the main floor.

IN THIS case the dining-room is made the "feature," with a little indoor garden closing the perspective at its farther end. The dining-table commands the outdoor garden at the rear, and the low windows on the gallery to the street front, the whole countering upon a simple fireplace of brick which combines with the comfortable breadth of fireplace in the living-room. The dining-room is so coupled with the living-room that one leads naturally into the other without destroying the privacy of either.

The living-room is still the heart of the house, and has access to both gallery and terrace, and gives an interesting glimpse of entry and stair landing.

The working department is roomy and convenient. The range is set within a brick-lined, brick-floored alcove, formed by the two fireplaces, the space overhead ventilated into a chimney flue. The servants' stairway reaches the landing of the main stairway, and the servants' room and bath are

situated over this landing, midway between the second and attic floors. The kitchen entry is from the side, and combines with the cellarway to avoid unsightly excrescences.

As the house is free in arrangement, and the main rooms large, a simplicity of material and treatment is necessary. The exterior is plastered with cement plaster. The interior, trimmed with Georgia pine, without mouldings, put on over rough plaster, together with the Georgia pine floors, is to be stained one coat. The outside woodwork, except shingles, is also to be stained. Paint and varnish are not used.

A COMBINATION hot-water apparatus would serve to heat the house perfectly, hot air in the main body of the house, and radiation in the dining-room and entry.

The cost of the house proper, exclusive of grading and walks, would approximate:

Masonry and Stone Water-Table	$1100.00
Plastering	600.00
Carpentry and Hardware	2950.00
Heating	375.00
Plumbing, Sewer and Gas Fitting	450.00
Staining and Glass	300.00
Electric Wiring	60.00
Total	$5835.00

The block plans at the lower corners of the page show two schemes for placing the house upon an inside, one-hundred-foot lot. One, as shown in perspective view, broad side to the street; the other alongside the depth of the lot.

EDITOR'S NOTE — As a guarantee that the plan of this house is practicable and that the estimates for cost are conservative, the architect is ready to accept the commission of preparing the working plans and specifications for this house to cost $5835.00, providing that the building site selected is within reasonable distance of a base of supplies where material and labor may be had at the standard market rates.

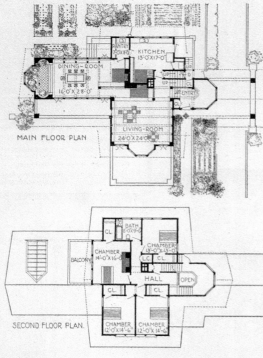

MAIN FLOOR PLAN

KITCHEN 13'-0"X17'-0"

DINING-ROOM 16'-0"X 28'-0"

LIVING-ROOM 24'-0"X24'-0"

SECOND FLOOR PLAN.

CHAMBER 14'-0"X16'-0"

CHAMBER 13'-0"X 13'-0"

HALL

CHAMBER 12'-0"X14'-6"

CHAMBER 12'-0"X 14'-0"

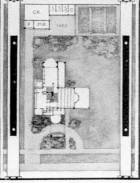

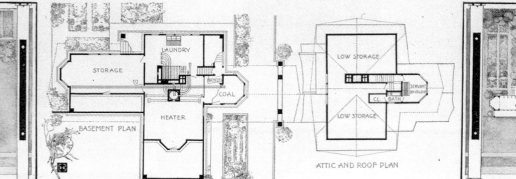

STORAGE

LAUNDRY

COAL

BASEMENT PLAN

HEATER

LOW STORAGE

SERVANTS 10'-0"X20'-0"

BATH

LOW STORAGE

ATTIC AND ROOF PLAN

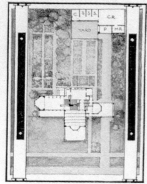

The Country Gentleman. A Journal for the Farm, the Garden, and the Fireside.

Launched in 1853, *The Country Gentleman* (above) became a national journal at a time when the West was being opened up and the prairie put under the plow. New farming methods were discussed in its pages, as were newly developed rootstocks, including the Concord grape.

During Edward Bok's distinguished tenure as editor, *The Ladies' Home Journal* published floor plans of well-designed, affordable houses such as this one (opposite), designed in 1901 by Frank Lloyd Wright.

them on women's role in society throughout history. Under the editorship of Sarah Josepha Hale — otherwise known as the author of "Mary Had a Little Lamb" — *Godey's* covered the issues of women's rights and advocated employment for women. At its peak, in the 1850s, *Godey's Lady's Book* sold 150,000 copies a month. Still, as the historian Sarah E. McBride observed of the magazines of the period, "Their primary function was helping the reader with her duties as mother and homemaker."

After the Civil War, magazines grew in several ways — in size, scope, style, and boldness. *North American Review, Harper's New Monthly Magazine, The Nation,* and *The Atlantic Monthly* became significant arbiters of literary taste and shapers of public debate. With their sophisticated mixture of poetry, fiction, essays, and serious journalism, they began to resemble their modern counterparts; urbane Americans could not consider themselves informed without at least a passing familiarity with the content of each issue. So important had magazines become to the culture of the growing nation that in 1879 Congress created special, low postage rates for them, the better to increase their nationwide distribution.

The relationship between magazines and society has always been intricate: Sometimes society leads and magazines follow; sometimes the reverse is true. As Americans moved West to the open prairies, farm magazines took on new importance. From publications like *The Cultivator* and *The Country Gentleman,* Americans learned of new inventions like Cyrus McCormick's "Virginia reaper." *The Country Gentleman* campaigned for the professional education of farmers before

Rural New Yorker was another outlet for the dissemination of farm news. In 1867 an "improved ditching machine" was prominently featured.

Long before the heyday of the muckrakers, cartoonists were savaging corrupt politicians, as in Thomas Nast's "The Tweed Ring's Brains," published in *Harper's Weekly* in 1871.

Ida Tarbell's attacks on John D. Rockefeller's Standard Oil, in *McClure's Magazine,* led to portrayals of the millionaire as "the king of combinations."

the Morrill Act set up land-grant colleges. It also suggested the need for a milking machine before one was invented. *The Country Gentleman* remained strong well into this century; in 1937 it was largely responsible for the Bankhead-Jones Act, which set up a national erosion-control program.

The Ladies' Home Journal, created by Cyrus Curtis in 1883, taught women home management and home economics. Under the editorship of Edward Bok, the *Journal* began publishing floor plans of functional, safe, well-designed houses that could be built for less than $2,000; the response was overwhelming. Architect Stanford White said that Bok "more completely influenced American domestic architecture for the better than any man in this generation." In the years that followed — under Bok and, later, Bruce and Beatrice Gould — the *Journal* campaigned against worthless patent medicines, crusaded for better maternal health, and pressed for truth in advertising. It created a model for the successful, responsible women's magazines of the twentieth century. (It also invented the modern advice column. Young women could write to Bok or the Goulds for counsel on courtship and marriage, child-rearing, and divorce. The common-sense answers reflected the social conservatism of the times.)

By the end of the nineteenth century, after the excesses of the Gilded Age and the rise of the robber barons, the nation was ready for a strong corrective, and muckraking magazines

Lewis Hine's photographs of children working in the mines (opposite) appeared in *The Survey* and other publications. Such photos helped spur Congress to enact legislation prohibiting child labor. Cartoonists, muckrakers, and photographers like Hine constituted a mighty coalition in the fight for reform.

provided it. The muckrakers, observed Walter Lippmann, "weren't voices crying in a wilderness, or lonely prophets who were stoned. They demanded a hearing; it was granted. They asked for belief; they were believed. . . . There must have been real causes for dissatisfaction, or the land notorious for its worship of successes would not have turned so savagely upon those who had achieved it."

Samuel S. McClure founded his eponymous magazine in 1893; a decade later, it had a circulation of 500,000 and a reputation built on muckraking. Not only did *McClure's* unleash Ida Tarbell to investigate Standard Oil; it set Lincoln Steffens to work on big-city corruption, commissioned Ray Stannard Baker to write on lynching, and inspired a legion of imitators. Publications like *Collier's*, *Hampton's*, *The Independent*, *Success*, *The American Magazine*, and *Cosmopolitan* jumped into the fray, sending writers to peer into the hidden recesses of corporations and political machines, prisons and hospitals and factories. At the height of their influence, Teddy Roosevelt became a sometimes critical friend and patron of several of the muckrakers, and built much of his own political career on their work, taking on the trusts and cartels they exposed. Not all muckrakers were writers. Lewis Hine's still-compelling photographs of child laborers and immigrants at Ellis Island showed America a side of itself that it had previously ignored. *McClure's*, *The Delineator*, *The Survey*, and even *The Red Cross Magazine* published his photographs.

In 1938, *Esquire*'s publisher, David Smart, and its editor, Arnold Gingrich, produced *Ken* (above), which billed itself as a "magazine of unfamiliar fact and informed opinion." Although the magazine lasted only two years, this 1939 cover on America's addiction to polls remains timely.

Reginald Marsh's haunting portrait (opposite) of Americans facing the prospect of another winter of the Great Depression occupied a full page in the September 1932 *Fortune*, and helped tell "the story of an industrial problem which charity has attempted unsuccessfully to solve."

Flaming Jets Drive Novel Aircraft

DRIVEN by blast nozzles, a rocketlike airplane designed by a French inventor is declared to make possible speeds of 600 miles or more an hour. A mixture of fuel oil and compressed air is fed to these nozzles and ignited, and jets of flaming and expanding vapor spurt rearward with terrific force, the recoil driving the machine forward. To supply air at high pressure, the inventor has devised a novel method that dispenses with conventional compressors. It employs, instead, a jet of steam from an oil-fired boiler, which entrains outside air and forces it under pressure into the supply system, the steam being condensed and the water drained off before the air reaches the burners. Since there are virtually no moving parts, the novel power plant is declared to offer practically no chance of mechanical failure. The plane has no motor in the accepted sense of the word.

Drawing shows design of new French plane which is driven by rocketlike jets of flaming oil spray

Popular Science, launched in 1872, lived up to its name, disseminating scientific knowledge and inventors' dreams, like this 1931 design of an aircraft "driven by rocketlike jets of flaming oil spray."

America's entry into the First World War prompted stirring displays of martial might, as exemplified by Paul Stahr's *Life* cover (top). It also prompted some flights of the imagination as with these armored aerial pods featured on the cover of a 1915 *Leslie's* (above).

By the end of the muckraking era, the Tweed gang in New York was smashed, the Standard Oil monopoly was broken, workman's compensation laws were instituted, the Pure Food and Drug Act was passed, life insurance companies and railroads were regulated, tenements in major cities were being cleaned up, and the first occupational safety standards were being devised around the nation. Never before or since have magazines had such a direct, sustained, and dramatic effect on American society.

And never have they provoked such violent reaction. Corrupt politicians howled, business people squealed, and John D. Rockefeller went to the unheard-of extreme of hiring a man named Ivy Lee to counsel him on what he called "public relations." The federal government took revenge in 1917 by raising postal rates for magazines. Forced to increase their subscription prices, the muckraking magazines subsequently experienced circulation declines. *McClure's* limped along for another twelve years.

As in the Civil War, magazines published during the First World War fell into step with the war effort. *Literary Digest*, for instance, abandoned its usual features to concentrate on war reporting. Even *The National Geographic*, already known for introducing Americans to parts of the world they had once only dreamed of, devoted its pages to maps of the front and articles on the geography of the nations at war.

After the war, magazines still affected society, but they sought a different level. Postwar publications generally did not attempt to remake government with broad strokes, as the muckrakers had done. Their fight was for humane values and the concerns of the unrepresented. Women's magazines distinguished themselves: *The Delineator*, originally just a compendium of sewing patterns, hired Theodore Dreiser as its editor in 1907. In its strongest years, it found homes for thousands of orphaned children, raised money to buy radium for Marie Curie, and rebuilt towns in France that had been destroyed by the First World War. During the war, *Good Housekeeping* and *McCall's* led the food conservation effort at home, and some publications even went so far as to suggest that women work in factories to free men for the front. Women's magazines also helped shape the national debate on alcohol, pointing out its devastating effects on the home — although, after the Volstead Act, many went on to question the wisdom of Prohibition.

The Jazz Age that followed the First World War was wild and fertile. F. Scott Fitzgerald first sold a short story to *The Saturday*

THE DELINEATOR CHILD-RESCUE CAMPAIGN ❧ · FOR THE CHILD THAT NEEDS A HOME, AND THE HOME THAT NEEDS A CHILD ❧ · · ❧

Since November, 1907, THE DELINEATOR has been conducting an educational campaign in the interests of the child without a home and the home without a child. It has strongly advocated the family home in preference to an institution as the best place to care for the normal dependent child, and has urged the cottage-plan institution for the temporary care of children. Largely through its efforts President Roosevelt called the recent remarkable White House Conference which unanimously indorsed everything that has been advocated by THE DELINEATOR on the subject. Much good has been accomplished. In addition to the children whose stories have been told, hundreds of children have been placed in excellent homes directly through the influence of this campaign, and many institutions have modified their methods. Thousands have enrolled as members of the National Child-Rescue League and are effectively working in the interests of dependent children. In response to many suggestions, arrangements have been made whereby, in addition to applications for the specific children whose stories and photographs are presented as types of hundreds of other children available for adoption, THE DELINEATOR will receive and refer to the proper agencies applications from any one desiring to take a child. Applications will be received from all parts of the United States. If you are willing to give some child an opportunity, please tell us of your wishes and we will give the matter immediate personal consideration.

THE EDITOR.

Charlie

Under editor Theodore Dreiser, *The Delineator* published distinguished fiction and took on such subjects as women's suffrage and underprivileged children, especially the treatment of children in orphanages. Dreiser was "the editor" who signed the child-rescue campaign notice reproduced here.

One technique *The Delineator* used to involve its readers was to offer prize money for letters. In this 1922 issue, the theme was "How I Worked My Way Through College." The prize: $500. By the late twenties, the magazine's circulation was more than two million.

Evening Post in 1920, and the nation's appetite for fiction seemed insatiable. *The Smart Set, Vanity Fair,* and a knowing new magazine called *The New Yorker* provided both showcase and training ground for writers of fiction and nonfiction. *The Nation* and *The New Republic,* though they never reached a mass audience, became shapers of opinion — in politics, the arts, and culture — among the nation's most influential citizens. Throughout the twenties, H. L. Mencken's *American Mercury* urged, goaded, flogged, and ridiculed Americans away from convention and conformism; one critic credits it with helping "to make the Roaring Twenties roar."

In 1923, two young men from Yale, Briton Hadden and Henry Luce, raised money from a small circle of friends to start what they called a "news magazine" — a publication that would digest the week's events and present them in a breezy,

The nation's magazines celebrated the first Fourth of July after America entered the Second World War by unfurling the flag.

Glamour

"UNITED
WE STAND"

JULY 1942 · PRICE 15 CENTS

Look photographer James Karales captured the spirit and determination of the civil rights movement in this image of a Southern protest march.

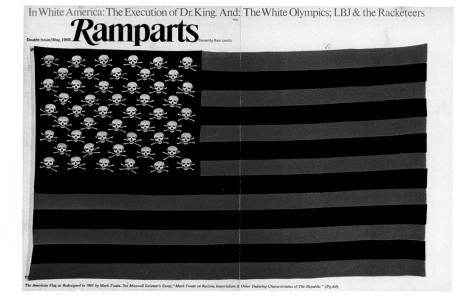

In White America: The Execution of Dr. King. And: The White Olympics; LBJ & the Racketeers

Ramparts

Double Issue/May, 1968

Seventy-five cents

The American Flag as Redesigned in 1901 by Mark Twain. See Maxwell Geismar's Essay, "Mark Twain on Racism, Imperialism & Other Enduring Characteristics of The Republic." (Pg. 64).

A flag for all seasons: *Ramparts* put it on the cover in May 1968 to protest the killing of Martin Luther King, Jr., and U.S. aggression in Southeast Asia. But credit Mark Twain for the flag's original design, which reflected his outrage at American racism and imperialism at the turn of the century.

engaging manner. The year before, a young husband and wife from New York, Lila and DeWitt Wallace, started a small-format magazine made up of articles culled from the rest of the press and condensed. *Time* and *Reader's Digest* grew into American institutions. Through the years, the voice of *Time* helped shape the course of American domestic and foreign policy; and *Reader's Digest*, by refusing to take cigarette advertising and by publishing more than fifty articles on the dangers of smoking, helped notify the nation about one of the century's most important health issues.

The years between the wars were productive ones; Henry Luce carried on after the death of Hadden, turning Time Inc. into a spawning ground of memorable magazines. At *Life* and *Fortune*, writers Archibald MacLeish and James Agee and photographers Margaret Bourke-White and Alfred Eisenstaedt captured the pain of a nation recovering from the Great Depression. Later, they documented the energy and pluck of a country going to war, a war that magazines proudly supported. *Life* and *Look*, among others, brought powerful images of that war home to the States.

The postwar years were generally prosperous and placid. Americans embraced those magazines that taught the hobbies and diversions that new-found leisure time allowed. *Popular Mechanics, Mechanix Illustrated*, and *Popular Science* became staples of the culture. Many magazines advised people on the ins and outs of settling into the suburbs, and by and large they served as arbiters of convention. Nevertheless, serious issues were not neglected. *Sports Illustrated* showed that real journalism could uncover the flaws and controversies of the locker room as well as of the board room. A 1947 special report in *Sports Afield* sounded one of the earliest warnings of pollution of the nation's rivers and lakes. From *Scientific American* to *The Bulletin of the Atomic Scientists*, magazines kept America informed of the wonders — and dangers — of science. Meanwhile, since 1936, *Consumer Reports* had been testing a wide variety of products to inform its audience about their quality and safety.

Other magazines were questioning and weighing the political judgements of the nation's leaders and U.S. policies, particularly abroad. *The Progressive, The Nation*, and *Ramparts*, for example, were early critics of the Vietnam War and of what they perceived as flaws in American society. Even some of the mainstream publications that enthusiastically supported the Kennedy administration and America's early involvement in

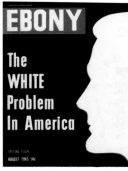

Each in its own way: With the issue of race relations front and center in the mid-sixties, news magazines weighed in with special reports on the subject.

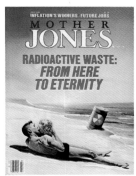

The women's liberation movement led to the creation of *Ms.* (above) in 1972. Muckraking flourished in the sixties and seventies with magazines like *New York, New Times, Mother Jones,* and *The Progressive* (below).

Vietnam eventually criticized the war. *Newsweek* devoted an entire issue to American involvement in Vietnam and raised serious questions about why we were there. *Life* brought home the cost of the war by publishing, in one issue, photographs of every American killed in Southeast Asia in a single week.

The cataclysm in American culture that attended the Vietnam War shook the magazine world as well. One happy result was a renewed daring, a willingness to break with the strictures of the past. Beginning in the mid-sixties, *Esquire* and *New York*, among others, helped reshape the way magazines were written. The New Journalism, as practiced by Tom Wolfe, Gay Talese, Tom Morgan, Gail Sheehy, and Jimmy Breslin freed magazine writing from many of the formulaic constraints it had acquired after the Second World War. Also in recent years, magazines as diverse as *New Times, Ramparts, Mother Jones,* and *The Washington Monthly* have provided an outlet for a new class of muckrakers, publishing investigations of government corruption and probing portraits of public officials — subjects from which more traditional publications have shied away. Feminism, which began to remake the face of society in the sixties, spawned *Ms.* in 1972. The women's magazines that already existed also helped bring the issues of equal rights and empowerment to the forefront in the seventies and eighties.

With the seventies came the rise of personality journalism, spearheaded by *People*, which interpreted the news of the day — in politics and medicine, sports and social trends, as well as entertainment — through profiles of the people making the news. That decade also saw wider acceptance of magazines like *Playboy* and *Penthouse*, which augmented their photographs of nude females with serious articles and fiction and campaigned for the repeal or relaxation of laws that restricted the private behavior of consenting adults.

Today, American magazines are diverse and hardy. They are tastemakers, guardians of culture, gossips, historians. Many modern magazines see their role as supportive, helping their readers cope with the stresses and demands of contemporary life. *Parents Magazine* pioneered in giving adults advice about the manifold challenges and opportunities of child-rearing. In 1987, *Good Housekeeping*, in conjunction with the American Academy of Pediatrics and the Bank Street College of Education, began an annual child-care supplement that provides parents with vital information about health care, education, and such practical subjects as allowances and household chores.

Philadelphia

NOVEMBER 1989

A CITY ON ITS ASS.

27 modestly outrageous
ways to get Philadelphia on
its feet again.
It's time, don't you think?

I HAVE A FRIEND WHO walks home from the office every night. She's used to the beggars, the vagrants, the crackheads who stick their hands in her face, demanding money, and then curse her when she ignores them. What she will never get used to is things like the sight of the bum who sat and defecated on Sansom Street around 6 o'clock one recent evening, right in front of her, leaning against a street sign, steadying himself. Doing his business on the curb like a dog. All the other pedestrians on that side of the block made a wide arc around him.

Other people I know feel compelled to report detailed horror stories about why they are leaving the city, fleeing the foulness of it all; many women who live or work in downtown Philadelphia say that what was once called "indecent exposure," and could get you locked up or at least slapped across the face, is now commonplace.

You would think that those of us who have to be downtown every day would, by now, be inured to all this, but we never get used to these things.

Over the last few months, literally hundreds of Philadelphians have called, written and personally button-

BY MIKE MALLOWE

PHOTOCOMPOSITION BY PHILADELPHIA MAGAZINE

Regional and city maga-
zines were created or
enjoyed a renaissance
during the seventies and
eighties. *Philadelphia* magazine, founded in 1908,
got fat in the eighties but
didn't go soft, as this
1989 article makes clear.

THE SECOND COMING

BY PAUL BURKA

With another Longhorn
having just moved into
the White House in 1989,
Texas Monthly attempted
to answer the question,
What's in it for Texans?

Longevity (above) is one of a number of magazines launched in the eighties for people concerned about good health and a long life. *People* (below) recounted the life of a brave young AIDS victim in 1988.

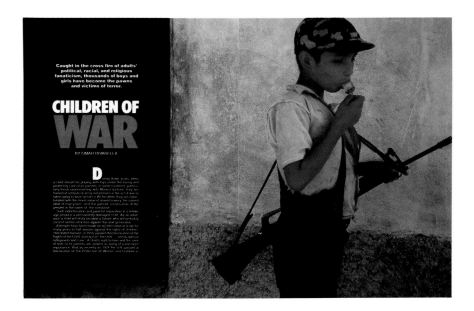

In a lengthy 1985 *Penthouse* essay (above), writer Omar Rivabella depicted the fate of thousands of children caught up in regional conflicts.

Cover

THE QUIET VICTORIES OF RYAN WHITE

Driven from his childhood, a courageous AIDS patient finds refuge and friendship in a small town with heart

Ryan White nearly died last January, one month past his 16th birthday. He was rushed to the hospital with pneumonia, the result of his AIDS: He has been taking AZT since last August, and it has helped him put on weight and generally improved his health, but it cannot stop his lungs from

At first surprised by his warm welcome, Ryan is now at home in Cicero. "People seem friendlier," he says.

sometimes filling with fluid or prevent other opportunistic infections brought on by the disease. Ryan is feeling better now, though, so he has agreed to travel to Omaha to talk about AIDS with reporters, a religion class at Father Flanagan's Boys Town and 100 adults at the Joslyn Witherspoon Concert Hall. He believes it is important to talk about AIDS; he feels people ought to know what he knows. But he is more comfortable discussing his illness with kids than with adults. "Kids listen," he explains.

"Are you afraid of dying?" asks a student at Boys Town.

"No," Ryan says. "If I were worried about dying, I'd die. I'm not afraid, I'm just not ready yet. I want to go to Indiana University."

"How does it feel knowing you're going to die?" another boy wonders.

"Someday you'll die too," says Ryan. The boy, about Ryan's age, looks shocked. "Things could always be worse," Ryan adds, not wanting to cause discomfort. "It's how you live your life that counts."

"DO YOU CRY?" a woman yells. Adults tend to talk at him that way. *"Kids don't talk to him like he's retarded,"* Ryan's mother, Jeanne, whispers. *"I wonder why adults do? Ryan can't figure it out."*

"I cry a lot for emotional reasons," Ryan answers. "Not for pain." At that the woman herself starts to cry. Ryan begs her not to. He's just fine, he assures her, and he's having lots of fun here in Omaha. Obediently, the woman stops crying.

"What was it like in Kokomo?" a girl asks. Kokomo is the Indiana city where Ryan was born and grew up. He was expelled from school there after he contracted AIDS 3½ years ago from a transfusion of contaminated blood. He, his mother and his sister, Andrea, now 14, fled Kokomo only a year ago.

"A lot of people would back away from me on the street," Ryan says. "They'd run from me. Maybe I would have been afraid of AIDS too, but I wouldn't have been mean about it."

"RYAN, HOW DOES YOUR CHRISTIAN FAITH HELP YOU WITH YOUR DISEASE?" bellows a minister.

"I've learned that God doesn't punish people," Ryan answers. "I've learned that God doesn't dislike homosexuals, like a lot of Christians think. AIDS isn't their fault, just like it isn't my fault. God loves homosexuals as much as He loves everyone else." The minister looks uncomfortable.

Afterward, a reporter asks Ryan what was the worst thing about Kokomo.

"I had no friends," Ryan says. "I was lonely. All I wanted was to go to school and fit in."

They say that fighter pilots are at their best in the heat of battle: Their reflexes are almost inexplicably quick, their choices of action far surer than in practice. Researchers know a biological cause for that—the surge of adrenaline provoked by any sudden, life-threatening danger. But the experiences of others, who look death in the eye under less dramatic circumstances, suggest a deeper reason. Having faced their own end, they become more graceful, more finely focused, wiser, seemingly purified of the petty dis-

"Here they were willing to educate themselves," says Ryan, in his bedroom. "And that made the difference, I guess."

tractions that plague and mess up most lives. The transformation is usually stunning and indelible, and it is never more wondrous than when it takes place in a child. Sage Volkman, 6 years old and terribly disfigured by a near-fatal fire (PEOPLE, Mar. 21, 1988), emanates just such

The women's magazines of the late twentieth century have been there when their readers needed them. They still offer advice on beauty, fashion, and home management; but now, they also guide women moving into the work force and tackle issues as difficult as divorce, single parenting, and surrogate motherhood. *Working Mother* and *Working Woman*, among many others, serve as advisors and advocates.

On the threshold of the twenty-first century, American magazines are more varied than ever. Every major city has its own magazine, as do most hobbies and many ethnic and special-interest groups. More than a few of these magazines, large and small, have displayed admirable courage. *Philadelphia* magazine made its name exposing corruption in the city's government and media; *Sports Illustrated* has tackled gambling in professional athletics. *Self, Prevention, Longevity,* and *In Health* have addressed the interests of Americans searching for healthier ways of living. Magazines like *Ebony* and *Essence* continue to voice the concerns of the African-American community. Others, like *The Advocate*, have sprung up around the country to meet the needs of the gay community.

Many magazines still try to shape the public discourse — sometimes courageously, even brilliantly. *The New Yorker* vividly dramatized the threat of nuclear extinction in its 1982 "Fate of the Earth" series. *Better Homes and Gardens* has devoted many of its pages to the issue of homelessness, and set up a foundation to help alleviate this shame of modern society. In the seventies, America's major women's magazines joined forces in an unusual way, agreeing to publish articles about the Equal Rights Amendment in the same month. In the past decade, magazines as different as *People, Rolling Stone,* and *Scientific American* have tried to increase public understanding of AIDS, portraying the human tragedies the disease creates and campaigning for more research funding.

William Lloyd Garrison, Ida Tarbell, Rachel Carson. Their names have become part of history, but their spirits belong to the present. Even as you read this, there are editors and writers throughout the nation willing to fight for their beliefs, to right wrongs and reach people's hearts with the power of the printing press. They may address issues undreamed of by Garrison, but they have this much in common with their distinguished forebear: They will not equivocate. They will be heard.

— *Michael Ryan*

Newsweek in a 1989 special issue (top) chronicled the end of the Berlin Wall and of the Cold War itself. *Vanity Fair* gave a human face to the tragedy of ecological destruction (above) with Alex Shoumatoff's 1989 investigation into the death of Brazilian environmental activist Chico Mendes.

The Magazine Cover

Art editor Eleanor Treacy gave Henry Luce's *Fortune* (opposite) — the magazine for the "aristocracy of our business civilization" — a look *The New York Times* called "sumptuous to the point of rivalling the pearly gates."

Although you can't judge a book by its cover, a magazine's cover tells you a lot. Its whole purpose is to communicate both explicit and subliminal messages about the riches within. Extraordinary amounts of time and effort go into the development of these showpieces. In the first decades of this century, artists and illustrators were paid handsome sums, even by today's standards, for cover drawings and paintings; now, some magazines have departments exclusively devoted to creating compelling covers.

Editors, art directors, and circulation managers have long battled over the words and images that might best work cover magic. Their strategies are diverse. *The New Yorker* eschews cover type that would herald its articles, while the *Reader's Digest*'s cover billboards the contents. Radically different approaches, perhaps, but each projects an identity and creates a familiar face for dedicated readers.

In the end, all covers invite: They invite readers to pick a magazine off a newsstand or grab it from the mail and explore what's inside. For 250 years, they've been just about the best invitations Americans could get.

"She has dared to blaze the earth's uncharted skyways," said *McCall's* of Amelia Earhart when her portrait, by Neysa McMein, appeared on the magazine's cover (above right). During the First and Second World Wars, James Montgomery Flagg's "I Want You" cover for *Leslie's* (right) appeared on more than 4.5 million posters.

Fortune

One Dollar a Copy   MAY 1938   Ten Dollars a Year

VOL. XX.—No. 515.　　　　NEW YORK, JANUARY 19, 1887.　　　　PRICE, TEN CENTS.

"What fools these Mortals be!"
MIDSUMMER-NIGHTS DREAM.

Puck

TRADE MARK REGISTERED 1878.

KEPPLER & SCHWARZMANN, Publishers.　　　　PUCK BUILDING, Cor. Houston & Mulberry Sts.

ENTERED AT THE POST OFFICE AT NEW YORK, AND ADMITTED FOR TRANSMISSION THROUGH THE MAILS AT SECOND CLASS RATES.

THE SENATE OF THE FUTURE—A CLOSE CORPORATION OF MILLIONAIRES.

Puck (opposite) used cartoons and satirical sketches to attack corruption and poke fun at society's foibles.

Sports Afield (above left) has had evocative covers since 1887. *The Masses* (middle) was suppressed by the government in 1917 for opposing the U.S. role in the First World War. *The New Yorker* (right) celebrated Earth Day 1990 with Atlas and a soiled world.

The Harper brothers started *Harper's Monthly* (below) in 1850 to advertise their books and make use of idle presses. *The Nation* (below right) commemorated the twenty-fifth anniversary of the Sacco and Vanzetti executions with this Ben Shahn portrait.

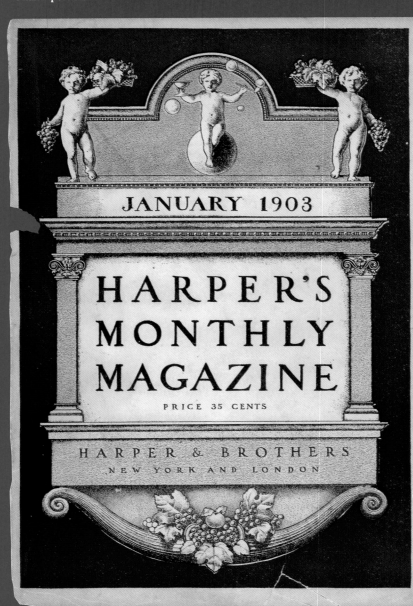

Photographer Anton Bruehl's 1937 *Vogue* cover (opposite) showed an independent woman as she prepared to fly to Cape Cod "just for the weekend."

H. L. Mencken and George Jean Nathan were co-editors of *The Smart Set*, subtitled "A Magazine of Cleverness," before moving on to found the *American Mercury* in 1924.

Frank S. Guild drew several animal covers for *The Ladies' Home Journal*, which began as a department in the *Tribune and Farmer* newspaper.

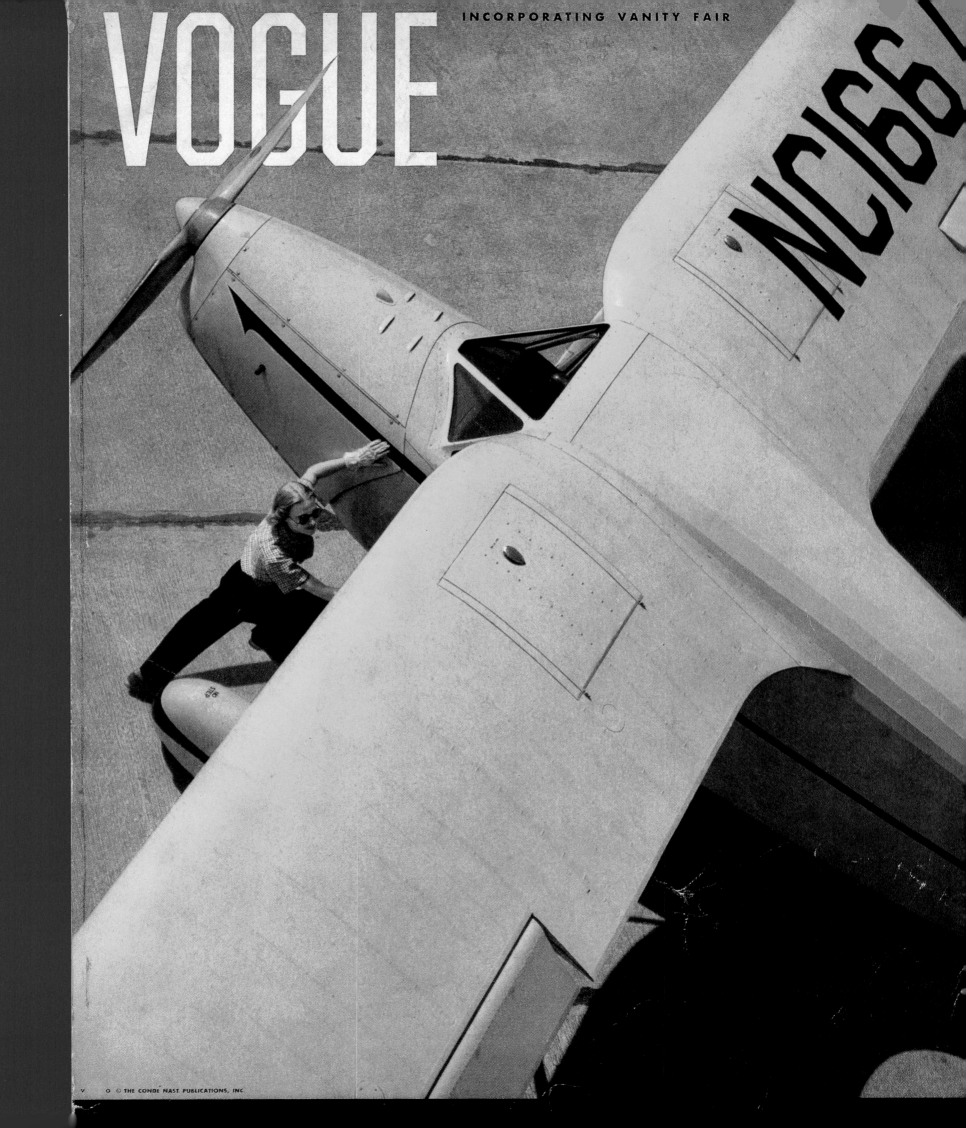

VOGUE

INCORPORATING VANITY FAIR

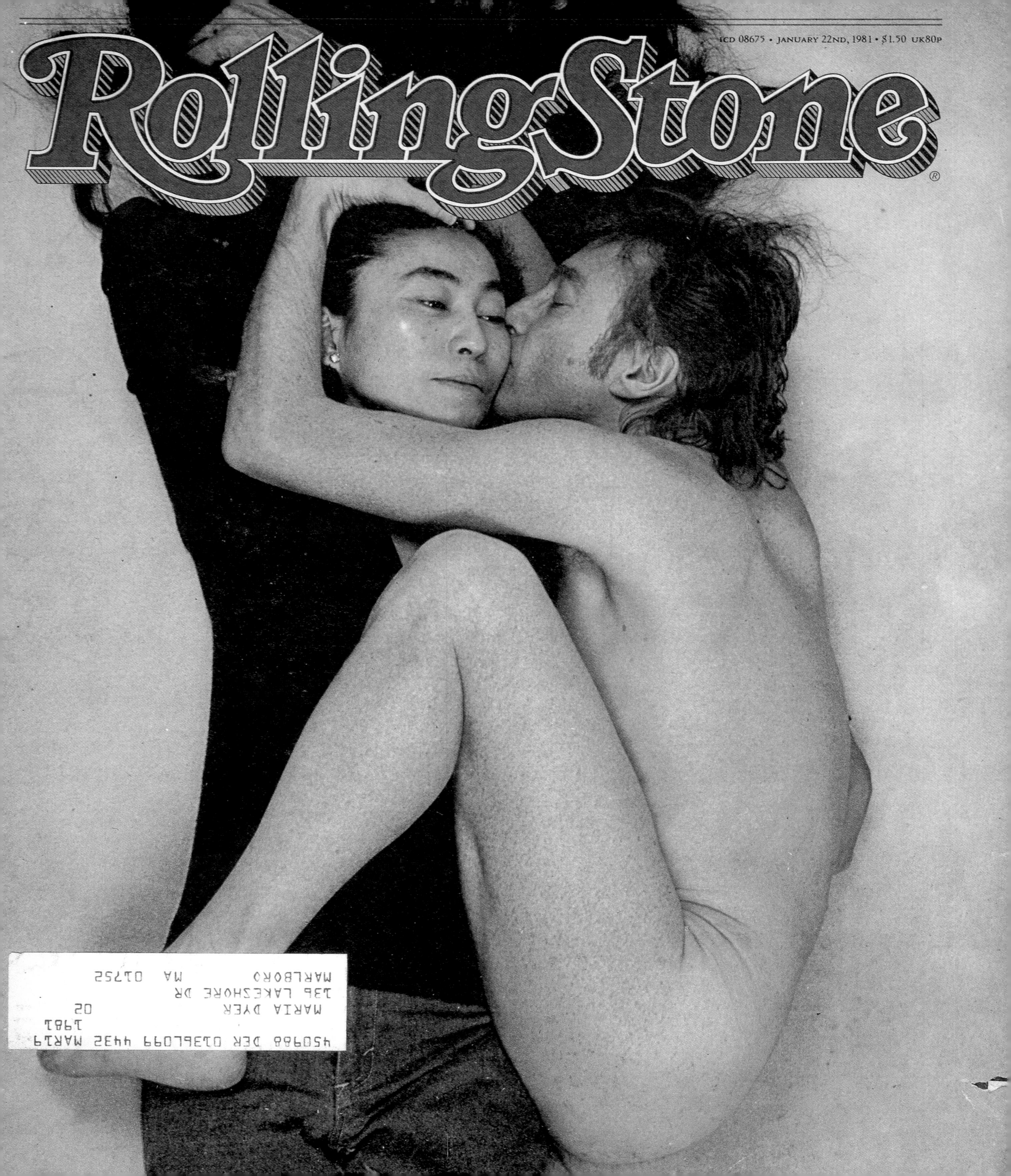

ICD 08675 · JANUARY 22ND, 1981 · $1.50 UK80p

RollingStone

George Petty drew Rita Hayworth for a 1941 cover of *Time* (right). His "Petty Girl" was a regular feature in *Esquire* during the thirties. Photographer Carl Fischer and art director George Lois signaled the decline of the Pop Art movement with their cover of Andy Warhol drowning in his famous can of soup (far right).

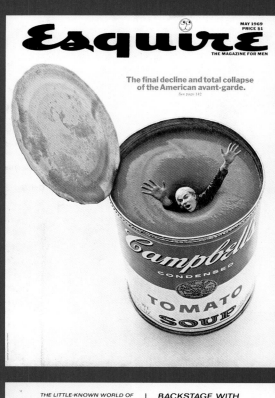

Henry Wolf created Old Glory out of Kennedys for the cover of *Show* (above left), owned by Huntington Hartford, heir to the A&P fortune. Between 1916 and 1963, Norman Rockwell contributed more than 300 covers to *The Saturday Evening Post* (above).

John Lennon thought Annie Leibovitz's portrait of Yoko Ono and himself (opposite) "captured our relationship perfectly." Lennon was killed shortly after this photo was taken.

New Republic

May 6, 1946 · Fifteen Cents

INFLATION

Milk—36¢ Butter—$1.20 Bacon—84¢

Eggs—$1.10 Bread—25¢ Gasoline—40¢

Herbert Croly, the first
editor of *The New Republic*,
wanted the magazine to
start "little insurrections"
in the minds of its readers.

Liberty (opposite), best
known for noting reading
time per article, paid tribute to America's war dead
with this 1945 cover.

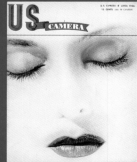

Gentry (right top), a lavish
men's quarterly, included
swatches of fabric and
packets of herbs with its
articles and ads. As interest
in photography soared in
the thirties and forties,
U.S. Camera (middle)
capitalized on the popularity
of America's newest hobby.
In its short life, *Wigwag*
(bottom) took a sometimes
humorous, sometimes
serious look at the arts,
science, and politics.

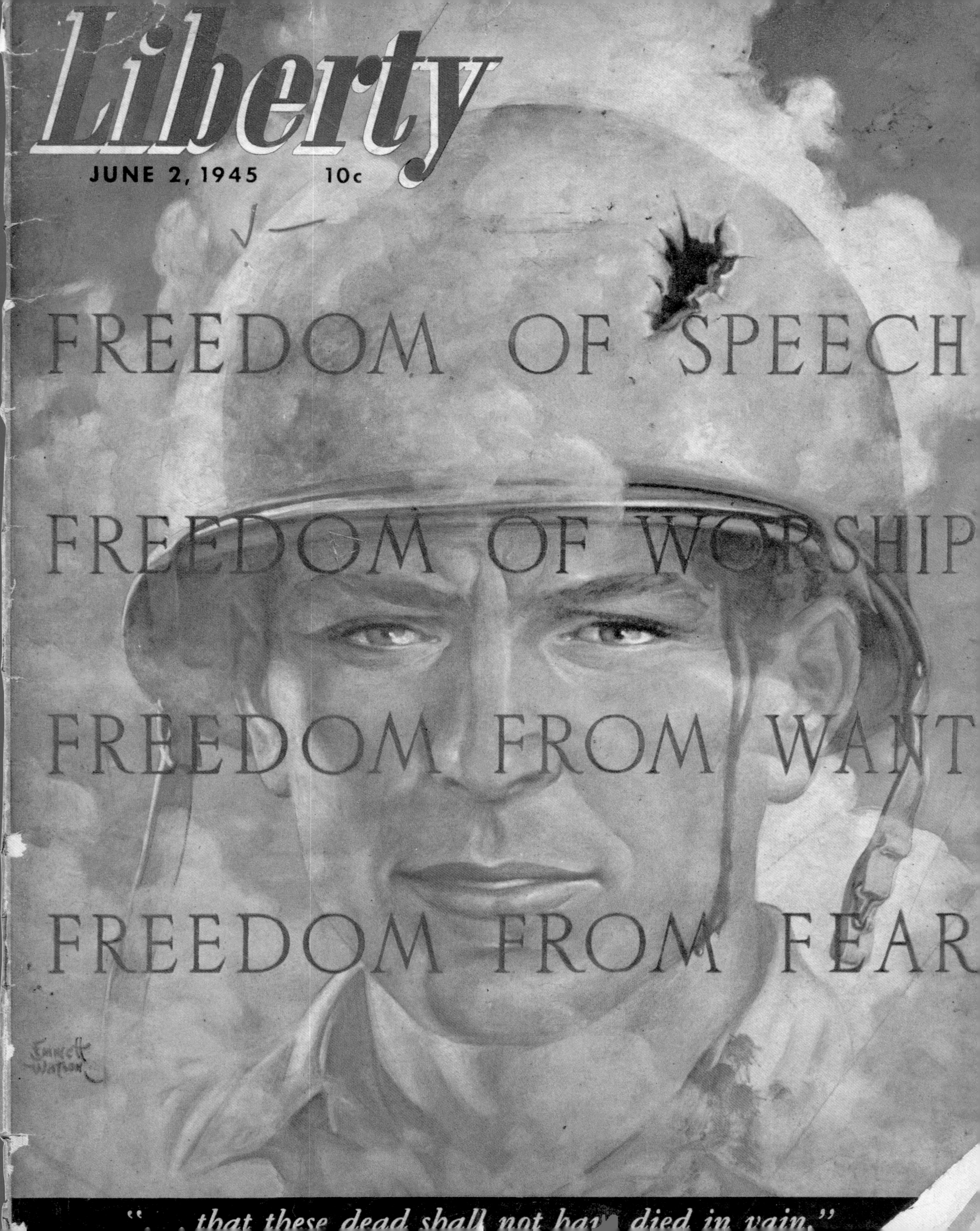

Liberty

JUNE 2, 1945 **10c**

FREEDOM OF SPEECH

FREEDOM OF WORSHIP

FREEDOM FROM WANT

FREEDOM FROM FEAR

" ... that these dead shall not have died in vain."

vacations … lots of fun for little money

woman's day

THE A & P MAGAZINE **7** *cents*

The cover of the May 1954 "vacation" issue of *Woman's Day* (opposite) captured the spirit of an America taking to the road with the interstate highway system under construction.

Ebony publisher John H. Johnson called this issue (top left) one of his most important. *New Times* (top middle) made Barbra Streisand bald — a reference to her affair with hairdresser Jon Peters. *Newsweek* takes a graphic departure from its normal cover style (top right). Designer Milton Glaser and art director Walter Bernard gave gossip life with this *New York* cover (above left). *Natural History* (above middle) investigated how Mickey keeps looking younger. Kinuko Craft illustrated *The Atlantic*'s 1990 cover story (above right) on Muslim resentment of the West.

Featuring "avant garb," *Details* began in 1982 as a unisex "downtown" Manhattan fashion magazine; it now focuses on men's styles.

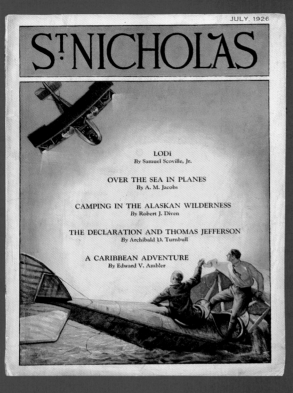

Among the children who read *St. Nicholas* (left) were F. Scott Fitzgerald, E. B. White, and Eudora Welty. Brooklyn Dodger Don Newcombe pitched his way onto the cover of *Sports Illustrated* (below left) in 1955.

Movie star Ann Sheridan graced *Glamour's* first cover (opposite) in 1939. For more than half a century the magazine has offered fashion and beauty tips to young working women.

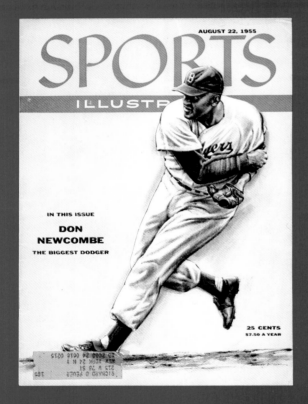

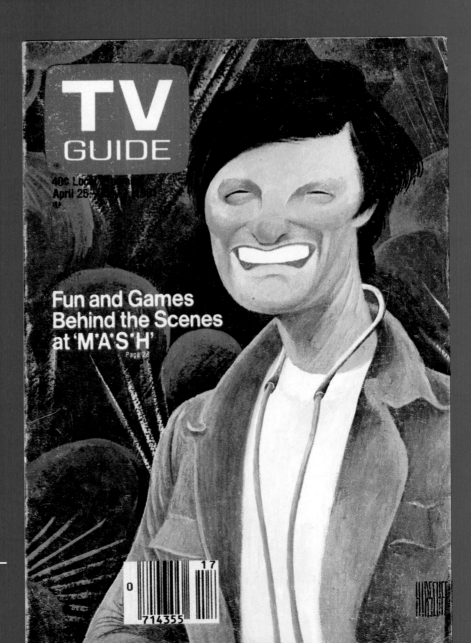

TV Guide turned to noted caricaturist Al Hirschfeld to portray M*A*S*H star Alan Alda for a cover in 1981.

glamour

OF HOLLYWOOD

ANN SHERIDAN

APRIL
15¢

A New Magazine

the Hollywood way to

Fashion · Beauty · Charm

POPULAR SCIENCE

FEBRUARY
15 CENTS
20 CENTS IN CANADA

FOUNDED MONTHLY *1872*

NOW 15¢

20 CENTS IN CANADA

NRA CODE

NEW INVENTIONS
MECHANICS
HOME WORKSHOP
MONEY MAKING IDEAS
350 PICTURES

Although *National Lampoon*'s shoot-the-dog cover wasn't a sell-out, it ranks among the most memorable of any magazine.

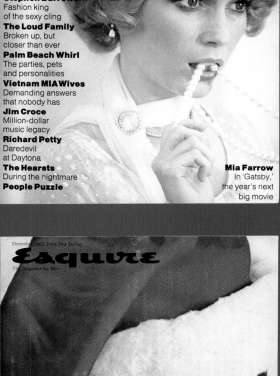

Founded in 1872 to spread scientific knowledge, *Popular Science* heralded new inventions and feats of the imagination such as this ski-parachute outfit on a 1935 cover (opposite).

Reporting on the "active personalities of our time," *People* (above right) put Mia Farrow on the cover of its first issue in 1974. *Esquire* (right) capped off 1963, a year of racial tension, with one of its most controversial covers — heavyweight boxer Sonny Liston as Saint Nick.

Mark Twain, Lincoln Steffens, and Robert Frost were contributors to *The Century*, which started out in 1870 as *Scribner's Monthly*.

Judge's owners started *Judge's Library: A Monthly Magazine of Fun* in 1887 (top) and devoted each issue to a single topic. Hugh Hefner used Marilyn Monroe for the 1953 premier issue of *Playboy* (above), which bore no cover date because Hefner feared it wouldn't generate enough cash to finance a second.

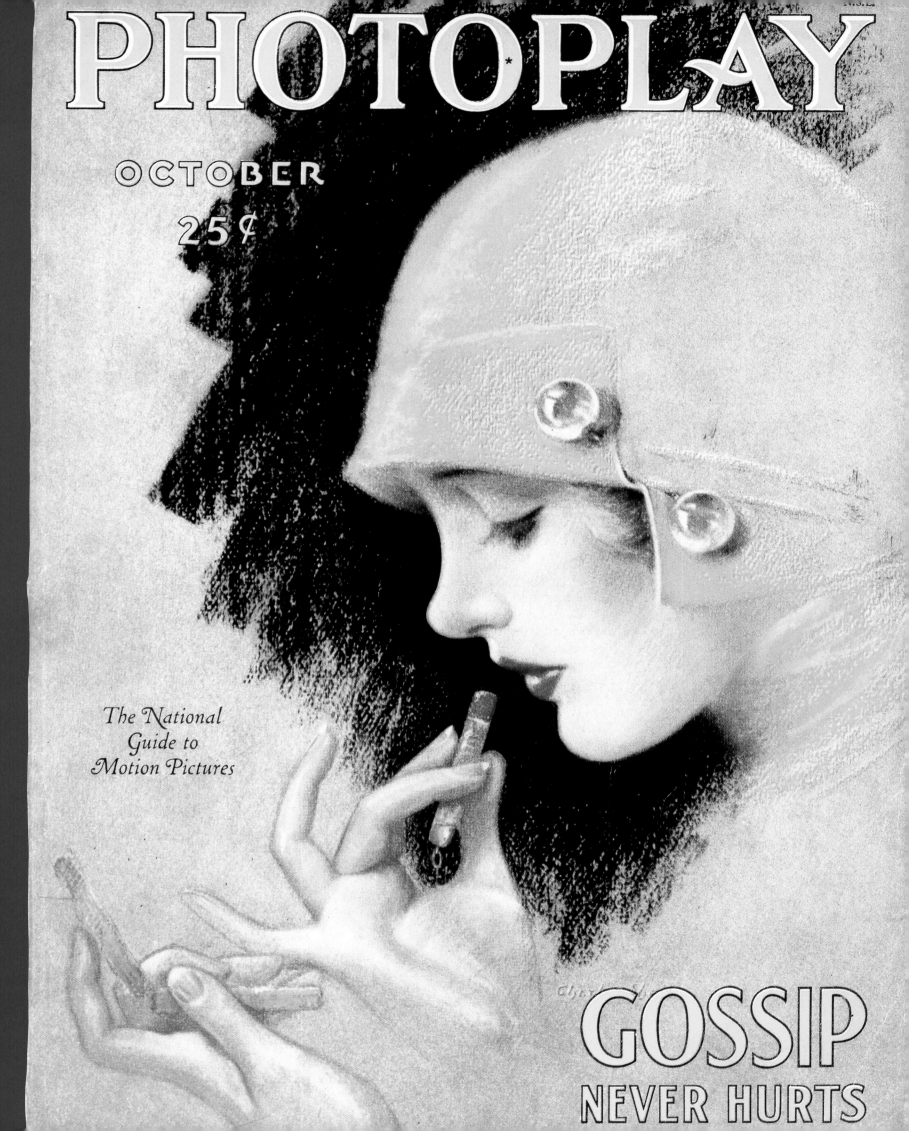

PHOTOPLAY

OCTOBER

25¢

*The National
Guide to
Motion Pictures*

GOSSIP
NEVER HURTS

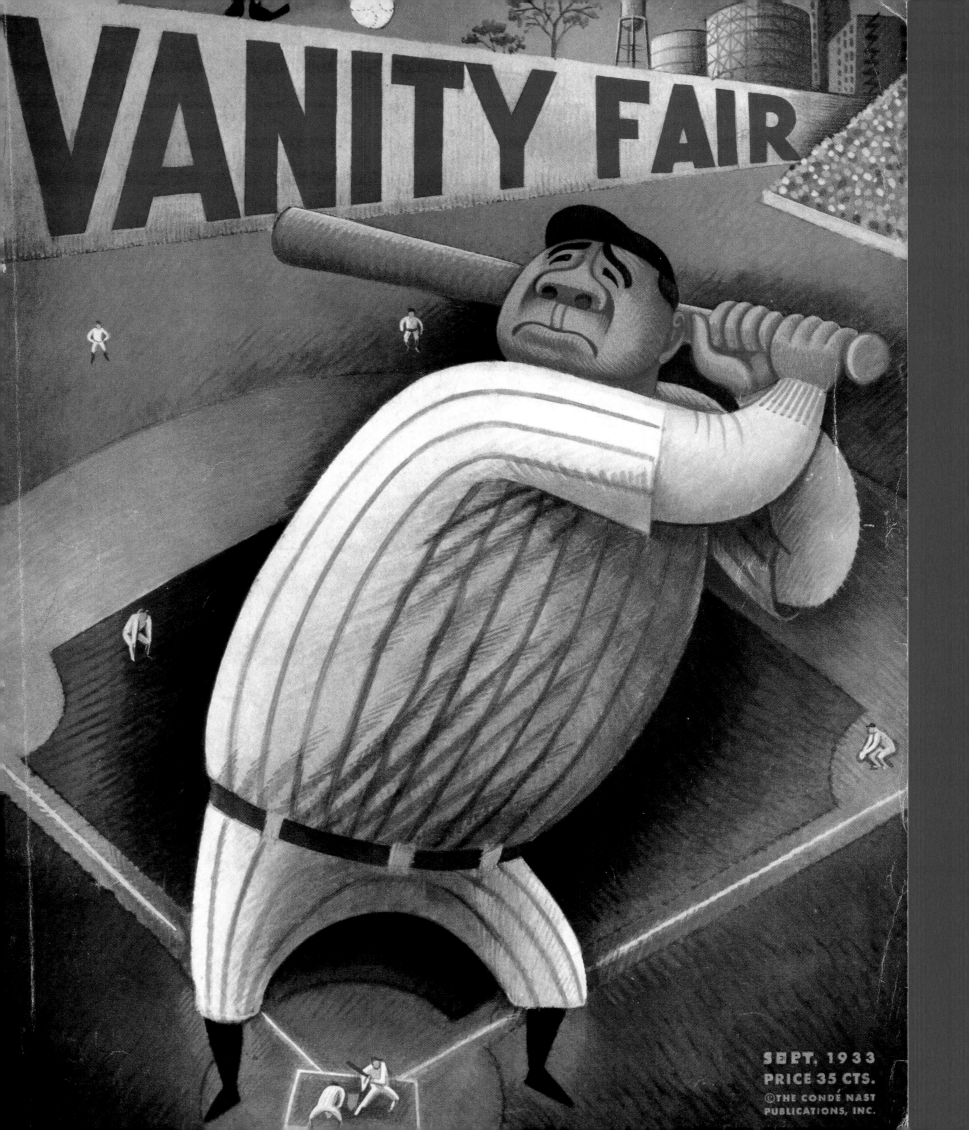

VANITY FAIR

SEPT, 1933
PRICE 35 CTS.

©THE CONDÉ NAST
PUBLICATIONS, INC.

AUGUST 4, 1921   **Life**   PRICE 15 CENTS

Copyright, 1921, Life Publishing Co.   COLES PHILLIPS

For Divers Reasons

The original *Life*, a humor magazine, started in 1883. When it fell on hard times in the thirties, Henry Luce bought it to transfer the name to his new picture-weekly.

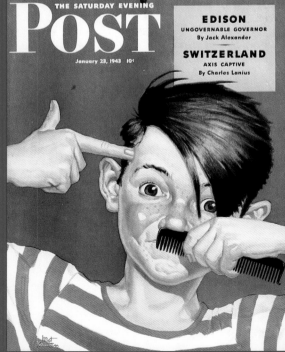

Vanity Fair's editor Frank Crowninshield wanted the magazine to be about "hot" topics. Certainly Babe Ruth filled the bill in 1933, when Miguel Covarrubias depicted the legendary hitter on the cover (opposite).

In its twenty-first year, *Essence* (above right) continues to give a sophisticated and positive view of black fashion and society. Halfway through the Second World War, *The Saturday Evening Post* (right) presented a child's perspective on the man responsible for the destruction of Europe.

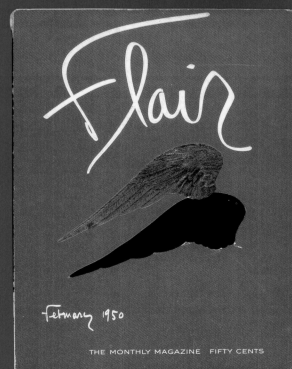

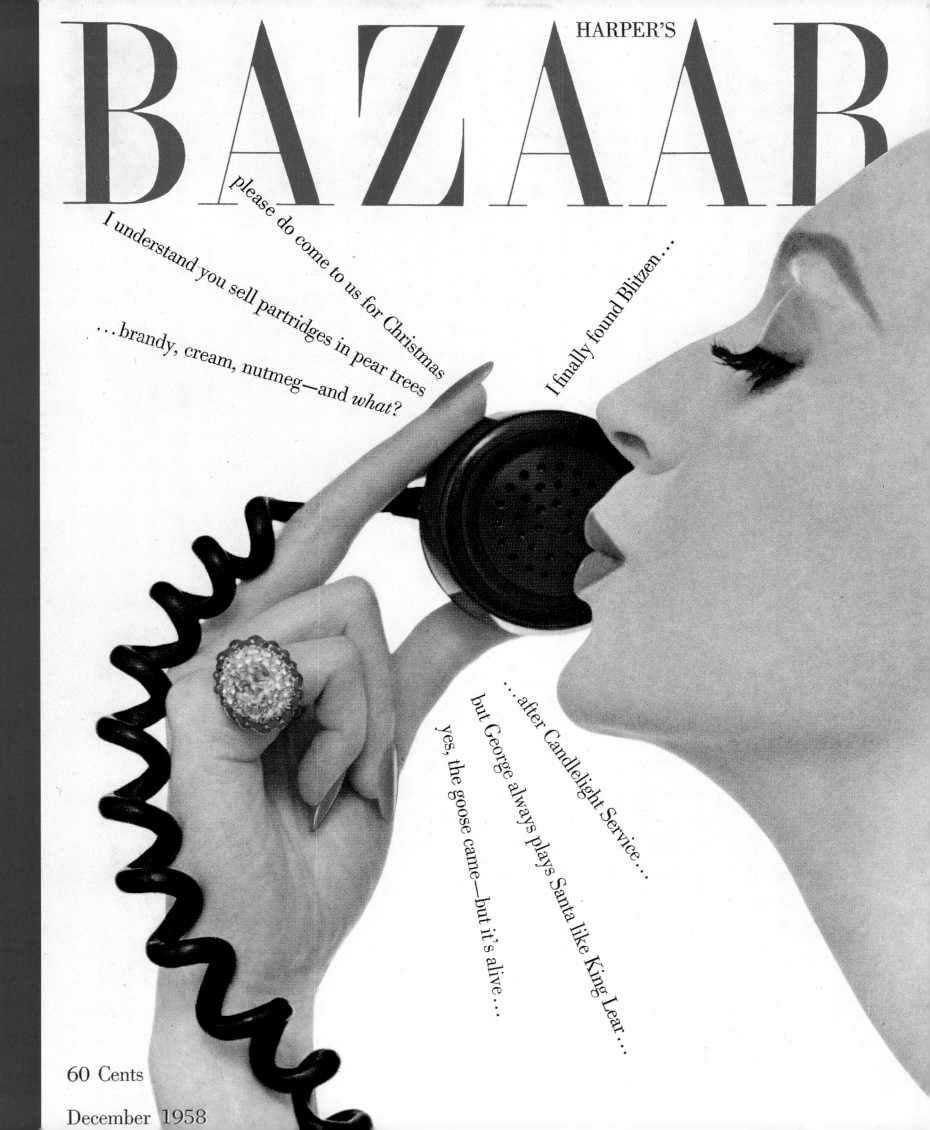

HARPER'S BAZAAR

please do come to us for Christmas

I understand you sell partridges in pear trees

...brandy, cream, nutmeg—and *what?*

I finally found Blitzen...

...after Candlelight Service...

but George always plays Santa like King Lear...

yes, the goose came—but it's alive...

60 Cents

December 1958

Mary Petty contributed thirty-eight covers to *The New Yorker* over twenty-six years. She often poked fun at the world of the rich, as with this 1942 cover (opposite), when war fears penetrated the homes of even the well-to-do.

Al Parker painted classy cover portraits of women — like this one for a 1937 *Ladies' Home Journal* (top left) — with a style soon imitated by his fellow illustrators. Francesco Clemente's self-portrait forms a striking 1988 cover of *Interview* (middle), founded by Andy Warhol. Polish-born W. T. Benda gave a luminous glow to this 1922 cover portrait for *Hearst's International* (bottom).

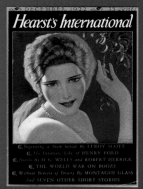

Founded in 1919, Bernarr Macfadden's *True Story* titillated readers with tales of common folk' love affairs. Supposedly they taught a moral lesson.

Magazine Personalities

MOLDERS OF THE MEDIUM

Ben Franklin, shown above as an apprentice carrying printing plates, went on to found *The General Magazine* in 1741.

"It is far better to be wrong than to be timorous," asserted H. L. Mencken (opposite), who in 1924 created *The American Mercury*.

Considering the history of American magazines, it seems remarkable that anyone ever chooses to enter the field in the first place. The mortality rate of magazines of every kind has always been high, no matter how great the genius of the editor or publisher; even Benjamin Franklin managed to sustain his ground-breaking publication for only six months. Almost always the odds against success were daunting, and the costs tended to be formidable. Even more formidable, however, was the determination of those who succeeded where others failed.

The history of magazines in America is a tale of men — and for at least two centuries, they were almost all men — driven by a unique vision to create something new for a market that no one else had discerned. Often these entrepreneurs started with virtually nothing, but their ambitions were so powerful that they triumphed over every form of adversity, from war to depression. They were typically gamblers at heart, the kind of men willing to risk ruination, not to mention their mother's mortgaged furniture or whatever else was handy, to pursue their ideas.

The editors and publishers who persisted in the face of such obstacles are a fascinating lot. Some were seemingly ordinary people who amazed everyone they knew by accomplishing the extraordinary, while others were genuine eccentrics whose determination to achieve the impossible was the least of many peculiarities. Many of them emerged from terrible poverty to build empires, and if their publications often peddled a Horatio Alger version of the American Dream, they themselves were the embodiment of it.

Even when magazines succeeded, most enjoyed only a brief heyday and then disappeared, eclipsed by changing times and tastes. A few venerable names that have survived their nineteenth-century origins include *Scientific American*, founded in 1845, *The Atlantic Monthly* (1857), *The Nation* (1865), *Popular Science* (1872), and *The Ladies' Home Journal* (1883). Many of the other magazines that flourished during the late nineteenth century and early twentieth are long gone, their once renowned leaders largely forgotten. Frank Munsey, a powerful magazine and newspaper publisher who established *Munsey's Magazine* in 1889, had left his job as a telegraph operator in Maine and come to New York with a grand total of $40 to his name. When he died in 1925, his fortune was estimated at $40 million, a vast amount in that day. He always made it clear that he was interested in money above all else, and he never bothered with literary niceties. "I can't spell cat," he acknowledged. "But then, why should I worry about this shortcoming when I can hire a good speller for ten dollars a week?" Munsey inaugurated the era of mass circulation when he reduced the price of *Munsey's*, "the flagship of the fleet," from twenty-five cents to a dime, and he exhibited an altogether modern ruthlessness as he bought newspaper after newspaper, only to merge or close the weak ones in an endless quest for efficient profit centers. The quintessential loner, he never married and had no heirs. He left his money to the Metropolitan Museum of Art — not because he had any particular interest in art, but because he had decided that the Met's board was reasonably honest and competent, in contrast to those of other charities. Cold and quixotic, Munsey was remembered after his death as "probably the most hated publisher that ever lived," as one observer put it, although many others have no doubt laid claim to that title in the years since.

Another leading publisher of the time was Samuel S. McClure, who came to America from Ireland with his widowed mother when he was nine years old. He was so poor that he went for days without anything to eat, but he worked his way through college and went on to establish the first American newspaper syndicate, in 1884. He also founded *McClure's Magazine*, a renowned muckraking magazine whose writers included Ida Tarbell, Lincoln Steffens, Ray Stannard Baker, and Willa Cather. Its coverage ranged from Marconi's discovery of the wireless to the "first authentic account" of the Wright brothers' "flying machine," but *McClure's* was best known for its exposés of municipal corruption, corporate malfeasance, and other abuses. Many of its crusades resulted in far-reaching reforms.

McClure had a sure instinct for good writers, and over the years he published the work of Rudyard Kipling, Sir Arthur Conan Doyle, Robert Louis Stevenson, Joseph Conrad, Mark Twain, O. Henry, and Jack London. At the age of eighty-two, he dispensed this advice: "Success is a matter of having the right ideas and the right people to help you." By then he had made and lost his fortune several times over; his famous magazine expired in 1929, but McClure lived for another twenty years, dining on a baked potato at the Automat every night, subsisting on the charity of a few old friends, and endlessly rereading a dog-eared copy of a 1910 article that described him as "an editor of genius" and "a staunch and sincere idealist."

Sarah Josepha Hale became editor of *Ladies' Magazine* in 1828 and, later, of *Godey's Lady's Book*, which she edited for forty years.

McClure's Magazine, 1905.

Gilbert H. Grosvenor recalled that when he edited his first issue of *The National Geographic* in 1899, he personally addressed the entire edition and carried it to the post office.

S. S. McClure (standing) chats with Willa Cather, Ida Tarbell, and Will Irwin in 1924. "Success," said McClure, who arrived in the United States virtually penniless in 1866, "is a matter of having the right ideas and the right people to help you."

Children "just want to have their own way over their own magazine," said Mary Mapes Dodge (above), who edited the monthly children's magazine *St. Nicholas* for thirty years.

George Horace Lorimer (opposite), hired in 1899 as a stop-gap editor of the moribund *Saturday Evening Post*, boosted its circulation to three million. In its covers and contents, the *Post* gave America a distinctive vision of itself.

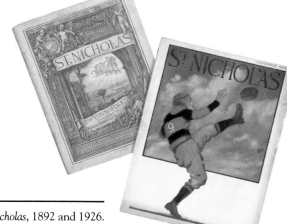

St. Nicholas, 1892 and 1926.

Despite the perennially high attrition rate in the magazine business, the arrival of the right editor at the right time could sometimes salvage even the most terminal case. *The Saturday Evening Post* was founded in 1821 as a family publication — "Neutral in Politics, Devoted to Morality, Pure Literature, Foreign and Domestic News, Agriculture, the Commercial Interests, Science, Art, and Amusement." As the turn of the century approached, the magazine was ailing; it was nearly defunct when it was purchased by Cyrus Curtis. Shortly thereafter, Curtis had the good fortune to be approached by George Horace Lorimer, an enterprising young man pursuing a cherished goal. Lorimer had established a flourishing career in the meat-packing business, but he wanted to go into journalism. He applied to Curtis for a job and was hired at a salary of $1,000 a year to keep *The Saturday Evening Post* alive while its publisher sailed to Europe to find a new editor. When Lorimer sent Curtis the next few issues of the magazine, Curtis was so impressed that he cabled Lorimer to put his own name on the masthead as editor-in-chief.

Lorimer held that position for the next thirty-eight years, eventually becoming chairman of the Curtis Publishing Company as well. During his tenure, he made *The Saturday Evening Post* a major part of the American landscape, boosting its circulation from around 2,000 to three million (the *Post* was the first magazine to break the one million mark) and publishing the work of such writers as Ring Lardner, F. Scott Fitzgerald, Sinclair Lewis, and Booth Tarkington, along with Norman Rockwell's wholesome, small-town scenes of America. Lorimer himself was modest about his role; one of his favorite maxims held that "the prime qualification of being an editor is being an ordinary man." When he died in 1937, his obituary in *The New York Times* hailed the magazine under his stewardship as having had "more influence upon the cultural life of America than any other."

Another Curtis protégé was Edward Bok, who left school at the age of thirteen to become an office boy for Western Union at the munificent salary of $6.25 a week. He was an enterprising teenager, writing letters to famous people — President James Garfield, General Ulysses S. Grant, General William Tecumseh Sherman — not only to learn about their lives but also to acquire a valuable autograph collection. Bok's early career was varied — he worked as a newspaper reporter, started a theater program, edited *The Brooklyn Magazine,* and founded a newspaper syndicate. He was publishing a literary

Edward Bok was twenty-five years old when he became editor of *The Ladies' Home Journal* in 1889, and he held that post for three decades. He also served for a time as the magazine's advice columnist.

letter for forty-five newspapers when he came to the attention of Cyrus Curtis, who needed an editor for *The Ladies' Home Journal*. Bok took on the job in 1889; seven years later, Curtis acquired a son-in-law as well, when Bok married Curtis's only daughter. Bok spent thirty years at the *Journal*, earning a place in history with some notably progressive positions, including his editorial stand in favor of conservation, his willingness to publish articles on venereal disease, and his refusal to accept patent-medicine advertisements. His crusade against those cure-alls contributed to the enactment of the Pure Food and Drug Act in 1906.

As an editor, Bok communicated very successfully with his female readers; in private, however, he was a misogynist who seemed ill at ease with women except his wife, his mother, and a few others. Although he advised millions of women on how to raise their children, he wasn't close to his own. He also disapproved of his readers' enthusiasm for the magazine's advice columns: "Let me tell you, mothers — there is something the matter in your home, something wrong with you when your daughter goes to an editor — an entire stranger to her — for advice." Bok's personal quirks notwithstanding, his influence was enduring; by the start of the First World War, he had implemented editorial ideas that have been used ever since by a wide array of women's magazines. *Ladies' Home Journal* survives, but the proud old weekly *Saturday Evening Post* closed in 1969, despite a circulation of 3.5 million.

If time appeared to pass some former trendsetters by, at least one turn-of-the-century publisher was far ahead of his era. In 1899, Bernarr Macfadden, who billed himself as a "kinestherapist," started *Physical Culture* magazine, dedicated to the maintenance of good health through exercise and diet. It reflected his own stern views when it called weakness a crime; later, in divorcing his second wife, Macfadden cited her failure to keep her body "beautiful, trim, and healthy." He went on to publish such magazines as *True Story*, *True Detective Mysteries*, *Master Detective*, *True Romances*, *Modern Marriage*, and *Ghost Stories*. He also owned ten newspapers, established a chain of health-food stores, and amassed a fortune estimated at $30 million. Wealth and success did nothing to soften Macfadden's commitment to the harsh disciplines he believed in so fervently: He slept on the floor, took long hikes barefoot, went nude as much as possible, believed in standing on his head regularly, and fasted for up to two weeks at a time. Macfadden, who believed that "old age is just a bad habit," was his own best advertise-

Maverick publisher Bernarr Macfadden, shown doing a headstand, insisted that "old age is just a bad habit." He promoted his ideas about how to stay fit in *Physical Culture* and made a fortune from *True Story*.

Physical Culture, 1933; *True Story*, 1933.

ment. Just before his eightieth birthday, he was married again, this time to a woman nearly half his age; he celebrated his eighty-third birthday by making a 2,500-foot parachute jump into the Hudson River, and he had great hopes of parachuting over Niagara Falls into the roiling waters below. That plan fell through, a disappointed Macfadden explained, only because "there was just too darned much red tape between the American and Canadian authorities." He died in 1955 at the age of eighty-seven. Had he survived a while longer, his fanatical commitment to exercise and nutrition and his genius for publicity would have made him even more at home at the end of the twentieth century than he was at its beginning.

Despite his boundless optimism, Macfadden ran into hard times during the Depression, and many others were ruined by it; *Munsey's* expired, along with *McClure's*, in the cataclysmic year of 1929. But even economic disaster failed to derail the destiny of Henry Luce and the empire he was building. Luce and Briton Hadden, a friend from Hotchkiss School and Yale, founded *Time* in 1923 because they were convinced that contemporary news coverage was inadequate. "People in America are, for the most part, poorly informed," they proclaimed, setting out to remedy this situation by compartmentalizing and condensing the news in a new format called the news magazine. Intended for "the busy man" with no time to waste, the publication featured a distinctively clipped, inverted writing style, which soon came to be called *Time*-ese.

Before Hadden died in 1929, he and Luce had also hatched the idea for *Fortune*, a deluxe magazine to cover business. Luce launched it in the inauspicious year of 1930, but it was a success from the beginning. He followed up six years later with *Life*, which specialized in photojournalism, boasted a circulation of 8.5 million at its height, and spawned *Look* as a competitor in 1937. Time Inc. introduced *Sports Illustrated* in 1954, *Money* in 1972, and *People* two years later. By that time, Luce's network encompassed radio and television stations, paper companies, Time-Life Books, and myriad other properties.

A political conservative with strongly anti-Communist views and an abiding faith in the free-enterprise system, Luce did not let the dictates of "objective" journalism control *Time*'s point of view. This approach incurred inevitable criticism. "The result of his rejection of the thesis of objectivity . . . has been the presentation of opinion and conjecture as straight news, without qualification or attribution," wrote Kenneth Stewart and John Tebbel in *Makers of Modern Journalism*. "To

Fortune, 1941; *Life*, 1936; *Time*, 1947.

Henry R. Luce, founder of Time Inc., and his wife, playwright Clare Boothe Luce, enjoy a relaxed moment in the sun during a trip to Spain in 1952.

Time Inc. president James Linen (left) and Luce (right) chat with colleagues at company headquarters in New York in 1964.

A few years before Luce launched *Fortune*, DeWitt and Lila Acheson Wallace (center) published the first issue of *Reader's Digest* from their Greenwich Village apartment. By the time this photo was taken in the fifties by Arnold Newman, the Wallaces' little magazine had become as ubiquitous as the Bible.

Reader's Digest, 1952.

those who find themselves in agreement with Luce, this practice makes his magazine a strong force for 'right thinking'; to those who disagree, the practice makes his magazines a deceptively harmful influence in the democratic process." Luce himself shrugged off such concerns. Asked how *Time* could call itself a news magazine when it was so full of opinion, he replied nonchalantly, "I invented the idea, so I guess I can call it anything I like."

Among Luce's contemporaries was another young man with a bright idea that would revolutionize the magazine world. DeWitt Wallace hardly seemed like a visionary; an indifferent student and incorrigible prankster, he repeated his first year of college because "the freshman year is more fun," and his exasperated father once wrote to another son, "It seems about hopeless to get a little business sense into DeWitt's head." After dropping out of college, Wallace knocked around in a series of jobs and hitchhiked through the West. He had just spent the day working in a Montana hay field when he had his grand idea — "a general digest of the best magazine articles." It took him several years to realize his dream. No one was interested in backing Wallace's project, which he called *Reader's Digest*, and eventually he sent out several thousand subscription appeals on his own with $5,000 borrowed from his father and brothers. The mailing netted 1,500 subscriptions at $3 each, enough money for Wallace and his new bride, Lila Bell Acheson, to put out the first issue from their Greenwich Village apartment in 1922. Using upbeat articles he himself had condensed, Wallace set the magazine's characteristic tone with such pieces as "How to Keep Young Mentally" and "Watch Your Dog and Be Wise." The *Digest* quickly turned into one of the greatest success stories in the history of journalism and the biggest seller since the Bible. After the Wallaces moved their operation to Pleasantville, New York, the mail got so heavy that the town had to build a bigger post office. Wallace's philosophy was straightforward and personal. "I simply hunt for things that interest me, and if they do, I print them," he said. Critics attributed the success of this formula to the mediocrity of Wallace's intellect, but when he died in 1981, at the age of ninety-one, *Reader's Digest* was the most successful monthly in the world, publishing in sixteen languages for more than 100 million readers.

Three years after the Wallaces started *Reader's Digest* and two years after Luce introduced *Time*, another legendary publishing figure began his own highly idiosyncratic magazine, one

In 1937, two months after Henry Luce started *Life*, Gardner Cowles, Jr., founded *Look*. Cowles is shown here on a honeymoon trip to Europe in 1933 with his third wife, Fleur, who edited his fashion magazine, *Flair*.

Harold Ross (left), who in 1925 created *The New Yorker*, was no city slicker but a rough-spoken, poker-playing former newspaper-man who was born in Aspen, Colorado, and began his journalism career in Salt Lake City. One of his early hires at *The New Yorker* was James Thurber, who later said that the magazine "has represented every damn decade in which it's been published."

The New Yorker, 1931
and 1976.

that was never to rack up comparable circulation bonanzas but that would exert an enduring influence on the literary intelligentsia of the nation. Harold Ross was an unlikely editor for *The New Yorker*; he did not pretend to be an educated man, and often astounded his more erudite employees with questions like, "Is Moby Dick the whale or the man?" Nevertheless, Ross knew precisely what he wanted: a sophisticated, humorous magazine that would "hate bunk" and would not be edited "for the old lady in Dubuque." Backed by Raoul Fleischmann, whose family had made its money in yeast, Ross established a legendary circle of writers and artists at *The New Yorker*. Its contributors have included E. B. White, James Thurber, A. J. Liebling, Robert Benchley, Ogden Nash, S. J. Perelman, Peter Arno, Dorothy Parker, Alexander Woollcott, Helen Hokinson, J. D. Salinger, John Cheever, John O'Hara, and John Updike.

When Ross died in 1951, he was succeeded by William Shawn, who remained as the magazine's editor until 1987. Although *The New Yorker* has always been regarded as a magazine for the elite, it has enjoyed an impact far beyond its limited circulation, publishing such important works as John Hersey's "Hiroshima," Rachel Carson's "Silent Spring," James Baldwin's

Herbert R. Mayes, lured away from *Good Housekeeping* to *McCall's* in 1956, made *McCall's* the leading women's magazine, in part by hiring top photographers to illustrate features on fashion, food, and décor.

Condé Nast bought *Vogue* in 1909 and turned it into the country's premier women's fashion magazine. Later acquisitions included *Vanity Fair* and *House & Garden*.

Vanity Fair, 1934; *House & Garden,* 1928; *Vogue,* 1927.

"The Fire Next Time," and Jonathan Schell's "The Fate of the Earth," all of which became books.

If Harold Ross unapologetically aimed his magazine at a small group of urban sophisticates, a contemporary publishing giant introduced the principle of "class publishing" — targeting a magazine to a specific group of readers — and ended up having a major impact on the masses as well. Condé Nast, who grew up poor in St. Louis, bought a struggling little society gazette called *Vogue* in 1909 and proceeded to build it into America's leading women's fashion magazine under the direction of its longtime editor Edna Woolman Chase. After purchasing *Vanity Fair* and *House & Garden* and incorporating his holdings as Condé Nast Publications in 1922, Nast became a symbol of wealth and glamour; just as his magazines instructed eager readers in the art of living well, Nast personified that goal with Gatsbyesque splendor, staging sumptuous Café Society parties in his thirty-room Park Avenue penthouse and cultivating the kind of lavish, peripatetic life-style another generation would describe as jet-set.

Nast had foreseen the importance of being able to single out the most desirable readers: His task was to "bait the editorial pages," he explained, "in such a way as to lift out of all the millions of Americans just the 100,000 cultivated people who can buy these quality goods." His own good fortune was not to last; he lost his money as well as the controlling interest in his company in the crash of 1929. Nast went on to found *Glamour,* aimed at young working women, in 1939, but he died in debt in 1942. Despite his disappointments, he understood that he had made a lasting contribution. Commenting on his long partnership with Edna Woolman Chase, he said, "Think of it. Between us, we have set the standards of the time. We showed America the meaning of style."

While Condé Nast was exerting his influence on the taste of American women, Arnold Gingrich played a comparable role for men at *Esquire,* founded in 1933. Gingrich had begun his journalistic career as the editor of *Apparel Arts,* a fashion magazine, later renamed *Gentleman's Quarterly.* It became so popular that its publishers decided to launch a new men's magazine that would cater to the "new leisure" that was supposed to come with the New Deal. *Esquire*'s salesmen started soliciting ads on the day that President Franklin Roosevelt closed the nation's banks, but Gingrich and his colleagues were undeterred.

Gingrich was nothing if not persistent; when his initial efforts to persuade Ernest Hemingway to submit a certain story to

Robert Rodale, editor of *Organic Gardening* from 1960 to 1990, and son David bike through the magazine's research farm in Allentown, Pennsylvania. Robert took over the editorship from his father, J. I. Rodale, who founded the magazine in 1942. It was one of the first magazines to call attention to the harmful effects of DDT and other pesticides.

Esquire proved unavailing, he continued to badger Hemingway, whom he had met at a bookstore in Chicago. Finally, the exasperated author suggested they decide the matter by seeing who could shoot down the most beer cans. Gingrich, who apparently had never used a gun before, won both the contest and the story. "I guess he was drunker than I was," he later explained. Hemingway, who also gave Gingrich letters of introduction to such well-known writers as Ring Lardner and John Dos Passos, became a regular contributor to the magazine, filing a monthly "Letter from Africa." To apologize for missing one deadline in 1936, he sent Gingrich "The Snows of Kilimanjaro."

Although *Esquire* was originally conceived as a vehicle for men's fashions, Gingrich made it into a veritable literary Who's Who, publishing Sinclair Lewis, William Faulkner, F. Scott Fitzgerald, James Baldwin, John Steinbeck, H. L. Mencken, Dorothy Parker, Tennessee Williams, Truman Capote, Vladimir Nabokov, Malcolm Muggeridge, John Updike, Dwight Macdonald, Saul Bellow, John O'Hara, and Philip Roth, among many others. Gingrich left *Esquire* in 1945 after a falling-out with its publisher, but four years later he was asked to come back; after resuming the editor's job, he became publisher and a vice president in 1952. When he reached the mandatory retirement age of seventy in 1974, Gingrich was named editor-in-chief, and he was designated the "founding editor" in 1976, the year he died. He had revealed the secret of his success eight years earlier, when the Magazine Publishers' Association gave him its highest award for individual achievement in magazine publishing. In his acceptance speech, Gingrich told the audience that the most important attribute for an editor is "a continuing sense of wonder."

As the first modern men's magazine, *Esquire* has had a lasting impact on the field, and although its readers have always included women, its focus has remained resolutely on men. Indeed, notwithstanding a few prominent female editors, the first 200 years of American magazine history were largely about the ideas and efforts of white men. By the middle of the twentieth century, however, a new generation of visionaries was beginning to show America the meaning of diversity.

John Johnson was only six years old when his father, a sawmill worker, was killed in a mill accident, and his mother went to work as a maid to keep her son in school. She raised an ambitious child who would triumph over the barriers of race and poverty to become one of the most successful black busi-

Jayne Mansfield (above) gets *Esquire*'s attention: (from left to right) Arnold Gingrich, John Smart, Fred Birmingham, Abe Blinder, and Sam Ferber.

Serving up elegance and style: Arnold Gingrich, *Esquire*'s founding editor, in his office in 1967 (opposite). Gingrich's magazine helped define the tastes and life-styles of a generation of American men.

Under the editorship of Norman Cousins, *Saturday Review*'s circulation rose from 20,000 in the early forties to 650,000 in the early seventies.

John H. Johnson started his first magazine, *Negro Digest*, with $500 in 1942 and, following its success, launched *Ebony* — "to provide positive images of blacks in a world of negative images" — and *Jet* and *Tan*.

Ebony, 1980.

nessmen in history.

"I don't want to destroy the system; I want to get into it," Johnson said during the militant sixties. He began his publishing career at the age of twenty-four; when bankers, who called him "boy," refused to give him a loan, he used his mother's furniture as collateral for a $500 loan and sent out a mailing of 20,000 letters offering a charter subscription to a new publication called *Negro Digest*. The magazine started out modestly enough in 1942, but the enterprising Johnson scored a major coup when he persuaded Eleanor Roosevelt to write one of a series of articles by white authors called "If I Were a Negro." With Roosevelt's contribution, the *Digest*'s circulation jumped from 50,000 to 150,000 in a single issue.

In 1945, Johnson launched *Ebony*, whose stated goal was "to emphasize the brighter side of Negro life and success." The magazine, which focused on black success stories and viewed its mission as inspirational, became an institution in the black community. Johnson went on to found the magazines *Jet* and *Tan* and to build Johnson Publishing into the nation's largest black-owned company. Along the way, he acquired a cosmetics company, became chairman of Supreme Life Insurance, and amassed a net worth of more than $200 million. Such success did little to soften Johnson's view of race relations in America, where he continued to see "a pattern of discrimination and denial." In 1990, at the age of seventy-two, he told a reporter, "I'm at the top, but not a day goes by without someone reminding me in some way that I am black." Not that that ever stopped him. "When I see a barrier, I cry and I curse," he said, "and then I get a ladder and climb over it."

Many of the magazine industry's modern success stories involve a forward-thinking publisher like Johnson who managed to identify a segment of the marketplace that had previously been ignored. Some latched onto the idea of selling a certain commodity. Hugh Hefner exploited changing sexual mores and an enduring male appetite for pictures of female sex objects to earn a fortune with *Playboy*, and Bob Guccione, quick to imitate Hefner's formula, followed suit with *Penthouse*.

Others tried to sell ideas. Gloria Steinem and Patricia Carbine broke new ground in 1972 with the founding of *Ms.*, a magazine run by women and aimed at an emerging generation influenced by feminist ideas and interested in consciousness-raising as an ongoing experience. (Women had long occupied positions of importance in the magazine business, but they had usually been editors rather than publishers, employees rather

Called the high priestess of fashion, Diana Vreeland (photographed by James H. Karales in 1965) was fashion editor of *Harper's Bazaar* from 1937 to 1962. Then she moved to *Vogue*, which she edited until 1971. "I loathe narcissism," she said, "but I approve of vanity."

Hugh Hefner (photographed in his element by Art Shay in 1961) quit his job in *Esquire*'s circulation department in 1952 and a year later, having raised about $7,000, started *Playboy*.

Playboy, 1964.

than owners.) *Ms.* was, Steinem said, a how-to magazine "for the liberated female human being — not how to make jelly but how to seize control of your life."

Although *Ms.* was quite influential for a number of years, the magazine fell on hard times and in 1990 was transformed into a subscriber-supported bimonthly without advertising. Today, the economics of the magazine business are tougher than ever; start-ups cost millions of dollars, and the attrition rate remains fearsome. General-interest magazines have largely given way to more specialized publications; the trend in recent years has been toward a narrower focus and a targeted audience, whether it be hot-rodders or gourmet cooks or computer hackers. The odds against success haven't improved, and the stakes are higher than they've ever been; even so, the right idea can still make a surprising dent in a market others have dismissed as saturated. As always, there is no substitute for a passionate dreamer with a good idea and the drive to see it realized.

— *Leslie Bennetts*

In 1972, after working as a free-lance journalist, then as a contributing editor and columnist of *New York*, Gloria Steinem (photographed by Jill Krementz) helped start *Ms.* and became its first editor. The premiere issue, she recalls, "was supposed to be on the newsstands for three months, and it sold out in eight days."

Helen Gurley Brown, *Cosmopolitan*'s editor, introduced the "Cosmo" girl for a generation of young readers primed for a new image and sense of themselves.

The Women's Magazine

From the *Lady's Magazine* of 1792 onward, women's magazines have spoken to and for American women about matters of concern to them and the nation at large. When Sarah Josepha Hale became the editor of *Godey's Lady's Book* in 1837, she set the mission for women's magazines: to inform, assist, and advise, and to keep women in touch with each other in a society that believed with Thomas Jefferson that "the tender breasts of ladies were not formed for political convulsion."

Tender, indeed! Always in the thick of the fight, women's magazines in the nineteenth century fought for women's suffrage, abolition, consumer rights, and improvement of working conditions. In the 1850s, the *Ladies' Repository* published a monthly column about news and national events even as it offered advice about homemaking and commitment to family values. In 1906, *The Ladies' Home Journal* pushed for the establishment of the Pure Food and Drug Act; and in 1907, *The Delineator* ran a children's rescue campaign. By the late thirties, *The Ladies' Home Journal* was publishing a column by Dorothy Thompson on political issues; soon after, Eleanor Roosevelt's opinions were appearing in *McCall's*, and Margaret Mead's column on public affairs was running in *Redbook*. *Good Housekeeping* employed a full-time national affairs department.

The covers of nineteenth-century women's magazines were sober and sentimental — witness this 1865 *Peterson's Magazine* cover (above left). By the turn of the century, elegant full-color illustrations were in use, like this 1911 painting of a swimmer by Coles Phillips (above right).

Not surprisingly, from their beginning, women's magazines have championed women's rights. In 1914, six years before U.S. women could vote, *Good Housekeeping* helped the cause by serializing the story of suffragist Emmeline Pankhurst's struggle for the vote in Britain.

By the late nineteenth century, almost all women's magazines had regular columns like this one from an 1890 issue of *The Ladies' World*, which published household hints and recipes.

Godey's Lady's Book is still remembered for fashion engravings like this one, of a slipper pattern, published in 1862. Large crews of women colored early drawings by hand.

The Delineator, competing with McCall's and similar magazines, sold dress patterns. A 1914 issue featured long tunics and low waistlines (above). As the First World War ended, The Woman's Magazine (below) offered sound financial advice.

NOTES AND NOTICES.

VASSAR COLLEGE! ! ! Our first note is one of exclamations, which, fully interpreted, mean that, on the 25th of June last, the Trustees of Vassar College, at their annual meeting, voted unanimously to drop the term "FEMALE" from the title of that Institution! ! !

Therefore, in our gratitude to the Trustees for this true chivalric deed of honor to the NAME OF WOMAN, we give three cheers (exclamations): the other three express our joy that the blot of animality is removed from this great Institution for Young Ladies, and our hope that all similar institutions in our country, having this blot now on their names, will soon follow the good example of VASSAR COLLEGE.

In 1867, Sarah Josepha Hale, Godey's editor, insisted that the term "female" was strictly biological and persuaded Vassar Female College to drop the word from its title. She put this notice in her magazine.

GIVING WOMEN A HEAD FOR BUSINESS

Miss Wylie Teaches the A B C of Finance to War-Workers, Wage-Earners and Home-Makers

BY BLANCHE FENTON

Photo by Champlain Studios, N.Y.

Miss Wylie is founder and director of "The Financial Center for Women," where all ages and classes come for business training

THE idea that a woman has "no head for business" is likely to figure among the notions that will not survive the war. Already in business circles it is being rapidly dispelled. When the call to arms came and men of military age left their desks and packed kits for camp, a number of

They were of the kind that required a quick "turnover," in the language of the Street. Her husband had been a speculator. Locked away from the giddy cavortings of the Market his "securities" were entirely swallowed up. The prudent widow found herself as penniless as the rash one. A little knowledge would have saved both of them.

The present need for women in business, imperative though it is, insists that they shall be trained. The average woman's abysmal ignorance of business is something the average man finds it hard to understand.

"Knowledge of a particular business is acquired by years of slow and perhaps painful growth. Countless details must be assimilated gradually. Any successful business man will tell you that it has taken years to develop the easy familiarity with figures and facts he now has.

"No matter if a woman has been president of her club, no matter if she has run an efficient and economical household, no matter how many college degrees she has

In all the financial Center classes the lessons are not learned; they are done. Notebooks are dispensed with. These business women must be independent; conscious of their knowledge and ability to take responsible positions and do the work required. With the new demand for business comes the demand for

WE'RE FOR CO-ED SCHOOLS...BUT WE'RE NOT

BY TONI TAYLOR
ILLUSTRATED BY HOWARD S. BEDELL

How Is Marriage Changing?

The same vows will be exchanged at the altar, but the problems of marriage will be different in the postwar world

BY PAUL DE KRUIF

Can We Now Fight Syphilis?

Women's magazines are — and always have been — in constant conversation with readers (left). In prefeminist 1945, *Seventeen* pointed out the pros and cons of coeducation. In the same year, *Redbook* told women to "give yourself to your husband and your children." In 1937, *Ladies' Home Journal* published Paul de Kruif's daring argument for fighting syphilis.

Ladies' Home Journal's series "How America Lives" was famous in its time. This 1945 story (below) by Elizabeth Janeway told harsh truths about postwar women. The picture was controversial, too.

VALENTINE NUMBER
WOMAN'S HOME COMPANION
FEBRUARY 1911
FIFTEEN CENTS

THE CROWELL PUBLISHING COMPANY

Woman's Home Companion, under editor Gertrude Battles Lane, gave its readers a mix of fiction, fashion, and food, and started a Better Baby Bureau to arouse interest in child health.

An excellent example of the service women's magazines can provide readers: the Good Housekeeping Institute staff shows the results of recipes it has tested.

By the seventies, when women's magazines were proliferating rapidly, they kept readers informed and involved in such national causes as equal pay for equal work, disarmament, access for women in politics, improved child care, adequate health insurance, a clean environment, racial equality, and the reduction of poverty and homelessness.

In July 1976 and November 1979, in an unprecedented show of cooperation among editors, more than thirty women's magazines, from *Ms.* and *Parents Magazine* to *Better Homes and Gardens* and *Bride's*, published articles simultaneously about the Equal Rights Amendment.

The basic service of women's magazines, however, is and always has been to help women care for themselves and their families. Today, with most women holding one paid job and sometimes two, the service these magazines offer is more vital than ever. The advice, information, and opinions they publish about child care and medicine; beauty, furnishings, and home care; craftwork; money and taxes; health, exercise, and nutrition; male and female relationships; fashion and design and cooking affect the way we live — men and women alike. Because women's magazines affect all of us, because they reach a greater audience than any other group of magazines, and because they represent not only individuals but families, they shape society in ways no other medium can.

— *Sey Chassler*

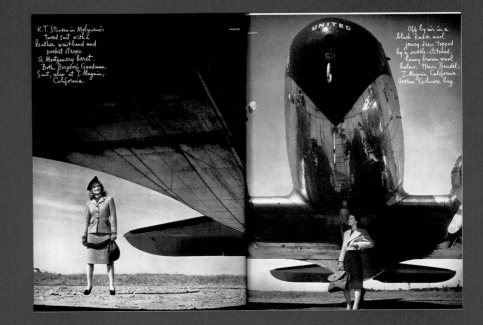

A golden age in magazine design blossomed during the forties, fifties, and sixties. Among the most innovative of art directors was Alexey Brodovitch of *Harper's Bazaar*. The two photographs juxtaposed above, by Martin Munkacsi, appeared in 1944.

Striking cover art was typical of the women's magazines of the twenties and thirties, as shown by the covers above of *The Bride's Magazine* (now simply *Bride's*) and the short-lived *Fashionable Dress*.

During the Second World War, *McCall's*, like many women's magazines, advised those on the home front. This newsletter from 1944 reported on rationing, saving fuel, and paper shortages.

One of the very first store-distributed magazines, *Family Circle* offered a mix of fashion, food and entertainment ideas, and usually a poignant cover to boot — like this one from 1949.

THE CASE OF THE CAMOUFLAGED PIN CURL

Although it appears quaint in the 1990s, *McCall's* solution (above) to the "curler look" was stylish in 1959. Ever practical, *Woman's Day* (left) sold patterns and helped readers save money in 1954.

one blouse — in 5 acts

Only one blouse and four quick-change collars provide a summer blouse collection. Make yours from Woman's Day pattern 5073 — in a heavenly shade of linen or cotton — and you'll be wearing it with literally everything from play shorts to summer evening skirts

MARGARET PARKER GARY
WOMAN'S DAY FASHION DEPARTMENT

1 A scoop-neck blouse plays the leading role in all five acts

2 Scalloped for a softer look.

3 Just a bit of you peeks through

4 Trim and tailored close-up

5 Crisp white in a Puritan collar

For pattern views, mail-order coupons and fabric information, see page 114

In 1950, *Family Circle* — competing in supermarkets with *Woman's Day*, and just as full of commonsense tips — advised women to share work.

FAMILY CIRCLE   OCTOBER 1950

"We whip through our cleaning," says Mrs. Hardinge

When she uses her vacuum with all its attachments, her sons eagerly help, too. Result: Even more time saved

By JESSIE BAKKER

MILLICENT and Franklin Hardinge Jr. of Evanston, Illinois, have shared an unusual marriage for a dozen years. They have been parted much of that time be—cause his work takes him all over the country. And it ... his family along when he travels. ... Frank, who lived in Chi—

"Gimma" holds her daughter's fur coat as the vacuum cleaner removes any loose light fur. Frank needn't fear ... bedding on his dark suit when the couple dines out ...time-consuming interests is knitting, ...eaters. Another is sewing, ...of the boys', and ...Dillon

When *Seventeen* started in 1944, it dared to admit that teenaged girls dated boys. It also was bold enough to say, even in the "uncombed sixties," that neatness counts, as it did in this 1967 fashion shot.

Edward R. Murrow: "One essential function of a woman is to deflate a man"

Maria Schell: "A woman, unlike a man, lives for her image of love"

Redbook published nontraditional features, including this offbeat dialogue in 1961.

WHAT DOES THE AMERICAN MAN EXPECT OF A WIFE?
BY MARGARET MEAD

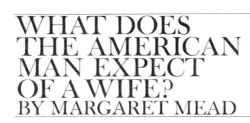

Anthropologist Margaret Mead wrote a *Redbook* column in the early sixties that dealt with everything from politics to marriage (above).

THANKS TO THE EARL OF SANDWICH

It was John Montagu, the fourth Earl of Sandwich, who discovered how much good eating could be tucked between two slices of bread. And wouldn't he be surprised to see the institution his invention has become?

Every day, in this country, thirty million sandwiches, from the tiniest tea size to the magnificent hero long as your arm, are consumed by all ages from kindergarten on. The dozens pictured give you a slight idea!

Our sandwiches on page 46 cover a wide field, too: hot and cold; with one or two or three slices of bread; some to eat soon as ready, some to freeze for future eating. You'll want to hold on to every last recipe.

Just a few tips when you make them: Keep spreads fairly soft. Use ready-sliced bread. Spread with a flexible spatula. Cut a stack of sandwiches at a time. Wrap each sandwich separately, to prevent odors' mingling.

GLAMOUR COLLEGE

THE 10 BEST-DRESSED COLLEGE GIRLS
100 GREAT FALL LOOKS
250 COLLEGE MEN'S ATTITUDES ON SEX AND VIRGINITY
IS STUDENT POWER REALLY MAKING IT?
HIGH SCHOOL INTO COLLEGE MAKE-OVER

More than simply a fashion magazine, *Glamour* has long dealt with social issues. In 1968, it became the first mass-circulation magazine to put a black woman, Katiti Kironde, on the cover (above). *McCall's* art director, Otto Storch, created this 1961 spread (left) of more than 400 sandwiches.

Ms. first appeared in 1972. It became one of the most discussed women's magazines in the world because of articles like the one featured on this 1977 cover.

Tuned to seventies graphics, Ms. was strong visually and intellectually. This 1972 article by Phyllis Chesler was illustrated by Barbara Nessim.

When a man quits his office job to find more fulfilling work or to find himself, it is understood and even admired. When a woman quits her household job for the same reason, it's considered unfeminine, selfish or downright crazy.

by Phyllis Chesler

WOMEN
&
MADNESS

In a 1984 *Woman's Day* reader survey (right) 120,000 women answered unequivocally that they wanted to be heard.

WHAT WOMEN VOTERS REALLY WANT

The results are here: A record-breaking number of you responded—nearly 120,000 impassioned voices speaking from the heart but thinking tough. What you reveal defies every stereotype about how mainstream American women think and makes it clear that women in our country have heartfelt political opinions that they want to be heard. Politicians, watch out!

The Unborn Have No FREEDOM of Choice

ENOUGH!

Abortion It's every woman's right!

I read banned books.

ERA YES

no nukes

In 1970, some 200 women occupied the *Ladies' Home Journal* offices until the editor agreed to publish this feminist section (left).

the new feminism

A SPECIAL SECTION PREPARED FOR THE LADIES' HOME JOURNAL BY THE WOMEN'S LIBERATION MOVEMENT

Hello to Our Sisters

I've often wondered if all rape victims become voyeurs locked into and away from the unbelievable trauma. I've looked at my own denial and I've wondered. Maybe the first step in approaching some understanding of the experience is to see the act behind the word.

THE 30 YEAR RAPE

Nearly 30 years ago, when rape was still a capital "R" felony (the R in rape keeps getting smaller), it happened that a 12-year-old girl came out of a hosiery store on an early Saturday evening onto a busy street in a small town in New Jersey where, without reason or warning, she was punched in the stomach by a young man who waited there. He seemed to her very tall. He forced her through the open door into the backseat of a parked car that held the driver and another male companion in the front and one other male in the backseat. The car took off. Ike and Tina Turner were singing a rhythm-and-blues accompaniment for the ride, which stayed well within the speed limit as the car cruised up and down streets and the streetlights came on. Her 12-year-old neighbors were probably settling down after dinner, after washing dishes, maybe to watch *Captain Video* on the DuMont Television Network. The victim listened to Ike and Tina on the car radio. Throughout her life she would associate Tina Turner with this violent ride through familiar streets during those last minutes of her childhood, when she was held by one man and raped by another.

Her rapist whispered threats about what would happen to her if she told anyone about them, what he would do to her if she told. He shook her shoulders roughly as one sometimes does to get a child's attention. He called her by name. She knew all four men. They were her neighbors. The one whispering in her ear was married, soon to be a father. The heady smell of sweet wine filled the backseat. The shock of it all forever dislodged her from the time fabric of the world of adolescence. She had no thoughts, no opinions, no voice. But she could hear. "Turn on the lights, man," the one who was holding her wrists said. Those were the only words spoken while he held her wrists in his hand over her head, which also rested in his lap. This was no time to get a ticket, so he told the driver: "Turn on the lights." Later that night, she would repeat the words to the detective at the police station. "He kept telling the driver to turn on the lights," she would tell him.

They didn't make her cry. They made her mother and her aunts cry. They made her younger sister cry, but she refused to cry—or to remember. She forgot the incident, locked it away for more than 20 years until it surfaced like one of those detailed instant replays at a football or basketball game. The encysted memory had, however, replayed itself in secret as it shaped the young woman in the girl.

When the details of that evening returned to me, I was in the bathtub almost catatonic with exhaustion. The memory had sprung loose from its trappings during the long process of mourning my mother's death the previous year; I had been defenseless against even small calamities since. Trains that were late and zippers that stuck reduced me to tears, exhaustion, then sleep. I had been hospitalized for "emotional [CONTINUED ON PAGE 96]

BY DORIS JEAN AUSTIN

JANUARY 1991 ESSENCE 59

Along with the food, fashion, and beauty tips, *Essence* gives its 850,000 readers revealing features, like the one above, that probe important personal and social problems.

In 1987, *Sassy* joined *Seventeen*, *YM*, and *Teen* in pursuit of the burgeoning youth market.

Whatever Happened to
GREAT SEX
(and the Single Girl)?

Will Eros survive the counter revolutionary eighties? AIDS, the man shortage, and new-style, go-slow seductions have brought about the drought—yet for the determinedly sexual, this can still be a fertile time!

By Shelley Levitt

When Cynthia thinks about Christmas, she thinks about Berkeley, California, and the winter of 1972. There wasn't a white Christmas in Berkeley then. There never has been. But Christmas will always evoke memories of Berkeley for Cynthia. That's where she spent her most lustful yuletide, if not her most traditional one.

On Christmas Eve, 1972, she and a dozen coworkers who were also transplanted to Berkeley from points east enjoyed a potluck dinner, complete with goose, stuffing, candied apples, and a wicked eggnog. In lieu of mistletoe, sprigs of homegrown marijuana were hung from the ceiling, and couples who found themselves under the "mistletoke" both smooched and smoked. By the end of the evening, a number of red-eyed romances had been born, including one between Cynthia and Jerry, an officemate for whom she'd long felt a keen attraction.

After a lovely, heated morning in bed, Cynthia said good-bye to Jerry, donned a Rudolph the Reindeer costume, and headed out to an offbeat masquerade party. Six hours later, her papier-mâché antlers were lying on her bedroom floor alongside the Santa Claus beard belonging to Eddie, an attractive new acquaintance. "I got just what I wanted for Christmas that year," recalls Cynthia, now a thirty-six-year-old public-relations executive, wife, and mother. "Great sex—and lots of it."

During the good old days of the sexual revolution—a mere decade or so ago—it wasn't unusual for a sexually adventurous woman to acquire the experience of back-to-back trysts, along with a copy of the *Kama Sutra*, a vibrator, and a collection of

Cosmopolitan made sex a hot topic in 1966 and continues to cover it from almost every angle.

87

"Hello, World!"

A sense-by-sense tour of your infant.

By Roberta Israeloff

Just being alive is a sensory experience for infants, who delight in each discovery.

Always alert to issues that affect readers, magazines like *Family Circle* (left) and *Glamour* (right) pull few punches.

Founded in 1926, *Parents Magazine* was one of the first magazines to find a successful niche within the women's market. It is joined today by *Child* and *Parenting*, among others.

Today, all women's magazines report the harsher facts of life. Even teen magazines like YM help clarify issues by exposing the human stories behind the tough news.

New York Woman, wise, witty and sophisticated, found a new approach to readers in 1986 with news, commentary, criticism, and reportage — but no recipes or household hints.

Celebrating Our Fourth Year!

"It's like a nightmare, but it's real."

BY CHRIS PHILLIPS

LIVING IN FEAR

One Girl's Terrifying Tale

Pop, pop, pop. That's what a gunshot sounds like. The noise is like a firecracker. But when you've heard it as many times as I have, you know it's no firecracker. Next you hear the ambulance sirens wailing, and people screaming and crying. It's like a nightmare, but it's real.

I live in Washington, DC, the "murder capital" of the U.S. My neighborhood of rundown row houses is filled with drug dealers and users.

It's like a war zone here.

I hear gun shots all the time. The shoot-outs usually start in the middle of the night. They still startle me. My heart stops.

I *never* go out to see what happened. It's too dangerous. A lot of innocent people have been killed in drug shoot-outs. A bullet doesn't have anybody's name on it. It'll hit me just as soon as it'll hit anybody else.

I'm afraid to go anywhere but to and from school. Sometimes it's dark when I leave school because I stay late for choir practice.

● *In a Washington, DC, drug zone, a 15-year-old boy was shot, execution style, by a 17-year-old. The slaying was over drugs.*

● *In Midlothian, TX, an undercover police officer who posed as a student and became part of the high school drug culture was shot twice through the head. Three students and a 23-year-old woman were charged in the case.*

● *In "Crack Heaven," a three-block area in Brooklyn, NY, children grow up under a reign of "narco-terror" while drug dealers shoot it out with each other to command street corners.*

Drugs have now infiltrated every part of the country, from middle-class suburbs to gang-plagued low-income neighborhoods to rural townships. To give you a close-up look at the toll drugs have taken on our neighborhoods, YM talked to Tania Lumpkin, a 20-year-old senior at Eastern High School, a tough inner city high school in northeast Washington, DC. Tania lives near school, in the middle of one of the worst drug-scourged neighborhoods in the nation. Here, in her own words, is the nightmare of drugs and despair she must face every day:

I run home as fast as I can.

The only other time I ever go outside my home is to go to the carry-out to get a burger. I have to pass a lot of drug dealers along the way. They'll ask me if I want to buy a "20-rock" or a "50-rock" — a $20 or $50

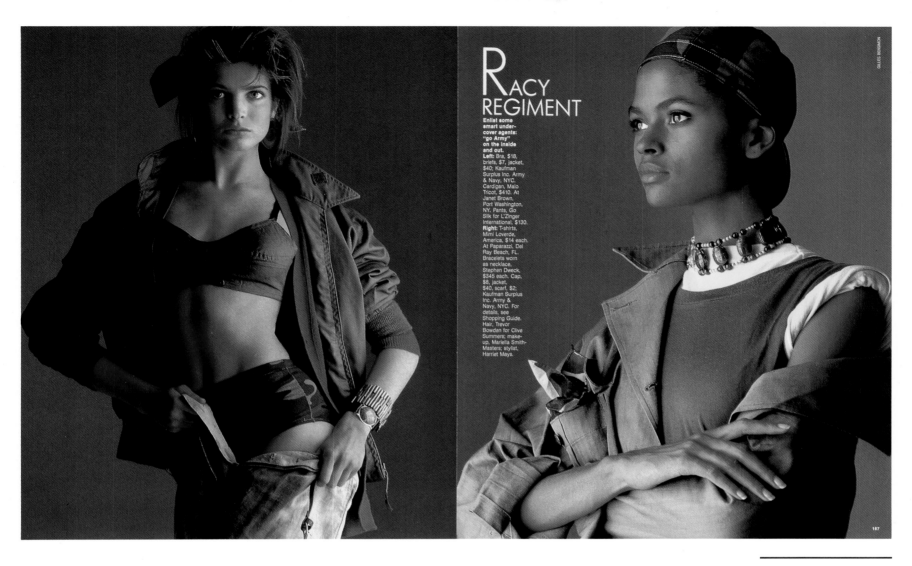

GILLES BENSIMON

Racy Regiment

Enlist some smart under-cover agents: "go Army" on the inside and out. **Left:** Bra, $18, briefs, $7, jacket, $40; Kaufman Surplus Inc. Army & Navy, NYC. Cardigan, Malo Tricot. At Janet Brown, Port Washington, NY. Pants, Go Silk for L'Zinger International, $130. **Right:** T-shirts, Mimi Loverde, America, $14 each. At Paparazzi, Del Ray Beach, FL. Bracelets worn as necklace, Stephen Dweck, $345 each. Cap, $8, jacket, $40, scarf, $2; Kaufman Surplus Inc. Army & Navy, NYC. For details, see Shopping Guide. Hair, Trevor Bowden for Clive Summers; make-up, Mariella Smith-Masters; stylist, Harriet Mays.

187

Elle, a French import with innovative graphics, design and photography — like this spread by Gilles Bensimon — burst on the scene in 1985 to challenge the U.S. fashion magazines.

In 1988, *Vogue* banished its slim goddesses for a twenty-first century U.S. ideal: the sexy, healthy, rebellious, active — and happy — woman.

With forceful graphics and elegant fashion photography, *Mirabella* debuted in 1989 with a new kind of service journalism for affluent women.

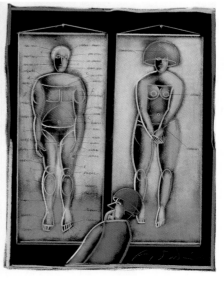

AUGUST

Metropolitan

Midsummer
Fiction
Number

20¢

Rolf Armstrong

The Imagined World

FICTION IN THE MAGAZINE

Mark Twain at the writer's desk in a 1911 silhouette inset from *The Ladies' Home Journal* (above).

Booth Tarkington's novel *The Magnificent Ambersons* was featured in this 1918 *Metropolitan* (opposite).

For two and a half centuries now, fiction and American magazines have managed to go along together, despite dire predictions for both. Time and again, as innovations came along — the car, radio, television — it was thought that each would decrease reading to such a degree that magazines would be put out of business. That hasn't happened, but the way magazines are read *has* changed drastically: These days, magazines are seldom read for entertainment of a narrative sort.

Fiction has always been more exploited than exalted in America's popular magazines. Short stories and serialized novels have served as adornments, come-ons, or concessions; have been dismissed as frivolous (and, in the old days, derided as "feminine") compared with what the best editors of our best magazines over the years usually considered their "serious" purposes: to inform, perhaps even to *re*form (in muckraking exposés), to educate and instruct, to influence, to guide, to provide service to the readers, whether for the home or office.

The good news is that, despite such editorial prejudices, an extraordinary amount of extraordinarily fine fiction has been published in American magazines over the years — although some of it appeared in very odd places. And there have been at least two long episodes in which individual magazines and their fiction managed to make a harmonious match.

From the very beginning — from, that is, the days when Ben Franklin and Andrew Bradford both claimed to have started the first American magazine, in Philadelphia, through Boston's newspaper-like quickies, to four-pagers like *The Independent Reflector* (1752) and *The Instructor* (1755), in New York City — the tone of magazines has been didactic and essayistic. News was for newspapers; essays were for magazines. Meanwhile, anything of a literary nature tended to be British — either just clipped and pasted from English periodicals or blatantly imitated.

For most of the magazines that came and went in America during the nineteenth century, literature in general and fiction in particular was merely an adjunct to their main functions. This was true even of magazines edited specifically for women, whose editors seem to have assumed that their readers were more interested in cooking and dress patterns and home decorating than in fiction. As a rule, the magazines started by book publishers serialized their own list of mostly foreign authors: *Appletons' Journal*'s serials were by British, French, and German novelists; *Harper's New Monthly Magazine* published Dickens

For years, many American magazines simply pirated British fiction. Here, *Harper's Weekly* boasts of having paid Charles Dickens $5,000 for reprint rights to *A Tale of Two Cities* in 1859.

and Thackeray and Hardy and Trollope; *Lippincott's Magazine* would sometimes do a novel complete in one issue, like Oscar Wilde's *The Picture of Dorian Gray* and Rudyard Kipling's *The Light That Failed*. None of these big magazines seems to have been much interested in the literary fiction of native authors like Washington Irving, Nathaniel Hawthorne, Herman Melville, or Edgar Allan Poe — although a magazine called *Graham's Magazine* did publish Poe's first detective story, "The Murders in the Rue Morgue," in 1841.

So, by and large, it was still mostly British Lit through the century, and even that was published what you might call sideways. There was a periodical called *Munsey's Magazine*, for instance, that sold sensationally in the 1890s, possibly because it displayed undressed female statuary, possibly because it sold for just ten cents. When it began to decline, after 1920, *Munsey's* started publishing a whole novel in every issue, to try to revive interest. But even the talents of Joseph Conrad, Arnold Bennett, P. G. Wodehouse, and George Barr McCutcheon (the author of the serialized novel *Graustark*) failed to do the job, and *Munsey's* passed away in 1929.

Another ten-cent publication, *McClure's Magazine*, published short stories by Thomas Hardy and Stephen Crane, and Kipling's *Captains Courageous*. What made *McClure's* famous, however, was not its fiction but the great pieces of muckraking it commissioned — notably, Lincoln Steffens's articles that were published in book form as *The Shame of the Cities* and Ida Tarbell's history of the Standard Oil Company. Still another of the big magazines around the turn of the century, the old *Cosmopolitan*, started serializing Tolstoy's last novel, *Resurrection*, deleting parts considered offensive, until finally the editors found the whole thing distasteful and dropped the project. Editors have always loved famous names (like Tolstoy), but the idea of putting the names of famous contributors on the cover apparently originated with George Graham, who paid big money for big names for his *Graham's Magazine*. His astuteness had its limits, however. Graham managed to put his magazine out of business in 1853 by writing a strongly negative review of *Uncle Tom's Cabin*. Harriet Beecher Stowe's sensationally successful and influential novel had been serialized the year before in an abolitionist journal called *The National Era* — a clear, if rare, example of how a work of fiction can serve a magazine's editorial purposes.

Between the Civil War and the turn of the century, changes in postal rates and innovations in printing processes encour-

SAMUEL L. CLEMENS (MARK TWAIN).

PUDD'NHEAD WILSON

A TALE BY MARK TWAIN

THERE is no character, howsoever good and fine, but it can be destroyed by ridicule, howsoever poor and witless. Observe the ass, for instance: his character is about perfect, he is the choicest spirit among all the humbler animals, yet see what ridicule has brought him to. Instead of feeling complimented when we are called an ass, we are left in doubt.— *Pudd'nhead Wilson's Calendar.*

A WHISPER TO THE READER.

A PERSON who is ignorant of legal matters is always liable to make mistakes when he tries to photograph a court scene with his pen; and so I was not willing to let the law chapters in this book go to press without first subjecting them to rigid and exhausting revision and correction by a trained barrister — if that is what they are called. These chapters are right, now, in every detail, for they were rewritten under the immediate eye of William Hicks, who studied law part of a while in southwest Missouri thirty-five years ago and then came over here to Florence for his health and is still helping for exercise and board in Macaroni Vermicelli's horse-feed shed which is up the back alley as you turn around the corner out of the Piazza del Duomo just beyond the house where that stone that Dante used to sit on six hundred years ago is let into the wall when he let on to be watching them build Giotto's campanile and yet always got tired looking as soon as Beatrice passed along on her way to get a chunk of chestnut cake to defend herself with in case of a Ghibelline outbreak before she got to school, at the same old stand where they sell the same old cake to this day and it is just as light and good as it was then, too, and this is not flattery, far from it. He was a little rusty on his law, but he rubbed up for this book, and those two or three legal chapters are right and straight, now. He told me so himself.

Given under my hand this second day of January, 1893, at the Villa Viviani, village of Settignano, three miles back of Florence, on the hills—the same certainly affording the most charming view to be found on this planet, and with it the most dream-like and enchanting sunsets to be found in any planet or even in any solar system—and given, too, in the swell room of the house, with the busts of Cerretani senators and other grandees of this line looking approvingly down upon me as they used to look down upon Dante, and mutely asking me to adopt them into my family, which I do with pleasure, for my remotest ancestors are but spring chickens compared with these robed and stately antiques, and it will be a great and satisfying lift for me, that six hundred years will.

Mark Twain.

CHAPTER I.

TELL the truth or trump —but get the trick.— *Pudd'nhead Wilson's Calendar.*

THE scene of this chronicle is the town of Dawson's Landing, on the Missouri side of the Mississippi, half a day's journey, per steamboat, below St. Louis.

In 1830 it was a snug little collection of modest one- and two-story frame dwellings whose whitewashed exteriors were almost concealed from sight by climbing tangles of rose-vines, honeysuckles and morning-glories. Each of these pretty homes had a garden in front fenced with white palings and opulently stocked with hollyhocks, marigolds, touch-me-nots, prince's-feathers and other old-fashioned flowers; while on the window-sills of the houses

stood wooden boxes containing moss-rose plants and terra-cotta pots in which grew a breed of geranium whose spread of intensely red blossoms accented the prevailing pink tint of the rose-clad house-front like an explosion of flame. When there was room on the ledge outside of the pots and boxes for a cat, the cat was there—in sunny weather—stretched at full length, asleep and blissful, with her furry belly to the sun and a paw curved over her nose. Then that house was complete, and its contentment and peace were made manifest to the world by this symbol, whose testimony is infallible. A home without a cat — and a well-fed, well-petted and properly revered cat—may be a perfect home, perhaps, but how can it prove title?

All along the streets, on both sides, at the

Mark Twain wrote this tale in 1893 for *The Century*, which started life as *Scribner's Monthly.* Other illustrious contributors were Jules Verne, Rudyard Kipling, and Henry James.

Appletons' Journal was launched in 1869 by a publishing house and offered a mixed bag of fact and fiction during its twelve-year existence.

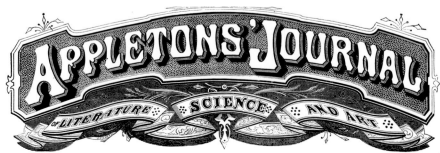

THE NATIONAL ERA.

L. P. NOBLE, PUBLISHER.   G. BAILEY, JUN., EDITOR; JOHN G. WHITTIER, CORRESPONDING EDITOR.   BUELL & BLANCHARD, PRINTERS.

VOL. II.   WASHINGTON, THURSDAY, JANUARY 27, 1848.   NO. 56.

From 1847 to 1860, poet John Greenleaf Whittier served as corresponding editor of *The National Era* (above), which published fiction by Nathaniel Hawthorne and Harriet Beecher Stowe, among others.

Rudyard Kipling's first "Just So" story was published in *The Ladies' Home Journal* in 1900; this one (opposite) ran a year later.

The National Era is best remembered as the abolitionist journal that in the 1850s serialized *Uncle Tom's Cabin*, by Harriet Beecher Stowe (below).

aged the proliferation of magazines; it has been estimated that more than fifty were nationally known and that some had a circulation of more than 100,000. They attracted national advertisers whose considerable expenditures made possible an even lower purchase price — ten or fifteen cents per copy — which in turn brought even greater readership and the emergence of a nationwide audience. The time was ripe for *The Saturday Evening Post*, selling for a nickel a copy, to become the nation's magazine.

The *Post* had come a long and wobbly way since its start in 1821 in the same printer's shop — legend has it — where Ben Franklin's 1728 newspaper, *Pennsylvania Gazette*, had been produced. By 1897, when Cyrus Curtis bought it for $1,000, it was on its last legs — in Irvin Cobb's words, "an elderly and indisposed magazine." Curtis infused it with a lot of the money he had made from *The Ladies' Home Journal*, and in 1899 he gave the editorship to a young man named George Horace Lorimer, who proved to be just what the doctor ordered. When Lorimer took over, only a few thousand people read the *Post*; when he retired thirty-eight years later, circulation stood at three million with a total readership of at least ten million. It was the largest weekly magazine the world had ever known.

"In every number," Lorimer wrote, "stories unite with the *Post*'s editorials and articles to portray American life." Indeed, everything in this remarkable magazine — from the Norman Rockwell covers to the illustrations for its articles and fiction — worked together to express and affirm Lorimer's conservative, complacent, small-town view of what America was or should be.

Post fiction was popular. Not made up of Victorian "classics" imported from England. Not written by big names to try to sell

THE LADIES' HOME JOURNAL

Vol. XVIII, No. 11   PHILADELPHIA, OCTOBER 1901   YEARLY SUBSCRIPTIONS, ONE DOLLAR
SINGLE COPIES, TEN CENTS

HOW THE LEOPARD GOT HIS SPOTS

BY RUDYARD KIPLING

Author of "The Jungle Book," "The Day's Work," "Kim," etc.

ILLUSTRATED BY FRANK VERBECK

IN THE days when everybody started fair, Best Beloved, the Leopard lived in a place called the High Veldt. 'Member it wasn't the Low Veldt, or the Bush Veldt, or the Sour Veldt, but the 'sclusively bare hot shiny High Veldt, where there was sand and sandy-colored rock and 'sclusively tufts of sandy-yellowish grass. The Giraffe and the Zebra and the Eland and the Koodoo and the Hartebeest lived there and they were 'sclusively sandy-yellow-brownish all over; but the Leopard, he was the 'sclusivest sandiest-yellowest-brownest of them all—a grayish-yellowish, catty-shaped kind of beast, and he matched the 'sclusively yellowish-grayish-brownish color of the High Veldt to one hair. That was very bad for the Giraffe and the Zebra and the rest of them; for he would lie down by a 'sclusively yellowish-grayish-brownish stone or clump of grass, and when the Giraffe or the Zebra or the Eland or the Koodoo or the Bush-Buck or the Bonte Buck came by he would surprise them out of their jumpsome lives. And, also, there was an Ethiopian with bows and arrows (a 'sclusively grayish-brownish-yellowish man he was then), who lived on the High Veldt with the Leopard: and the two used to hunt together—the Ethiopian with his bows and arrows, and the Leopard 'sclusively with his teeth and claws—till the Giraffe and the Eland and the Koodoo and the Quagga and all the rest of them didn't know which way to jump, Best Beloved. They didn't indeed.

After a long time—people lived for ever so long in those days—they learned to avoid anything that looked like a Leopard or an Ethiopian; and bit by bit—the Giraffe began it—(his legs were longest) they went away from the High Veldt. They scuttled for days and days till they came to a great forest, 'sclusively full of trees and bushes and stripy, speckly, patchy shadows, and there they hid: and after another long time, what with standing half in the shade and half out of it, and what with the slippery-slidy shadows of the trees falling on them, the Giraffe grew blotchy and the Zebra grew stripy and the Eland and the Koodoo grew darker with little gray lines on their backs like bark on a tree-trunk; and though you could hear them and smell them you could very seldom see them, and then only when you knew precisely where to look. They had a beautiful time in the 'sclusively speckly-spickly shadows of the forest, while the Leopard and the Ethiopian ran about all over

the 'sclusively grayish-yellowish-reddish High Veldt wondering where all their breakfasts and their dinners and their teas had gone. At last they were so hungry that they ate rats and beetles and rock-rabbits, the Leopard and the Ethiopian, and then they had big tummy-ache, and then

"AND THE TWO USED TO HUNT TOGETHER"

they met Baviaan—the dog-headed barking Baboon, who is quite the wisest animal in all South Africa.

Said Leopard to Baviaan (and it was a very hot day): "Where has all the game gone?"

And Baviaan winked. *He* knew.

Said the Ethiopian to Baviaan: "Can you tell me the present habitat of the aboriginal Fauna?"

And Baviaan winked. *He* knew.

Then said Baviaan: "The game has gone into other spots, and my advice to you, Leopard, is to go into other spots as soon as you can."

And the Ethiopian said: "That is all very fine but I wish to know whither the aboriginal Fauna has migrated."

Then said Baviaan: "The aboriginal Fauna has joined the aboriginal Flora because it was high time for a change; and my advice to you, Ethiopian, is to change as soon as you can."

That puzzled the Leopard and the Ethiopian, but they set off to look for the aboriginal Flora, and presently, after ever so many days, they saw a great, high, tall forest full of tree-trunks all 'sclusively speckled and dotted and splashed and slashed and hatched and cross-hatched with shadows.

"What is this," said the Leopard, "that is so 'sclusively dark and so full of little pieces of light?"

"I don't know," said the Ethiopian, "but it ought to be the aboriginal Flora. I can smell Giraffe and I can hear Giraffe, but I can't see Giraffe."

"That's curious," said the Leopard. "I suppose it is because we have just come in out of the sunshine. I can smell Zebra and I can hear Zebra, but I can't see Zebra."

"Wait a bit," said the Ethiopian. "It's a long time since we've hunted 'em. Perhaps we've forgotten what they were like."

"Fiddle!" said the Leopard. "I remember them perfectly on the High Veldt, especially their marrow-bones. Giraffe is about seventeen feet high, of a 'sclusively fulvous golden-yellow from head to heel; and Zebra is about four and a half feet high of a 'sclusively gray-fawn color from head to heel."

"Umm," said the Ethiopian, looking into the speckly-spickly shadows of the aboriginal Flora. "Then they ought to show up in this dark place like ripe bananas in a smoke-house."

But they didn't. The Leopard and the Ethiopian hunted all day, and though they could smell them and hear them they never saw one of them.

"For goodness sake," said the Leopard at tea-time, "let us wait till it gets dark. This daylight hunting is a perfect scandal."

So they waited till dark and then the Leopard heard something breathing sniffily in the starlight that fell all stripy through the branches: and he jumped in the

"WHAT HAVE YOU AT YOUR END OF THE TABLE, BROTHER?"

"WHEREVER THE FIVE FINGERS TOUCHED THEY LEFT FIVE LITTLE BLACK MARKS"

For decades, *The Saturday Evening Post* provided millions of readers with a treasure trove of popular fiction — more than 200 short stories a year, plus novels and novellas (above). The *Post* was also giving members of its famous roster of writers special billing (below).

extra copies. Not highbrow, to improve the magazine's image for the advertisers or to upgrade the readership demographics. But truly popular, the way a song is when it sweeps the nation. Popular the way radio became for a while when the whole country tuned in to hear Jack Benny every Sunday night. Popular the way television came to be. *The Saturday Evening Post's* weekly editorial package of features, fiction, service, humor, and reportage, in fact, very much resembled the format (or formula) for a week of network programming. The *Post* represented perhaps the first example of what came to be known as mass culture.

And, Lord, there was a lot of it, just the way there is of television. One historian of the magazine counted for the year 1924 alone: twenty-one serialized novels, eleven novelettes, and more than two hundred short stories. Lorimer had the idea of assembling a group of regulars, writers who would sometimes contribute articles, sometimes stories. This created a coherence of tone and attitude. Although big-name writers, as different as F. Scott Fitzgerald and Booth Tarkington, often wrote for the *Post*, they weren't part of the permanent team. The regular contributors created characters who reappeared, over the weeks

and months and years, sometimes in short stories, sometimes in novelettes, and sometimes in serialized full-length novels.

There were the dog stories of Albert Payson Terhune. There were Octavus Roy Cohen's stories about urban blacks, lovable and comic. There were P. G. Wodehouse stories and novels about Jeeves and the whole Blandings Castle crew. There were the Tugboat Annie stories, by Norman Reilly Raine. There were boy-meets-girl stories by any number of writers. There were stories about Perry Mason, Mr. Tutt, Mr. Glencannon, Mr. Moto, Scattergood Baines, and a raft of other beloved characters, including the devilish Alexander Botts, ace salesman for the Earthworm Tractor Company. Millions may still remember these stories at least faintly; only trivia experts could tell you the authors' names.

Eventually this whole system of popular entertainment was translated to television — mysteries, Westerns, buddy dramas, family comedies, Lassie — the whole ball of cotton candy was taken right over. It's odd, and sad, that the TV sitcoms and series dramas of the past live on from generation to generation in reruns; but the memory of once oh-so-beloved magazine fiction fades, both with the aging individual readers and with the culture as a whole, and will disappear entirely in time.

The *Post* went to its heavenly reward in 1969, to be followed in quick succession by the two remaining general-interest, mass-audience magazines — *Look* in 1971, *Life* in 1972. *Collier's* had folded in 1957. Like the *Post*, *Collier's* — founded in 1888 — published fiction. One of the first serials to appear in its pages was Henry James's *The Turn of the Screw* (can you believe it?). Editorial concern at *Collier's* turned for a time to muckraking until, in 1924, its editor at the time, William Chenery, declared that fiction was "the backbone of mass circulation." It was nice of him to say it, and although he published Sinclair Lewis and Willa Cather, mostly it was slick stuff — Mary Roberts Rinehart mysteries, Zane Grey Westerns, and Fu Manchu serials.

Thanks to *Collier's* and the *Post*, a huge audience read a huge amount of fiction — perhaps a thousand short stories a year. Even if the overwhelming majority of what they published was formulaic stuff — what used to be called "magazine fiction" — one nevertheless has to lament its demise, if only as a training ground now lost to young, aspiring writers. Not to mention the loss (to television) of new young readers.

In the years since the Second World War, the role of fiction in magazines has declined substantially. During the war,

It lasted only a decade — from 1925 to 1935 — but while it flourished, *The Golden Book Magazine* was a gem (top). Willa Cather, Ring Lardner, "Saki," and Sherwood Anderson all appeared in its pages. *Collier's*, like *The Saturday Evening Post*, churned out fiction for a huge readership — more than three million in the forties (above).

Editorial Bulletin

Saturday, April 25, 1908

"You all did see that on the Lupercal
I thrice presented him a kingly crown,
Which he did thrice refuse."—Julius Cæsar.

Mr. Shaw Refuses

An entertaining aftermath of our quarterly fiction awards is the following, recently received from Mr. G. Bernard Shaw, whose story, "Aerial Football—The New Game," was printed in Collier's for November 23, 1907 (Thanksgiving Number):

"*10 Adelphi Terrace, W. C.*
"*14th March, 1908.*

"EDITOR COLLIER'S:

"DEAR SIR.—What do you mean by this unspeakable outrage? You send me a cheque for a thousand dollars, and inform me that it is a bonus offered by Messrs. P. F. Collier & Son for the best story received during the quarter in which my contribution appeared. May I ask what Messrs. P. F. Collier & Son expected my story to be? If it were not the best they could get for the price they were prepared to pay, they had no right to insert it at all. If it was the best, what right have they to stamp their other contributors publicly as inferior when they have taken steps to secure the result beforehand by paying a special price to a special writer? And what right have they to assume that I want to be paid twice over for my work, or that I am in the habit of accepting bonuses and competing for prizes?

"Waiving all these questions for a moment, I have another one to put to you. How do Messrs. P. F. Collier & Son know that my story was the best they received during the quarter? Are they posterity? Are they the Verdict of History? Have they even the very doubtful qualification of being professional critics?

"I had better break this letter off lest I should be betrayed into expressing myself as strongly as I feel.

"I return the cheque. If you should see fit to use it for the purpose of erecting a tombstone to Messrs. P. F. Collier & Son, I shall be happy to contribute the epitaph, in which I shall do my best to do justice to their monstrous presumption.

"Yours faithfully,
"(Signed) G. BERNARD SHAW."

Happy Mr. Shaw, at one stroke thus to disburthen your mind of its Olympian scorn and your purse of our unwelcome thousand. To what noble uses shall that now historic check be put? Shall it go toward the erection of a Shaw-Shakespeare Memorial at Stratford? Or for the foundation of the Shaw Chair of Advertising at Oxford? Or shall we lay it by against the day when our impatient readers clamor for more Shaw and we are compelled (with a reluctance only known to publishers) again to pay "a special price to a special writer"? However, you must be right about "Aerial Football—The New Game." The awarding of that offensive thousand to your story was a mistake. It will not occur again. The responsible "readers" for that quarter were out of town, and the verdict lay with the Sporting Editor, who happens to be a devotee of Football, a Vegetarian, a Socialist, a Misanthrope, a Misogynist, in short, a true disciple of the incomparable G. B. S. You will be glad to know that the young man has been discharged, and that a portion of that contemned "bonus" will be devoted to the support of his family and his own education in a correspondence school of advertising.

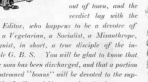

Not your average free-lance writer. George Bernard Shaw let his *Collier's* editors know what he thought of getting special payment for his literary efforts and they responded in this exchange of letters.

Collier's, the *Post,* and other magazines turned away from fiction, choosing instead to report extensively from the battlefield. After the war, many of the magazines that had published fiction went out of business; some of those that previously published fiction dropped it; and most of the new magazines decided not to publish fiction in the first place. Practically none of the postwar magazines were general-interest — that is, designed for both men and women and not about a single particular subject.

Holiday, for example, was a special-interest magazine devoted to travel. Launched by the Curtis Publishing Company in March 1946, it published literary authors of great renown but did not publish fiction — a policy that seems to have been adopted by the various travel and leisure magazines that followed. *Sports Illustrated,* launched by Time Inc. in August 1954, seldom if ever published fiction. In all the wild proliferation of so-called city magazines inspired by Clay Felker's *New York,* very few have published fiction. Fiction about travel or sports, or stories set in the cities the magazine represents, would seem a logical supplement to the regular editorial mix. But we have no fiction about "Brides," no stories about "Outdoors" or "Tennis" or "Motor Boating" or any other interest that isn't "general."

Of the general-interest magazines that survive, none are "mass audience" in the sense that *Collier's* and the old *Saturday Evening Post* were. But luckily, three still publish fiction to some degree: *Harper's Magazine, The Atlantic,* and, most important, because it is a weekly, *The New Yorker.*

For decades, *The New Yorker* has run two short stories in most issues, stories that are more or less literary. *New Yorker* fiction has not been in the American grain of realism and naturalism. Hemingway, Faulkner, and Fitzgerald, for instance, were never published in *The New Yorker* (and were probably not wanted there anyway), nor were most of the American writers of the twentieth century now considered "major." Its fiction has been sophisticated and very popular: In 1941, four comedies based on *New Yorker* material — *Pal Joey, Life With Father, My Sister Eileen,* and *Mr. and Mrs. North* — were all running on Broadway at the same time. There were admittedly years when the memoirish upper-class fiction seemed not to be stories with proper beginnings and middles, and many readers (careless ones, mostly) may have missed the sense of a real ending. But authors appeared — John Cheever and John Updike preeminently — who by the magic of their language

Among the magazines that carried fiction early in the century were *The Munsey, The Blue Book,* and *Ainslee's Magazine,* which called itself "A Magazine of Clever Fiction."

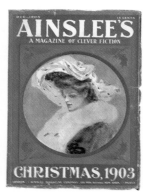

One of the most prolific writers of magazine fiction during the first half of the twentieth century was Booth Tarkington, whose fiction won him two Pulitzer Prizes.

Painting by C. E. Chambers   *Illustration for "The Turmoil"*

THE HOME-COMING OF BIBBS

HARPER'S MAGAZINE

Vol. CXXIX   AUGUST, 1914   No. DCCLXXI

The Turmoil

A NOVEL

BY BOOTH TARKINGTON

CHAPTER I

THERE is a midland city in the heart of fair, open country, a dirty and wonderful city nesting dingily in the fog of its own smoke. The stranger must feel the dirt before he feels the wonder, for the dirt will be upon him instantly. It will be upon him and within him, since he must breathe it, and he may care for no further proof that wealth is here better loved than cleanliness, but whether he cares or not, the negligently tended streets incessantly press home the point, and so do the flecked and grimy citizens. At a breeze he must smother in whirlpools of dust, and if he should decline at any time to inhale the smoke he has the meager alternative of suicide.

The smoke is like the bad breath of a giant panting for more and more riches. He gets them and pants the fiercer, smelling and swelling prodigiously. He has a voice, a hoarse voice, hot and rapacious, trained to one tune: "Wealth! I will get Wealth! I will make Wealth! I will sell Wealth for more Wealth! My house shall be dirty, my garment shall be dirty, and I will foul my neighbor so that he cannot be clean—but I will get Wealth! There shall be no clean thing about me: my wife shall be dirty and my child shall be dirty, but I will get Wealth!" And yet it is not wealth that he is so greedy for: what the giant really wants is hasty riches. To get these he squanders wealth upon the four winds, for wealth is in the smoke.

Not quite so long ago as a generation there was no panting giant here, no heaving, grimy city; there was but a pleasant big town of neighborly people who had understanding of one another, being, on the whole, much of the same type. It was a leisurely and kindly place—"homelike," it was called—and when the visitor had been taken through the State Asylum for the Insane and made to appreciate the view of the cemetery from a little hill, his host's duty as Baedeker was done. The good burghers were given to jogging comfortably about in phaetons or in surreys for a family drive on Sunday. No one was very rich; few were very poor; the air was clean and there was time to live.

But there was a spirit abroad in the

THE Old Man
AND THE Sea

by Ernest Hemingway

He was an old man who fished alone in a skiff in the Gulf Stream and he had gone eighty-four days now without taking a fish. In the first forty days a boy had been with him. But after forty days without a fish the boy's parents had told him that the old man was now definitely and finally *salao*, which is the worst form of unlucky, and the boy had gone at their orders in another boat which caught three good fish the first week. It made the boy sad to see the old man come in each day with his skiff empty and he always went down to help him carry either the coiled lines or the gaff and harpoon and the sail that was furled around the mast. The sail was patched with flour sacks and, furled, it looked like the flag of permanent defeat.

The old man was thin and gaunt with deep wrinkles in the back of his neck. The brown blotches of the benevolent skin cancer the sun brings from its reflection on the tropic sea were on his cheeks. The blotches ran well down the sides of his face and his hands had the deep-creased scars from handling heavy fish on the cords. But none of these scars were fresh. They were as old as erosions in a fishless desert.

Everything about him was old except his eyes and they were the same color as the sea and were cheerful and undefeated.

"Santiago," the boy said to him as they climbed the bank from where the skiff was hauled up. "I could go with you again. We've made some money."

The old man had taught the boy to fish and the boy loved him.

"No," the old man said. "You're with a lucky boat. Stay with them."

"But remember how you went eighty-seven days without fish and then we caught big ones every day for three weeks."

"I remember," the old man said. "I know you did not leave me because you doubted."

"It was papa made me leave. I am a boy and I must obey him."

"I know," the old man said. "It is quite normal."

"He hasn't much faith."

"No," the old man said. "But we have. Haven't we?"

"Yes," the boy said. "Can I offer you a beer on the Terrace and then we'll take the stuff home."

"Why not?" the old man said. "Between fishermen."

They sat on the Terrace and many of the fishermen made fun of the old man and he was not angry. Others, of the older fishermen, looked at him and were sad. But they did not show it and they spoke politely about the current and the depths they had drifted their lines at and the steady good weather and of what they had seen. The successful fishermen of that day were already in and had butchered their marlin out and carried them laid full length across two planks, with two men staggering at the end of each plank, to the fish house where they waited for the ice truck to carry them to the market in Havana. Those who had caught sharks had taken them to the shark factory on the other side of the cove where they were hoisted on a block and tackle, their livers removed, their fins cut off and their hides skinned out and their flesh cut into strips for salting.

When the wind was in the east a smell came across the harbour from the shark factory; but today there was only the faint edge of the odour because the wind had backed into the north and then dropped off and it was pleasant and sunny on the Terrace.

"Santiago," the boy said.

"Yes," the old man said. He was holding his glass and thinking of many years ago.

"Can I go out to get sardines for you for tomorrow?"

"No. Go and play baseball. I can still row and Rogelio will throw the net."

"I would like to go. If I cannot fish with you, I would like to serve in some way."

"You bought me a beer," the old man said. "You are already a man."

THE AUTHOR is shown at a Cuban fishing village like the one used by the "old man" of his story.

35

In 1952, *Life* proudly presented Hemingway's powerful new novella. The author's fame played no small part in the editors' decision to take this plunge into fiction.

were able to transmute accounts of suburban-exurban goings-on into literary art of great beauty. Then, too, there were the Glass-family stories of J. D. Salinger and the innovative fiction of Donald Barthelme. To put it simply: A lot of *New Yorker* fiction had a sameness about it — unless it didn't, in which case it was likely to be very different and really remarkable.

Much of the regular fiction for *The New Yorker*, though, was (and to a lesser degree still is) produced in much the same way as at the old *Saturday Evening Post* — it was written by a group of writers close to the editors, almost a coterie, familiar with the magazine's needs and modes, who would sometimes contribute fiction and sometimes nonfiction. Many of these writers were staff members, or on some sort of retainer or drawing account. In this way the magazine's "voice" was set and perpetuated. Fiction "fit" in *The New Yorker* just as it had in *The Saturday Evening Post* in its glory years.

Harper's and *The Atlantic* are the other two general-interest magazines that still publish fiction. Both, of course, have venerable literary traditions. *Harper's New Monthly Magazine*, begun in 1850, published all the great British writers from its very inception — Dickens, Thackeray, Eliot, Hardy, Trollope, and so on. It was called "a great foreign magazine" but went on to run fiction by Mark Twain, Bret Harte, Stephen Crane, and others. *The Atlantic Monthly*, established in 1857 in Boston, began with all the great New England authors — Emerson, Hawthorne, Longfellow, Oliver Wendell Holmes, Whittier, Thoreau. Later, it too published pieces by Mark Twain, as well as fiction by Hemingway (the boxing story "Fifty Grand" was his first appearance in a national magazine), Welty, Saroyan, Faulkner, and a host of others.

To their credit, both magazines have retained fiction throughout their comparatively long lives. *The Atlantic* is especially conscientious in regularly publishing short stories, often by new writers, whom it occasionally puts in print for the first time, with its "*Atlantic* First" series.

Neither monthly is in any sense a mass-audience magazine, so the influence of each in literary matters is supportive rather than supporting. They can't keep a whole stable of writers going the way the *Post* did. They can't suddenly wash over the whole nation with a wave of literature, the way the old *Life* did when in 1952 it published Hemingway's *The Old Man and the Sea* complete in one issue. Like *Life*, *Rolling Stone* can pay huge amounts of money for fiction on a one-shot basis — as it did for Tom Wolfe's *The Bonfire of the Vanities* and Norman Mailer's CIA novel, *Harlot's Ghost*. Then, as at *Life*, fiction will disappear from its pages until some other hot property comes along. *Harper's* and *The Atlantic*, born literary, remain committed to fiction, for which we can all be grateful.

The only other national magazines that publish fiction are edited primarily for men or for women. Historically in America, magazines edited for women have published a generous amount of fiction — novels running serially and lots of short stories, often written especially for what was considered a special audience. Little of this could be considered literature. Still, it is sad that the great majority of magazines today that are edited for women run no fiction at all, or very little and then very seldom.

The cover says it all: *Harper's* excerpt of William Styron's 1967 novel gave readers an empathetic glimpse into the world of the American slave in the 1830s.

The Atlantic featured a lengthy excerpt from James Dickey's novel *Deliverance* in this 1970 issue.

There was a wonderful time in the fifties when Marguerita Smith was the fiction editor of *Mademoiselle* and published work by her sister, Carson McCullers, by William Faulkner, Tennessee Williams, Katherine Anne Porter, and a young writer she discovered, Truman Capote, as well as many others. In the same period, Alice Morris was the literary editor of *Harper's Bazaar* and published the work of Christopher Isherwood, Eudora Welty, Colette, Jean Stafford, and other fine writers regularly. Now, *Bazaar* runs no fiction at all, and *Mademoiselle* publishes very little, although it continues to conduct a fiction contest for young writers.

The history of *Redbook* — or *The Red Book Magazine* as it used to be called — is another case in point. From its origins in 1903, when it was edited for both sexes, it billed itself as "the Short Story Magazine," but it soon dropped the label. When it became a magazine for young women, in 1964, under the guidance of fiction editor Anne Mollegen Smith, it had a glorious period of publishing first-class fiction by such writers as Joyce Carol Oates, Alice Walker, Tim O'Brien, John Irving, Mary Gordon, and Toni Morrison, and it won National Magazine Awards for fiction in 1970 and 1975. Now, with a change of editors or a change of times, fiction at *Redbook* is gone, except for an occasional romantic novelette.

Cosmopolitan, founded in 1886 and not originally a women's magazine, was at one point co-edited by no less a literary figure than William Dean Howells. It had a long history of publishing fiction, including the writings of Jack London and H. G. Wells, before it went through a period of muckraking, after which it was transformed again in the twenties and thirties under the editorship of Ray Long. Under Long, *Cosmopolitan* became *primarily* a fiction magazine, publishing all the big names of the time — Edna Ferber, Rafael Sabatini, Fannie Hurst, Ring Lardner, Louis Bromfield, and so on. Finally, *Cosmo* was sensationally and successfully repositioned in 1966 by Helen Gurley Brown, author of *Sex and the Single Girl*. The magazine continues to run fiction; but, as might be expected, the fiction, like most of the other features, concerns itself with sex and dating.

Neither of the huge supermarket magazines — *Family Circle* and *Woman's Day* — runs any fiction at all. *Ladies' Home Journal*, which for decades published vast quantities of fiction, now publishes none. Of the remaining women's magazines, *Lear's* and *Mirabella* will print fiction very occasionally, and *Seventeen* still publishes stories (bless its young heart), but most

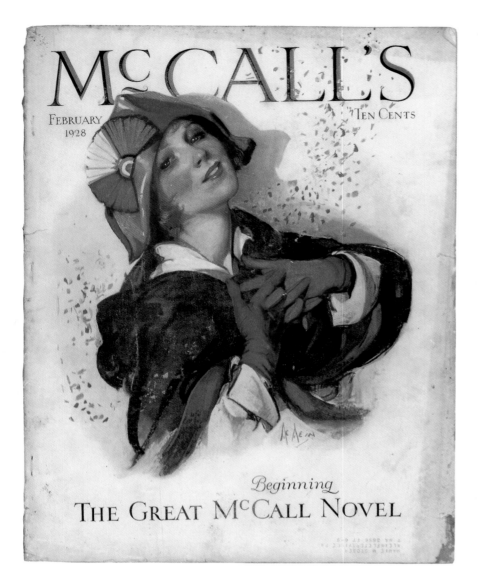

Over the years *McCall's* has published fiction by many famous writers, but romances like this 1959 tale by Eileen Herbert Jordan (with illustrations by Coby Whitmore) have predominated.

Otis Lee Wiese became editor of *McCall's* in 1928, ushering in a time when fiction by such writers as Faith Baldwin, Heywood Broun, and J. P. Marquand was a staple.

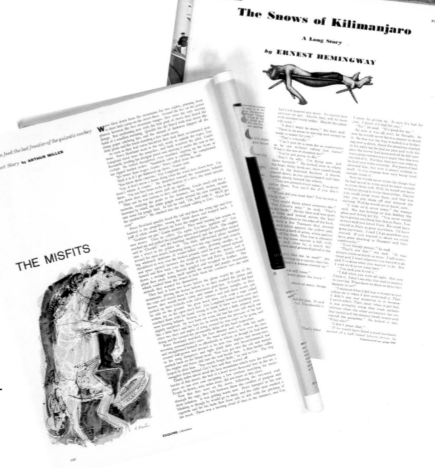

Esquire editor Arnold Gingrich scored many coups, including getting Ernest Hemingway and Arthur Miller to contribute important works of fiction.

Playboy has often featured fiction by leading American writers, among them Saul Bellow and Jules Feiffer.

no one could look at him without loving him—yet, when he looked out at the world, he wanted still more, and still more . . .

a novel by JULES FEIFFER part one   HARRY,   THE RAT WITH WOMEN

Esquire played a role in acquainting the general public with the science fiction of Ray Bradbury, whose gripping tale of a tattooed freak appeared in 1950.

THE ILLUSTRATED MAN

Here is a story of strange power that you'll never forget. It's about a hideously fat man, the ghastly pictures tattooed on his body, and the woman that he loved—to death. You'll retell it over and over. . . .   by RAY BRADBURY

"HEY, the Illustrated Man!"

A calliope screamed, and Mr. William Philippus Phelps stood, arms folded, high on the summer-night platform, a crowd unto himself.

He was an entire civilization. In the Main Country, his chest, the Vasties lived—nipple-eyed dragons swirling over his fleshpot, his almost feminine breasts. His navel was the mouth of a slit-eyed monster—an obscene, insucked mouth, toothless as a witch. And there were secret caves where Darklings lurked, his armpits, adrip with slow subterranean liquors, where the Darklings, eyes jealously ablaze, peered out through rank creeper and hanging vine.

Mr. William Philippus Phelps leered down from his freak platform with a thousand peacock eyes. Across the sawdust meadow he saw his wife, Lisabeth, far away, ripping tickets in half, staring at the silver belt buckles of passing men. Mr. William Philippus Phelps' hands were tattooed roses. At the sight of his wife's interest, the roses shriveled, as with the passing of sunlight.

A year before, when he had led Lisabeth to the marriage bureau to watch her work her name in ink, slowly, on the form, his skin had been pure and white and clean. He glanced down at himself in sudden horror. Now he was like a great painted canvas, shaken in the night wind! How had it happened? Where had it all begun?

It had started with the arguments, and then the flesh, and then the pictures. They had fought deep into the summer nights, she like a brass trumpet forever blaring at him. And he had gone out to eat five thousand steaming hot dogs, ten million hamburgers, and a forest of green onions, and to drink vast red seas of orange juice. Peppermint candy formed his brontosaur bones, the hamburgers shaped his balloon flesh, and strawberry pop pumped in and out of his heart valves sickeningly, until he weighed three hundred pounds.

"William Philippus Phelps," Lisabeth said to him in the eleventh month of their marriage, "you're dumb and fat."

That was the day the carnival boss handed him the blue envelope. "Sorry, Phelps. You're no good to me with all that gut on you."

"Wasn't I always your best tent man, boss?"

"Once. Not any more. Now you sit, you don't get the work out."

"Let me be your Fat Man."

"I got a Fat Man. Dime a dozen." The boss eyed him up and down. "Tell you what, though. We ain't had a Tattooed Man since Gallery Smith died last year. . . ."

That had been a month ago. Four short weeks. From someone, he had learned of a tattoo artist far out in the rolling Wisconsin country, an old woman, they said, who knew her trade. If he took the dirt road and turned right at the river and then left . . .

He had walked out across a yellow meadow, which was crisp from the sun. Red flowers blew and bent in the wind as he walked, and he came to the old shack, which looked as if it had stood in a million rains.

Inside the door was a silent, bare room, and in the center of the bare room sat an ancient woman.

Her eyes were stitched with red resin-thread. Her nose was sealed with black wax-twine. Her ears were sewn, too, as if a darning-needle dragonfly had stitched all her senses shut. She sat, not moving, in the vacant room. Dust lay in a yellow flour all about, unfootprinted in many weeks; if she had moved it would have shown, but she had not moved. Her hands touched each other like thin, rusted instruments. Her feet were naked and obscene as rain rubbers, and near them sat vials of tattoo milk—red, lightning-blue, brown, cat-yellow. She was a thing sewn tight into whispers and silence.

Only her mouth moved, unsewn: "Come in. Sit down. I'm lonely here."

"You came for the pictures," she said in a high voice. "I have a picture to show you, first."

She tapped a blind finger to her thrust-out palm. "See!" she cried.

It was a tattoo-portrait of William Philippus Phelps.

"Me!" he said.

Her cry stopped him at the door. "Don't run."

He held to the edges of the door, his back to her. "That's me, that's me on your hand!"

"It's been there fifty years." She stroked it like a cat, over and over.

He turned. "It's an *old* tattoo." He drew slowly nearer. He edged forward and bent to blink at it. He put out a trembling finger to brush the picture. "Old. That's impossible! You don't know *me*. I don't know *you*. Your eyes, all sewed shut."

"I've been waiting for you," she said. "And many people." She displayed her arms and legs, like the spindles of an antique chair. "I have pictures on me of *(Continued on page 152)*

of the recent magazines edited for younger women avoided getting into it in the first place. *Good Housekeeping* and some others may do novelettes advertised as "romantic," but only *Ms.*, proudly feminist, seems to think literary fiction could interest a female readership.

In the men's magazine field, it's only the fashion magazines for men, rather than the outdoors, sports, or other more macho ones, that publish fiction. *Esquire* seems to have set this pattern, begun in 1933 by Arnold Gingrich, who happened to be interested in literature — and clothes and cars and jazz and so on. All these interests went into the magazine he published. Several magazines that appeared after the Second World War cast themselves in *Esquire*'s image — notably *Playboy*, *Penthouse*, and *Gentleman's Quarterly*. *Playboy* in particular made an effort to attract well-known literary writers by offering big money for stories that emphasized sex.

From the very first issue, *Esquire* featured literary authors. Sometimes they would contribute fiction, sometimes nonfiction, sometimes a strange mixture of the two. Erskine Caldwell, Hemingway, Fitzgerald, Thomas Wolfe, Sherwood Anderson, John Steinbeck, Sinclair Lewis, John Dos Passos, and just about any writer you can think of in that generation appeared in the glossy, oversized pages of what began as a giveaway item in men's clothing stores. *Esquire* has traditionally paid authors so parsimoniously that there has never been the tendency (or opportunity) to build the sort of stable of regulars found at *The New Yorker* and *The Saturday Evening Post*. But in the postwar years, the great American contemporaries continued to appear in its pages — Mailer, Bellow, Styron, Capote, Updike, Roth, Malamud, Singer, Barth, Barthelme, Heller, Friedman, Welty, Oates, Walker, Kesey, Stone, and DeLillo. Often, some of these distinguished authors have felt their work resided a bit uneasily among all the men's clothing ads and service features on, say, grooming or dining out. In recent decades, too, the magazine has gone through an unsettling sequence of changes in owners and editors. It became briefly a fortnightly, and it changed editorial direction repeatedly, exchanging the New Journalism for New Age thinking (or lack of it) for a while. Yet, through all the extraordinary transformations, *Esquire* continued to publish serious literary fiction. From its very beginnings, the magazine has found literature useful, even if it's only for commercial reasons or to class up its act.

To be truly committed to fiction — to publish fiction for its

One of *Esquire*'s literary draws: Tennessee Williams' simmering drama debuted in its pages in early 1962, several months before being published in book form.

Ramparts packaged Kurt Vonnegut like a superstar when it published excerpts from his latest book in 1973.

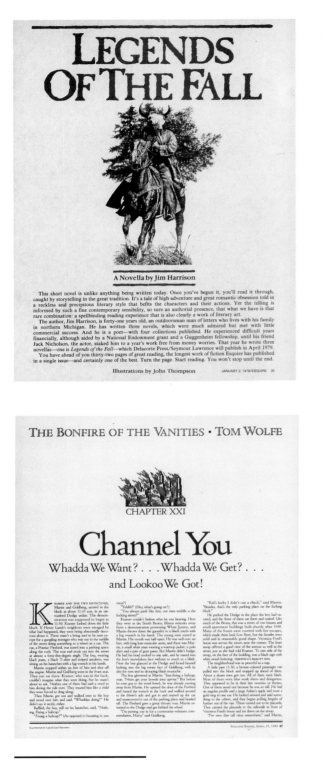

In 1979, *Esquire* (top) devoted an unprecedented thirty-two pages to a short novel by Jim Harrison. Tom Wolfe's celebrated novel *The Bonfire of the Vanities* first appeared serially in *Rolling Stone* in 1985 (above).

own sake — a magazine would either have to be devoted to some special kind of fiction (science or detective or mystery fiction, say, or romance or adventure fiction) or it would have to be totally noncommercial, in which case it would probably have only a tiny circulation. There have been a lot of the latter. It is an often-cited statistic that 80 percent of the literary authors who came to prominence after 1912 were first published in the so-called little magazines. These periodicals, most of them quarterlies with a short life expectancy, traditionally publish experimental and innovative work by new writers. The species is still with us, thank goodness, but many of today's literary magazines must be thought of as an accommodation for the vast graduate-writing programs that have proliferated at colleges and universities across the country. Their "workshop" method of teaching writing requires the production of vast quantities of short stories weekly. As a result, what's sometimes called "workshop fiction" has largely replaced what used to be called "magazine fiction" as the training ground for young writers.

One way or another, fiction seems always to find some way to get published, despite perennial fears that it is "dying." If anything is dying, it's not fiction but *reading* — and that's not the fault of magazines. The truth of the matter seems to be that fiction in American magazines does not have any future at all unless it is literary in its nature and excellent in its quality. There seems no reason for a magazine to publish anything else anyway.

— *Rust Hills*

SHOT

If she could follow the strange sound
to where it came from, maybe
it would finally stop haunting her

Loneliness sharpens the senses. In this new place where her parents had come to work the girl slept poorly and woke each morning at dawn, or before dawn, to a strange noise in the near distance—shouting, or loud singing, or a dog's repetitive hysterical barking. She lay in bed without moving or breathing and without thinking, listening to the sound with its serrated edges, the texture of mica-studded rusty earth, yet there was something moist and eager about it too, a shameless percussive rhythm that could belong to no machine, only to life. The sound called to her. She dreaded it entering her sleep.

Gradually, with morning, other noises intervened. Diesel trucks on the highway, construction crews building new homes close by, bulldozers, chain saws, garbage trucks, jet bombers from the air force base at the edge of the desert. In the girl's own household there was likely to be uninterrupted quiet since neither her mother nor her father believed in television or radio news or inconsequential chatter in the crucial hour before they left for work but when, the single time the girl inquired of them if they'd heard that strange noise, ''off in the distance, like someone calling for help,'' the noise had faded or ceased or been drowned out by other noises, so her mother said, after seeming to listen, that she couldn't hear anything out of the ordinary, and her father, annoyed by the question but making an effort to be polite, merely smiled, and shook his head no, not having made much of an effort to listen at all. As always, his thoughts were elsewhere where no one, not even his wife, was encouraged to follow.

One morning in midsummer when the family had been living in the new house for about a month and the girl was again wakened by the sound, she decided to track it to its source. Barefoot, in her pajamas, she went downstairs and stood on the bare concrete terrace at the rear of the house, listening intently, and fixing the sound at approximately eleven o'clock in terms of her position. It could not have been more than a mile away, probably less. This morning **by Joyce Carol Oates**

the sound was a harsh careless sobbing that grated against her nerves. She thought, I don't really want to know what it is!

Her parents left for work at eight o'clock: Though they were not assigned to the same project, they worked in the same complex of government buildings known locally as the Institute, and they drove together in the same car. Shortly afterward the girl bicycled out of the subdivision, along the coyly curving asphalt drives past the stucco ranch houses with Spanish-style roofs, and grassless lawns, houses virtually identical to the one the girl's father had bought for them, and as she approached the highway she could hear the sound only intermittently, like a radio station fading, and returning, and fading again, but she knew she was going in the right direction.

She left San Jacinto Estates and after a little difficulty crossed the busy highway and pedaled until she came to an unpaved road where instinct told her to turn. To her left was a deep irrigation ditch in which brackish water glinted; to her right were shabby little bungalows and tar-paper shanties, places at which it seemed rude to stare, small children playing in the dirt oblivious of her passing. It was early but the desert-dry air was warming minute by minute. The girl knew that the world through which she moved was composed of what her father called structural fictions—ideograms—for where she saw light, color, texture, solid shapes, and experienced herself as one, there existed nothing but a cascade of ever-shifting and -changing atoms and molecules, substanceless as hieroglyphics on a computer screen, in some mysterious way linked to the rhythms of the human brain; yet, for all her knowing, for all her having been trained to know, she did not somehow believe.

Now the sound resumed and the girl heard it for what it was, distinctly: a dog's barking.

A dog's barking!—so commonplace after all.

But there was a special urgency to it. A sound as of words in a nightmare scramble. Where you hear, but can't understand——you ▶

132   133

JAMES CORBETT

Among *Seventeen*'s roster of distinguished contributors are Sylvia Plath, Chaim Potok, Ursula K. LeGuin, and Joyce Carol Oates, whose short story "Shot" ran in 1990.

MOTHER JONES   MOTHER JONES

JULY'S PEOPLE

BY NADINE GORDIMER ·————ILLUSTRATION BY SUE COE

Editor's note: Nadine Gordimer is South Africa's finest writer of fiction. As an outspoken critic of apartheid, however, she could be the first to point out the unfairness of that characterization. Censorship and other hurdles are incomparably greater for writers who come from the 84 percent of South Africa's population that is nonwhite; the great artist in their midst will not fully emerge until the long struggle for racial justice is won.

Gordimer, the author of seven novels and six volumes of short stories, has had her own run-ins with her country's authorities. Her best-known novel, Burger's Daughter, *was banned by the South African censor, soon after its publication in 1979. Finally, after protests from writers around the world and after the novel won much praise in Europe and the United States, the government lifted the ban. Her next novel, an excerpt of which appears on the following pages, seems headed for more trouble with the censors.*

July's People, *which Viking Press has just published in the United States, takes place as the final cataclysm in South African arrives and the country is divided in civil war. By focusing on a white family who flee their Johannesburg home,* July's People *appears on the surface to address the question of revolution as whites now frame it. When it happens, will we survive? But gradually, ironically, Gordimer uses the Smales family's flight as a subtle prism through which to see relations between whites and blacks. Before the upheaval, the Smales knew July only as their dutiful, condescension house servant, after, as they take refuge in the village of which he is the leading figure, he is their only chance of staying alive.*

The book's plot reminds one slightly of James Barrie's play about class reversal among a shipwrecked party of English aristocrats, The Admirable Crichton, *in which a rich family's butler is shipwrecked and, under the rigors of life on a desert island, their resourceful butler takes command. When a rescue ship appears on the horizon, Crich-*

ten reverts to his old role and dons his butler's uniform once again. But is Nadine Gordimer's novel—as in South Africa's future—the ending is far different.   —A.H.

''You like to have some cup of tea?''
July bent at the doorway and began that day the tea for them as his kind has always done for their kind.

The knock on the door. Seven o'clock. In govern-ment residences, commercial hotel rooms, shift houses company bungalows: master bedrooms en suite—the tea-tray in black hands smelling of Lifebuoy soap.

The knock on the door
no door, an aperture in thick mud walls, and the sack that hung over it looped back for air, sometimes during the short night. *Bam, I'm telling; her voice raising him from the dead,* he staggering up from his exhausted sleep.

No knock, but July, their servant, their host, bringing two pink glass cups of tea and a small tin of condensed milk, jaggedly opened, specially for them, with a spoon in it.

—No milk for me.—
—Or me, thanks.—

The black man looked over to the three sleeping children hooked-down on seats taken from the vehicle. He smiled conformation—They all right.—

—Yes, all right—he dipped out under the doorway.
—Thank you, July, thank you very much.—

She had slept in round mud huts cooled in thatch like this before. In the Kruger Park, a child of the shift how and his family on leave, an enamel basin and ewer among their supplies of orange squash and biscuits on the table, coming twice at this morning light came. Roundavels adapted to Bam's vacation on his Bozo role from the huts of the blacks. They were a romantic tour to the continent; before air-conditioning, everyone praised the natural insulation of

JULY, 1981
48

COE

Mother Jones excerpted South African writer Nadine Gordimer's novel *July's People* in 1981, giving readers a look at the tensions in black-white relations under apartheid.

107

The Telling Anecdote

Clay Felker, the genius who created *New York* magazine, was the first editor I ever worked for. The first thing I noticed about him was that he had an incredibly short attention span. He got bored faster than anyone I've ever met. When you'd bring a story idea to Clay, he would stare at you with a half smile for a few seconds, then — almost immediately, turn, run his fingers through his thin hair, and make a noise that sounded like "eeeeaugh" (part moan, part sigh, part elephant trumpet). Then he would walk away, usually into the art department, while you stood there with your mouth half open and your last sentence half finished. Clay didn't mean to be rude; you just hadn't held his attention well enough for him to remember that he was supposed to be listening to you. Maddening as it was at the time, his behavior was probably the reason so many talented editors, writers, and art directors got their start at *New York*. People learned quickly that to get Clay to listen to an idea, it had to be sharply defined and explained in a way that would hold his interest for more than ten seconds. Once you had learned to achieve this miracle of timing and concision, everything else — editing articles, writing headlines, and deciding on graphics — was a cinch.
Elizabeth Crow, president/editorial director, Gruner + Jahr USA Publishing

MAY 6, 1966   40 CENTS
'Adam Smith' on
Wall Street's Trading Binge: Euphoria or Panic?

New York

Soap Opera Digest regularly runs a column called "Cooking with the Stars." One time, an actress gave us two recipes: one for barbecued chicken, the other for cake icing. Two weeks after they ran, a reader wrote in: "Thank you for that wonderful recipe. At first when I read about chicken with icing, I was a little unsure, but all the other recipes in *Soap Opera Digest* were so good, I thought what the heck. Boy, did my kids love it! I served it to the ladies in my card club and they raved! Even my husband thought it was the greatest. Thank you *Soap Opera Digest*, I can't wait to try it with chocolate icing!"
Meredith Berlin, editor, *Soap Opera Digest*

For several years, I worked for Henry Robinson Luce. I knew him as a man of no slight curiosity. When he traveled abroad, the heads of his local bureaus were said to go out and reconnoiter the paths he would travel so that they might respond in a very knowledgeable way on the monuments he would pass. Still, I was not prepared for the display of curiosity I encountered one night walking with him from the Time-Life building at Rockefeller Center to the Waldorf Towers where, for a time, he lived. That curiosity shone forth as we passed a building with a sign on a second-floor window advertising a private detective agency:

"I'd like to know what they investigate," he said.

"How much do you suppose they charge?

"Do they have some special training? Detective schools?

"I suppose they spend a lot of time tracking down wives and husbands and their behavior. That must be rather interesting.

"I'd like to know how often they find out what they are hired to get."

That was only the beginning. As we arrived at the Waldorf, he said, "I wonder if we shouldn't do a story on the private detective business."

By then, I had come to think so too.
John Kenneth Galbraith, Harvard University

•

One of my best moments was when *Essence* won the National Magazine Award for fiction. *Texas Monthly* was also a winner that year, and Bill Broyles came by the office to join the celebration and help us work our way through several cases of champagne. Here we were, white Texans and black New Yorkers, two of the newest kids on the block, neither truly part of the old publishing establishment, carrying home the prize! Despite the industry's liberal posturing, I knew that black publications were not taken as seriously as their white counterparts, that black editors and writers were not sought out with the same zeal. My goal for *Essence* was that it be considered not only the best black women's magazine, but also one of the best women's magazines in the nation. Winning that award (for a short story called "Isom," by Hortense Spillers) was an incredible morale boost for the entire staff. It also made all those late nights I'd spent reading my way through an Everest-like mound of submissions, many of them truly awful, seem worth it. Despite the loss of sleep, it was a labor of love and hope. Hungry for fiction by African-American women, I just knew that one night I was going to find a new star. When

I came across that particular piece, which like so many others had been sent in cold, I knew I'd finally found her.
Marcia Ann Gillespie, former editor-in-chief, *Essence*

•

It was May 1945. I was in Paris as a war correspondent for *Newsweek*. I was also supervising the printing and distribution of "Battle Baby," a trimmed-down edition of the magazine for American military forces in Europe. Each weekend, *Newsweek* sent us from New York a packet of film containing the

following week's edition for use by the printer. Ordinarily we started distribution on Monday. Early one weekend, though, we learned that the Germans were about to surrender. Joe Evans, our bureau chief, secured the exact terms in return for a promise that we would not distribute that week's issue until the following Wednesday at 1:00 P.M. — the embargo date for all media. Until then, we could not mention the surrender to anyone.

We cabled New York for permission to hold up distribution for forty-eight hours without, of course, being able to tell them why. We were immediately told not to delay but to get the edition out on time. Deciding to disobey these instructions, we prepared a new cover showing a German soldier with his hands up, surrendering. In place of the lead article we substituted the full story of the surrender with the exact terms of the document itself.

Getting the magazine out was no easy task, for everyone at the printer's wanted to celebrate. With a couple of cases of champagne, though, we convinced them to go ahead, and thousands of copies were readied for distribution in Paris and elsewhere. At 1:00 P.M. Wednesday the bells rang and Paris went crazy. A couple of trucks drove through the the city, distributing copies to American soldiers. We sat back and waited for word that we'd been fired. Later that day, however, congratulatory wires and phone calls began pouring in. We had scooped the world.
Gibson McCabe, former president, *Newsweek*

•

It helps to keep things in perspective. About three years ago, the American Institute of Graphic Arts held a symposium on magazine design. In one panel, some of the nation's top editorial art directors were asked, if given the opportunity, would they dare to attempt to redesign the hallowed *New Yorker*. Most members of the panel stated in reverential tones that they wouldn't because of the long-standing success of the magazine's design format. Finally, Ron Campisi, who was art director of the award-winning *Boston Globe* magazine, said, "Hell, yes, I'd do it. It's just a magazine."
D. J. Stout, art director, *Texas Monthly*

•

I had closed my first issue as managing editor of *Rolling Stone* and was sitting in a bar on First Avenue with Will Hearst when the news that John Lennon had been shot came on the television. I went immediately back to the office and started making calls. Jann Wenner naturally was doing the same thing. The unique relationship that Lennon had had with both the magazine and Jann made the next week the most intense I have ever experienced as an editor — much more so than anything I went through at *Newsweek* or the numerous other places I have worked. People would break into tears in meetings. Jann did that when I was describing an eyewitness account of how much Lennon had been bleeding. Just a week earlier, Annie Leibovitz had taken a great shot of John and Yoko in bed. We put it on the cover with no words. No one even suggested a headline. It was Jann's finest hour. We found out later that because Lennon was naked in the picture we couldn't get distribution in many parts of the country.
Terry McDonell, editor-in-chief, *Esquire*

•

In the summer of 1989, we were preparing our eleventh straight "Best & Worst" cover. What was there left to say about pizzerias and politicians? Then my next-door neighbor invited me to say hello to her new springer spaniel puppy. When I told her how cute it was, she observed that her springer was much cuter than the President's dog, Millie. We decided to put Millie on the cover as the ugliest dog in Washington. When the issue appeared, President Bush went public with his displeasure. "Imagine picking on a guy's dog," he told reporters. "I know now how Roosevelt felt with that attack on Fala." When showing off Millie to visitors, Barbara Bush made a point of saying what a beautiful dog she was. The Associated Press and Reuters picked up the story and Jay Leno joked about it. Overall, we got more news coverage from Millie than from anything else we've published in twenty-five years.

The moral: Be looking for an idea even when a puppy is biting at your shoelaces.
John A. Limpert, editor, *Washingtonian*

By John Sansing

BEST & WORST

The Annual Guide to What's In and What's Out, What's Great and What's Not—Plus, Readers' Favorites

It was late on a Friday afternoon in March 1974, and I had just returned to my home in Mt. Kisco from a trip to Washington, D.C. My wife, Janet, greeted me with the news that my boss, DeWitt Wallace, the founder of *Reader's Digest*, urgently wanted me to call him. I went right to the phone, ready to discuss article ideas.

"Wally, this is Ken. You called." "Oh, yes," he said in his somewhat shy fashion. "The Mt. Kisco railroad station is a mess. Could you be there at nine tomorrow?"

"Yes sir," I replied, not completely sure what this editorial genius had in mind. Could it be some railroad scandal?

"Good," Wally replied. "And please bring a couple of trash bags."

I was there at nine sharp. Wally and half a dozen other ranking editors were already there, including Hobart Lewis, the president and editor-in-chief of *Reader's Digest*. Each was stuffing arm-loads of trash into bags.

Every piece of paper and plastic was wet and slimy from a heavy rain the night before. I was astonished at how many empty liquor bottles and other unmentionable items had accumulated on either side of the tracks. Fortunately, Bob Bischoff, one of our best-organized editors, had brought some extra bags.

We'd taken all but two of the bags to a nearby lot to be picked up when suddenly an express train thundered through the station. The entire contents of both bags were littered far and wide. "Oh no," we moaned.

"I guess we have some more work to do," declared Wally.

We finally finished about noon. We had filled at least twenty-five bags. I had never seen Wally, then in his mid-eighties, looking more healthy and happy. Clearly, he and his *Digest* gang of pollution-fighters had won the day.

"Thanks to one and all. You are an outstanding group of volunteers," he announced and headed for his 1954 Chevy.

A couple of days later, Wally passed the word that there would be no publicity given to his cleanup, nor to another he had organized at the Chappaqua train station.

It has been ten years since Wally died. I don't think he would mind my telling the story now.
Ken Gilmore, former editor-in-chief, *Reader's Digest*

•

I got into the magazine business on a bet twenty-five years ago. One of a group of college newspaper editors invited by *Life* to attend an early space launch, I spent a week with the astronauts and Time Inc. executives at Cape Kennedy. One night over too many beers, a group of us began reciting poetry. Dick Coffey, the longtime, great promotion director of *Life* — who was referred to in the industry as "Mr. Print" — was reciting a stanza from the A. E. Housman poem "When I was One and Twenty." He said, ". . .Give crowns and pounds and rubles, but not your heart away." I said it was "guineas" and not "rubles," and reminded him I was, after all, twenty-one. He insisted he was right and bet me a dollar. When I returned to Louisiana, I sent him a copy of the poem. He sent back a terse letter. It said, "Dollar enclosed. How would you like a job?" It was to be the only job offer I received, and one which started me on a twenty-five-year love affair with magazine publishing. It was the best bet I ever made.

Thomas O. Ryder, president, American Express Worldwide Publishing

•

In May 1974, *New Times* published a cover story called "The ten dumbest congress-men." The cover pictured William Scott, a U.S. Senator from Virginia, with the headline, "The dumbest congressman of them all," proclaiming the unfortunate Scott to be at the head of the list.

A few days after the magazine came out, Scott called a press conference to deny the charge. The Washington press corps reacted with glee, and the story received major coverage across the nation.

The issue enjoyed one of the largest newsstand sales *New Times* ever had. And, aside from Scott, I never heard anyone question the accuracy of our story.

George A. Hirsch, publisher, *Runner's World* and founding publisher, *New Times*

•

It all began in the winter of 1978, when I took Calvin Trillin to lunch and proposed that he write a weekly column for *The Nation*. He liked the idea, provided that we had a "no diddling clause," which meant no changes without consultation, and provided that he could "make fun of the editor" (me). When, after a sumptuous cheeseburger, he had the bad taste to ask what we were going to pay him, I said, "We are thinking of something in the high two figures." Trillin put his agent on the case, and before we knew it, he had us up to $100 per column — twice our normal rate!

One of Trillin's first columns was about "Dinner at the de la Rentas" — a parody of a *New York Times Magazine* piece about how the fashion couple was famous for inviting one celebrity per category to their dinners: the novelist Norman Mailer, the investment banker Felix Rohatyn, etc. Trillin reported that when the name of Henry Kissinger was suggested as a last minute fill-in, Mrs. de la Renta objected, "But we already have one war criminal."

Soon after, Trillin was asked to appear on the Johnny Carson show. Instead of talking about the de la Rentas, he talked about how he was paid "in the high two figures by the wily and parsimonious Victor Navasky" to an audience

of millions of puzzled viewers who, of course, had never heard of *The Nation* or its editor.

Trillin's successes mounted. He became a regular on the Carson show, started a syndicated column, and got a one-man show at the American Place Theater. And with him went his repertoire, including his repeated references to his wily and parsimonious editor. As the word went forth on stage and screen, my children were asked by their classmates how it felt to be the offspring of a wily and par-simonious man. One night my ninety-year-old father happened to be watching the Carson show and who should come on but Calvin Trillin.

Johnny: How would you describe *The Nation*?
Trillin (after a short pause): Pinko.
Johnny: And how would you describe its editor?
Trillin: Are you referring to the wily and parsimonious Victor Navasky?

When Trillin finally published a collection of pieces that neglected to mention *The Nation* or its editor, the reviewer in the *New York Times Book Review* went out of her way to point out that he was paid "in the high two figures" by "the wily and parsimonious" one. It got to the point where, in my own travels on totally unrelated business, I was asked to sign programs and other ephemera with "the wily and parsimonious" Victor Navasky, or sometimes simply "w. and p."

I finally figured out how to thwart Trillin. I took him to his second sumptuous lunch in ten years and told him we intended to double his salary. As he wrote in his next column, "He says he is going to double my pay. I figure he has to be up to something. I resign. He tells me my share of the check is $13.38."

Victor Navasky, editor, *The Nation*

•

The New Yorker traditionally kept a firm separation be-tween its advertising and editorial functions. A. J. Russell joined the advertising staff in its early years and rose to become advertising director and eventually company president. I once asked him how well acquainted he was with his longtime associate, the founding editor Harold

Ross. "Not very," he said. "I would see him at our company birthday parties. I sometimes saw him in the elevator. But he didn't like to talk in the elevator, so we didn't speak."

Theodore Peterson, historian and author of *Magazines in the Twentieth Century*

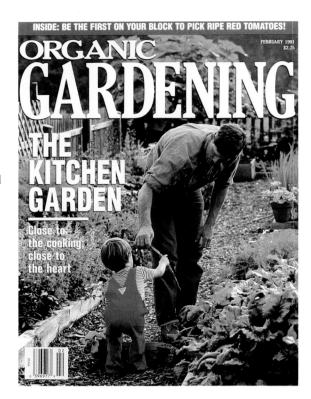

Organic Gardening gets so much unusual mail that we ran a notice in the magazine asking readers not to send "insects, plant specimens, or anything that would tend to break down in the mail." But this notice obviously isn't followed to the letter by all of our subscribers.

Walking past OG's Readers' Service Department last summer, I was stopped by one of our editors, who was holding a shoebox filled with a white ash-like substance that appeared to be potash. "What do you think this stuff is?" he posed.

Well, I replied, it appears to be potash or some sort of soil conditioner. Visibly shaking, he handed me a note that was enclosed with it.

"Throughout our marriage, my husband Harry devoted every spare cent we had on Rodale magazines and books. Even when there were things I had to have for the house or children, Rodale publications always came first. It was Harry's final request that he be cremated and his ashes be sprinkled on the Organic Farm. You have my best wishes and Harry."

Was this a hoax or a prank? There was no return ad-dress, but the cancellation indicated it came from Kansas. Without bothering to have a sample tested, we dutifully fulfilled Harry's last request and spread either him or someone's fireplace by-product on the compost pile. We just didn't want to know the truth.

Robert J. Teufel, president, Rodale Press

•

I am often asked — well, once I was asked — "What does an editor do?" Perhaps the best way to answer is to describe a typical day:

Because the school bus picks my kids up in the middle of the night, I get to the office early. I wash down a sesame bagel with a cup of coffee — regular, two sugars — give the obituaries in the *Times* a quick once-over, and settle in at my computer to begin wreaking havoc on some unsuspect-ing wretch's perfectly good copy. The staff starts drifting in around 9 and by 9:10 somebody's pestering me about this or that. As far as I'm concerned, it's high time.

If more than a few minutes go by without somebody coming in to bother me, I'll go into the hallway and bother someone else. Or I'll sort the mail, or wander into the art department in search of a layout I can fiddle with. But I never stay long. I'm always anxious to get back to turning someone's golden rhetoric into dross. It's a lucky man who loves his work.

As a general rule, the better the writers, the happier they are with my editing. "Uncanny skill," Alistair Cooke said of what I did to his piece on Winston Churchill. Really, I have it in writing: "I did feel that somebody had exercised uncanny skill in deleting just those passages that were thoughtful or original." That's a quote.

Joe Morgenstern said my editing of his piece on the movie *The Grapes of Wrath* reminded him of Joseph Conrad and Vladimir Nabokov. Okay, his actual words were that he felt it had been edited by someone for whom English was not a first language. But who else could he have meant?

Sometimes I go out to lunch, have a glass of wine, and am totally useless for the rest of the day. But more often I'll just grab a sandwich or get a couple of franks with sauerkraut at the Nathan's across the street. Who said being an editor isn't glamorous?

Around four o'clock I have a fade. In the old days before we hired a fact checker, I used to make an afternoon coffee run. But the fact checker we hired fades a little earlier than I do, so I no longer make coffee runs or worry about facts.

I'm usually out of gas by 6:00 P.M. and spend the next hour or so trying to decipher the reader mail, signing invoices or staring at my shoes and muttering incoherently.

I like to get home after Dan Rather has signed off but before my kids do. A *little* before. I usually dine on Ben and Jerry's ice cream before slipping quietly into a coma in front of a television turned to the least objectionable program. My wife kicks me awake around midnight and I stagger into bed for a few hours of fitful sleep. It's a wonderful life.
Carey Winfrey, editor-in-chief, *American Health* and founding editor, *Memories*

When I was text editor of *Sports Illustrated* — probably the most delightful job I ever held in publishing — I hired George Foreman, then heavyweight champion of the world, to do a first-person story. The promised fee was $10,000.

This was the early seventies, when Time Inc. was converting to computers and checks were no longer drawn by hand. Publishing companies did not play the float then,

and we had a tradition of paying our writers promptly. Within a week. And if a writer was hungry, within two days.

My secretary requisitioned the check for Foreman. Three weeks went by and he began phoning. No check had arrived. The cash disbursements department had misplaced the requisition. They said do it again. We tried. Still, the money did not arrive, and Foreman's anger flared. We made a third try, and by now I was on the phone to the company treasurer. After three months I still did not have a check to send Foreman.

One morning George Foreman was waiting for me when I arrived at the office. He is a very big man. And he was a very angry man. He was accompanied by his handlers. Also very big, very angry men.

Like a criminal, I placed one phone call. It was to Bill Bishop, the company controller. I said, "Bill, I have a problem. Remember, we discussed that George Foreman has not been paid. Mr. Foreman and I are coming up to see you about this matter. Now!" George Foreman was paid within an hour.
Pat Ryan, former managing editor, *People* and *Life*

•

In July 1969, when Neil Armstrong made his "giant leap for mankind," I was determined to display on *Newsweek*'s cover an actual photograph, not just an artist's rendition, of the first man on the moon. We kept the magazine open a couple of extra days that historic week and stationed photographers in front of television sets in Dayton, Tokyo, and London (our major printing locations). They were all instructed to shoot continuously as the fantastic moon story unfolded on their TV screens.

At about 1:00 A.M., New York time, I was shown a hundred or so pictures shot off the screen by our photographer in New York. These were supposed to show us what the other three photographers, near our printing plants, were shooting. As I bent over the contact sheets with a magnifying hand viewer, I was seized with gloom: The quality of the pictures was very poor.

Finally I selected one shot that I thought might be usable. It showed an astronaut in the foreground, walking away from the camera, the left side of his backpack in the shadow, the right side in the light. I had the picture cropped and blown up until the astronaut's helmet obliterated the final two "e's" in the *Newsweek* logotype. I knew we had a serviceable black-and-white domestic cover — provided our photographer in Dayton had shot the same scene at just about the same moment.

It turned out he had. But what about the overseas editions, to be printed in London and Tokyo? At about 2:00 A.M., our London bureau chief called in and described the one shot, out of scores that he and his photographer thought might be used. It was almost exactly the same picture as the ones taken in New York and Dayton. Half an hour later, a similar call from Tokyo.

So it was that *Newsweek* was able to appear that week, in Asia and Europe and North America, with seemingly identical shots of Armstrong on the moon — but actually

three different pictures, taken at almost precisely the same split second, at three different locations around the world and cropped on the basis of a fourth picture snapped in New York.

A final, vulgar, competitive note: *Time* appeared on the newsstands that week with an artist's rendering of what the moon walk *probably* looked like.
Osborn Elliott, former editor-in-chief, *Newsweek*

•

I remember firing a young man for using the word failure. "Nothing personal," I said, "but I'm too insecure myself to have people around me who believe that failure is a possibility. Failure is a word I don't accept."

The word I wanted to hear, then and now, was *success*. The energy I sought, then and now, was the energy that comes from focusing all your powers, like a beam, on a single point. I used to say to myself, "John Johnson, you can make it. John Johnson, you can make it. John Johnson, you can and *must* make it!

When things got real tough, I'd call my mother and she would say, "You can make it."

I told her one day in perhaps the worst week of my life, "Mother, it looks like I'm going to fail."

"Son," she said, "are you trying hard?"

"Yes."

"Real hard?"

"Yes."

"Well," she said, closing the conversation, "whenever you're trying hard, you're never failing. The only failure is failing to try."
John H. Johnson, publisher, *Ebony*

•

Every February, more than 100 chief editors, managing editors, and art directors make their way to the World Room of the Journalism Building of Columbia University. They come not just from midtown Manhattan but from Washington, D.C., and Boston and Texas and Iowa. Their mission: To be screeners for the National Magazine Awards. Their job description: To read themselves blind for two-plus days, then discuss and evaluate the more than 1,200 entries submitted each year to the NMA.

Picture this: In the World Room, a space about half the size of a basketball court, are eight tables, each about forty feet long, stacked edge to edge with magazines of every size and description. Along the walls, a long line-up of chairs, and in the chairs sit the screeners, reading, reading, reading, motionless except when they toss out a blow-in card that's got in their way. Now and then, a snort of laughter breaks the silence.

Most editors cherish the task of judging, and do it year after year after year. Phyllis Wilson, founding editor of *Self*, wanted to be a screener even in the last year of her life. One morning I interrupted my World Room reading to go to the ladies' room. There I found Phyllis, straight from a visit to her cancer doctor. She was drinking from a large plastic container. "What's that?" I asked. (It looked like a day's worth of liquid protein diet food.)

"My chemotherapy," she answered, finished it off, and went back to the World Room to read more magazines.
Ruth Whitney, editor-in-chief, *Glamour*

It was a magazine, not a newspaper or TV program, that showed the world what the assassination of President John F. Kennedy looked like. A Dallas garment manufacturer named Abraham Zapruder had taken his 8-mm home movie camera to Dealey Plaza and, through a combination of luck and courage, caught the entire grisly sequence in a few seconds of film.

Several hours after the assassination, I arrived in Dallas from Los Angeles, where I was *Life*'s bureau chief, and learned from one of our stringers at police headquarters that someone had photographed the bloody event. Eventually I got an approximation of the name "Zapruder," and, finding it in the phone directory, called every fifteen minutes for hours until finally reaching the man at midnight.

I persuaded Zapruder to let me see the film early the next morning. Knowing that *Life* must have it, I convinced him that the magazine would present his pictures in a tasteful way and thus show a confused world what had happened that Friday afternoon. We signed a makeshift contract turning the print rights over to *Life* for $50,000. Two days later, Zapruder, besieged by reporters, gratefully turned over all remaining rights for an additional $100,000.

The magazine ran the sequence in its report on the assassination and several times after that as the controversy over the assassination heated up. And, since the film was crucial in determining the timing, number, and direction of the shots fired at Kennedy, we made copies available to the Warren Commission.

In 1975, Time Inc. returned the original film to the Zapruder heirs (Abraham had died in 1970) for one dollar. They, in turn, donated it to the National Archives in Washington, where it currently resides.
Richard Stolley, editorial director, Time Inc. Magazines

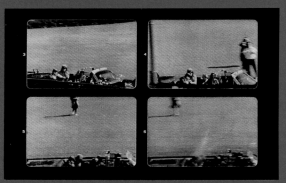

Why are we editors often pictured as churlish, uncompromising, self-destructive curmudgeons and revolutionaries? Because we are. We are not *mal*contents, but we are *dis*content to leave anything the way we find it. And if we ever told you we would be easy to get along with, we lied.

Take John Pekanen, writing his exhaustive study of emergency rooms for *Washingtonian*. A successful tactic for the tireless Pekanen is asking "the dumb question."

When questioning the surgeon who removed the assassin's bullet from President Reagan, he asked, "Why did you take the bullet out of the President?" The surgeon replied, "There was no medical reason for doing it, but I thought, What the hell is the media going to say if I leave the bullet in?"
John Mack Carter, editor-in-chief, *Good Housekeeping*

In the early seventies, when I was editor of *Apartment Life* (now *Metropolitan Home*), Dorothy Kalins was my executive editor. She was young, smart, and dedicated, and she made up in enthusiasm what she lacked in experience.

She became very concerned when she failed to see *Apartment Life* on the newsstands in midtown Manhattan. She complained to Jerry Ward, our circulation director, "Jerry, those corner newsstands are where some of our most important readers have a chance to see our magazine. And influential people from the advertising business will see us there as well. We're just a fledgling magazine. We need that exposure!"

Jerry assured Dorothy that *Apartment Life* had plenty of copies on midtown newsstands. "I'll prove you're wrong," Dorothy said. "When we have our operations meeting next month, we'll just take a little tour of newsstands, and you'll see!"

Several weeks later, Dorothy and Jerry set out on their tour. Each newsstand they visited was festooned with at least twenty-five copies of *Apartment Life*. After about the third one, Jerry owned up. He had passed out a few bucks to the newsstand owners to make sure that *Apartment Life* would greet Dorothy everywhere they went.

Dorothy learned that day what all editors learn sooner or later: Leave circulation to the circulation directors.
**David Jordan, editor-in-chief,
*Better Homes and Gardens***

•

Arnold Gingrich, the publisher and founding editor of *Esquire*, was my first boss. When I asked him to explain the magazine business one day, he said it was all very simple: "Being the publisher of a magazine is quite easy — as long as you *never* forget that *all* of your assets get in the elevator and go home at night."
Steve Florio, publisher, *The New Yorker*

•

In twenty-three years of publishing, I've been subjected to pressure — sometimes subtle, sometimes very direct — to put certain stars, musicians, or celebrities on the cover. One incident that stands out took place in the fall of 1969, when the magazine was two years old and I was twenty-four. We had managed to get an interview with legendary producer Phil Spector, and our then-chief photographer, Baron Wolman, and I flew from San Francisco to Los Angeles to do the piece. We had been given instructions by Spector, a man known for his secretive and eccentric life-style, to meet him in front of his office on Sunset Boulevard on a Sunday night. We were sitting in the Volkswagen bug that Baron had rented when a very long black limo pulled up and parked right behind us. The driver told us to park our car around the back and get in the limo. We got in expecting Spector, but it was just the burly driver and bodyguard, who pulled a screeching U-turn on Sunset and headed

up into the hills. When we arrived at Spector's mansion, the majestic gates opened mechanically and we proceeded down a long driveway.

The bodyguard left us sitting in the living room and went off, we assumed, to find his boss. When he came back, his jacket was off and there, plain as day, was his shoulder holster and a gun. He explained that Mr. Spector was watching *Star Trek*, but he wanted a few questions answered first. He pulled out a notepad. The first question: "Now this *will* be a cover, won't it?"
Jann S. Wenner, editor and publisher, *Rolling Stone*

•

Before launching my first magazine, I sought out the counsel of an old Tibetan Buddhist monk. I asked him if he thought magazine publishing could be spiritual work, i.e., work that contributes to the alleviation of suffering and the enlightenment of readers. He just looked at me and laughed for what felt like an eternity. Then he said, "The Tibetan word for 'news' is the same as the word for 'illusion.' Go ahead and publish your magazine. Just remember that in dealing with news you are dealing in illusions."
**Eric Utne, editor-in-chief,
*Utne Reader***

•

It was twenty years ago this past Christmas, and the Vietnam War was tearing America apart. Particularly disturbing was the subject of our prisoners of war who seemed to have vanished off the face of the earth. At *Ladies' Home Journal*, we decided to try to do something dramatic. The *Journal* regularly ran a "Power of a Woman" feature that encouraged readers to become more active in civic and political affairs. In our December 1970 issue, we printed a petition for readers to sign and mail in. It was an open letter addressed to the three major Vietnam factions asking for relief for the POWs and the release of those who were sick and wounded. Sign this petition, we said, and we'd get it to the Viets.

Readers responded in droves, sending in 65,000 petitions — enough to fill a small office. Meanwhile, it had been announced that the Viets would be attending a peace conference in April in Paris. We decided to put in an appearance. A delegation of four was chosen: John Mack Carter, the editor-in-chief; Myrlie Evers, widow of the slain civil rights leader; Virginia R. Allan, a Republican women's leader who later joined the State Department; and me. We planned to make our presence felt by leaving behind a huge leather-bound presentation titled "The Women of America Speak Out On the Prisoners of War and Peace in South East Asia."

In Paris, we were not able to meet formally with the Vietnamese leaders, but we were able to catch a few of them on steps and in courtyards, and we managed to leave our cards with the Hanoi group, the Vietcong, and the Lao Patriotic Front. Every day at the peace talks there was a press conference — the only event that didn't require military clearance to attend. One morning, Myrlie got so fed up that she simply rose to her feet, interrupted the general at the podium and in her throbbing contralto (with our interpreter catching every nuance), cut through the bureaucratic mush with a ringing recitation about the realities of pain and suffering, the pointlessness of war, and women's hope for some flexibility.

There was absolute silence while she spoke. When she had finished, Nguyen Thanh Le, the press representative from Hanoi, delivered a twenty-five minute diatribe but later said through his interpreter that this had been the most human exchange at the entire conference. Coming down to the floor, he said to me as he passed, "Talking is very important if wars are to end."

Later, we sat at the Hotel Raphael bar with Bernard Valery, the Paris correspondent for the New York *Daily News*. "I know you folks started this all as some kind of magazine promotion, and we all were kind of amused at your naiveté," he said over his cognac. "But the joke's on us. There are some rumors floating around that you may be used as a neutral communications bridge for opening new talks."

The next morning, however, it was reported that President Nixon had just resumed the bombing in Vietnam, and all the doors slammed shut. Myrlie's little speech got two paragraphs in the *International Herald Tribune*. We were exhausted and devastated. Still, we had tried. And we had lived up to the promise we had made to readers. Successful or not, we believed we had made a difference.

Lenore Hershey, former editor-in-chief, *Ladies' Home Journal*

•

To see life; to see the world; to eyewitness great events; to watch the faces of the poor and the gestures of the proud; to see strange things — machines, armies, multitudes, shadows in the jungle and on the moon; to see man's work — his paintings, towers and discoveries; to see things thousands of miles away, things hidden behind walls and within rooms, things dangerous to come to; the women that men love and many children; to see and to take pleasure in seeing; to see and be amazed; to see and be instructed. . . .

Henry R. Luce in 1936 on the "mission" of *Life* magazine

"A good reason to be famous...is so you can read all the big magazines and know everybody in all the stories."
–Andy Warhol

A few years ago, the American Society of Magazine Editors sponsored a panel whose theme was something like: "I've been up and I've been down, and up is better." The panelists gave wry accounts of their experiences of suddenly finding themselves without a job — a magazine sold from under them, a new editor bringing in her own team, a blowup with the publisher. I remember thinking, as I listened, how generous the panelists were to share their experiences of such confidence-destroying events.

From then on, whenever I spoke to young people starting out in the magazine field, or any field, really, I reminded them that everyone whose career path they admired, whose success and good fortune they envied, had certainly been unemployed at some point and had probably been fired at least once, and that the trajectory of a professional life takes shape only in retrospect.

And soon it happened to me. In 1988, *Ms.* magazine, where I had spent seventeen years, was bought by an Australian team, and soon I was out there consulting, free-lancing, and trying to convince publishers that the *Ms.* experience had left me with some transferable skills. What was memorable about that period, though, is that I experienced firsthand that same generosity of spirit I had admired in those ASME panelists. Every editor I knew checked in regularly with leads and lunch invitations. I don't think a single editing job came up in New York during those eight or ten months that I didn't hear about twice over. Each editor confirmed in word and deed that being without an affiliation was part of the game and did not make one an outcast. As competitive as we may be at the newsstand, the collegial bond is there when we need it. Which leaves me with an edited version of the panel title I mentioned earlier: "I've been up and I've been down and up is better, but when you're down, belonging to the community of magazine editors sure helps."

Suzanne Braun Levine, editor, *Columbia Journalism Review*

•

On my first Saturday working at *Yankee* magazine in 1958, I was upstairs at our eighteenth-century office building. My uncle Robb Sagendorph, founder of the magazine, was in the bathroom on the first floor near the stairs, reading *The New York Times*.

At some point, I became aware of a group of women wandering about downstairs. "Hello-o," they were crying out, "anybody home here?" I'd started down to help them when one of the voices suddenly exclaimed, "Oh, you're Robb Sagendorph! We never expected to find *you* here." Another voice chimed in, "We've seen you on 'What's My Line?' and 'I've Got a Secret!' "

As I reached the bottom of the stairs, I could see Robb, sitting — his pants crumpled about his shoes, the newspaper spread over his lap — surrounded by three or four nicely dressed elderly ladies who, totally oblivious to the situation, expressed their desire to subscribe to the magazine. Never one to turn down business, Robb meticulously wrote down their names and addresses, utilizing the pad and pencil he always kept in his shirt pocket. Then he accepted their money, even providing change fetched from his pants pocket on the floor. At this point, I tiptoed back upstairs.

Ten minutes later, Robb trudged up to the second floor while the ladies, still happily chatting, were getting in their car. "You know, Jud," he said, settling his six-foot-four frame at his desk, "we really ought to provide something for visitors to do here — especially on Saturdays when no one's working downstairs."

So began our gift shop, which we've been operating successfully ever since. And, in another change, the various bathroom facilities in our expanded offices here in Dublin are now plainly labeled as such. Then again, we seldom work on Saturdays anymore.

Judson D. Hale, Sr., editor, *Yankee* and *The Old Farmer's Almanac*

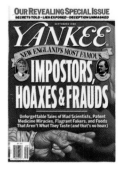

CENTURY

JANUARY 1919

Confronting Reality

NONFICTION IN THE MAGAZINE

Near the end of the last century, a new sound was heard in magazine offices: the clack of typewriters like this 1894 Densmore (above).

Shortly after the end of the First World War, *Century* examined the origins of the conflict (opposite).

T he great *New Yorker* writer A. J. Liebling once said in self-appraisal, "I can write faster than anyone who can write better, and better than anyone who can write faster."

What a lovely, judicious boast — an epitaph under which anyone who spent a life around magazines might gratefully slumber.

For the most part, nonfiction magazine writing is very much of the moment and to the point. Magazines live in the here and now. Paradoxically, that makes old magazines precious to us; with their unapologetic appetite for a present that is now long gone, they capture the particularity of another age.

Much magazine writing of course transcends its moment in history. Certainly that was the case with Emerson's essays, which appeared in such magazines as *The Atlantic Monthly* and Margaret Fuller's *Dial*. Yet even those pieces had the electricity of newness, of ideas crystallized from the air. They were written not only for their time but for an audience. That is another thing about writing for magazines; unlike a book, which is often a cry in the wilderness, a magazine piece more nearly resembles a letter to friends. It is written to a community of readers whose identity is more or less understood.

In the nineteenth century, the community of cultivated men and women was more easily definable than it is today. A succession of strong, reflective, and principled magazines served that audience. The best magazines nourished (and were nourished by) most of the leading writers of the day: Emerson, Thoreau, Twain, Howells, and James, among others.

The North American Review, founded in 1815, had a dignified, Anglophilic, and rather sleepy existence for a number of years. Emerson remarked that one could hear the "snores of the muse" in its pages, but, not one to worry about a foolish consistency, he was occasionally published there. Thoreau boasted of *not* appearing in its pages. Decades into its life, *The North American Review* became a much livelier magazine and at various times enjoyed the editorship of James Russell Lowell, Charles Eliot Norton, and Henry Adams. Its best years occurred after it was bought by a young man named Allen Thorndike Rice, who moved it to New York. In a short time, the *Review* published Whitman's thoughts on the future of poetry; Twain's devastating meditation on missionaries, "To the Person Sitting in Darkness"; and Andrew Carnegie's essay "Wealth," in which the industrialist argued that private fortunes are rightfully a public trust. "The man who dies thus

John Muir's article on "The New Sequoia Forests of California," published by *Harper's* in 1878 with illustrations by various artists, had a powerful effect: It led to the establishment of the Sequoia and Yosemite National Parks.

rich dies disgraced," he wrote.

Culture seemed a cozy, if serious, thing in Boston when *The Atlantic Monthly* was founded, in 1857. An early editor could say with serenity that all the best writers in America lived "within twenty-five miles of the Massachusetts statehouse." Pride of place and its underside, insularity, characterized *The Atlantic* during its early years, but the magazine did deliver the best of what was then the cultural center of America, in the persons of Emerson and Thoreau, for instance. It boasted the immensely popular "Autocrat of the Breakfast Table" series by Oliver Wendell Holmes and the political writings of James Russell Lowell, its first editor. In its pages, Harriet Beecher Stowe denounced the pernicious influence of Lord Byron on the American reading public (and, it is said, increased his popularity sevenfold). Toward the end of the century, Boston lost some of its grip on *The Atlantic*, and though the magazine always looked warily on New York, it paid close attention to the South and West. Mark Twain's lavishly entertaining "Old Times on the Mississippi" appeared in the magazine, as did "The Freedman's Case in Equity," a searing essay on Reconstruction by George Washington Cable.

The 1880s and 1890s were glorious days for serious magazines. *The North American Review* flourished, and *The Century* (though it soon failed) overtook *The Atlantic*, with a remarkable circulation of 200,000. *The Century* published one of the most successful articles in American magazine history with its "Battles of the Civil War" series, written by Generals Grant, McClellan, and Sherman, and by some 200 other participants of all ranks. *Harper's New Monthly Magazine*, started at midcentury and heavily dependent at first on English imports, came into its own in these years. It began jostling *The Atlantic* with such pieces as John Muir's account of the discovery of the great sequoia forests of California.

In their earliest years, American magazines depended on the contributions of their editors and of gifted and/or passionate amateurs. The writers who came to prominence and lasting fame during the nineteenth century had multiple means of support: books, lecturing, and professorships, in addition to magazines. But not long into the century there appeared another sort of writer, inglorious at first, though he may be seen as the progenitor of the modern free-lance writer. Around 1830, it became possible for a few writers to make their living writing for the coarser magazines. These writers became known as "magazinists." The first of the type to be identified

The Real Reason for High Prices

By Samuel Hopkins Adams

EDITOR'S NOTE.—"Thus far shalt thou go and no farther!" When the people of this big, hustling nation of ours become angry enough or determined enough to cry this command from the housetops at the great predatory trusts *and to see to it that the command is enforced literally and without favoritism*—on that day the first real step forward will be taken toward the solution of the gravest and most vital problem now confronting us. For years we have stood by like helpless children, watching the trusts cinch their hold upon national affairs. They have and they maintain the power to fix prices. The consumer pays. Further and more insolent still, tribute, like the famous blood and land tributes of the old feudal barons, is demanded of every one of us to help pay interest on the billions of dollars of the trusts' watered stocks—nine billions in railroad securities alone. How long will it last? Doesn't it seem about time to make a change, to *really wake up?* Such an awakening is all that is needed to put into force a very simple and a very effective remedy in the interest not of a few but of all the people.

SOME years ago Mr. William Allen White, the obscure editor of an obscure paper in the obscure town of Emporia, lifted up his voice to inquire "What's the matter with Kansas?" The query went echoing across the country. It reëchoed back to the state which originally voiced it. Kansas sat up and took notice. What *was* the matter with Kansas, anyway? Because it put that question to itself insistently and earnestly, that former commonwealth of cranks, malcontents, and long-haired visionaries who needed just that irritating incitement to "stop raising hell and go to raising corn" is one of the most progressive, educated, and self-representative states in the Union. Which is cited merely as evidence that when any considerable body of Americans can be brought to look a question in the face, they are likely to furnish the answer.

Some millions of whites, blacks, browns, greens, grays, and assorted hues and shades of Americanism are to-day asking "What's the matter with America?" They began by asking it timorously, next dubiously, then anxiously. Now they're asking it fearfully. Soon they will be asking it angrily, for fear breeds wrath in the blood of a free people. And in that day it will go hard with our leaders if they formulate no better reply than did William H. Taft to that unknown voice in Cooper Union, demanding to know what a man was to do, who, being out of work and able to work, could find no work. "God knows," said Mr. Taft sadly. "I don't."

Many men of many minds have made answer to the national riddle, in the COSMO-POLITAN'S symposium [June and July numbers], on the advanced cost of living. All agree upon one point: that the cost of existence has swollen like a river in flood. But that, of course, diagnoses not the disease itself, but only a symptom. And, as I run over the list of the contributors to the symposium, I seem to discern in the editorial mind behind the publication a subtle implication that these men are in some sense responsible for the ailment. The COSMOPOLITAN might have said to these eminent gentlemen (with one or two exceptions) and, I suspect, did say within its editorial self: "You are the guiding minds of this nation, you professors of economics who educate our youth to think, you financial editorializers who voice the theories upon which we act, you capitalists who determine our prices and trim our laws to fit, you millionaire merchants who direct our trade, you labor leaders who declare war or make peace for the great army of toil, you politicians who represent some of us all of the time, if not all of us some of the time. Let us hear what you've got to say about it."

And they say their say, and the result is turned over for analysis and report to me, who am neither economist, politician, employer or controller of labor, nor, Heaven knows, capitalist or millionaire, but only an interested and implicated observer, the man in the street; in short, that disregarded, discountenanced, voiceless, leaderless, and groping nonentity, the consumer. Whatever conviction or conclusion I advance is offered modestly as the view of a man who has to pay one-ninety-millionth part of the bill, and finds it increasingly hard to meet that growing obligation.

Here, then, are the principal diagnoses of the many men of many minds. Overproduc-

460

Drawn by Horace Taylor

THE GREAT TRUSTS ARE TREMENDOUSLY OVERCAPITALIZED; IN TERMS OF VALUE, THREE FOR ONE, FOUR FOR ONE, EVEN FIVE FOR ONE DOLLAR ACTUALLY INVESTED OR REPRESENTED BY ANYTHING OTHER THAN THEIR POWER TO OVERCHARGE THE PUBLIC

Cosmopolitan was one of the leaders of the reform movement in the latter days of muckraking. This attack on "the great trusts" was published in 1914.

The magazine that made muckraking famous: *McClure's* featured this photograph in Ida Tarbell's tough look at Standard Oil, which appeared in 1903.

by historians appears to have been Nathaniel Parker Willis, who was famous for his dandified dress and for his versatility (he could move easily from lyric verse to travel pieces to satirical sketches). Writing for *Graham's Magazine*, *Godey's Lady's Book*, *New-York Mirror*, and *Ladies' Companion*, Willis earned in excess of $1,500 per year. If he was more prominent, he was no more prolific than Lydia Sigourney, who thought of herself as a poet but who contributed some 2,000 articles to magazines before she stopped counting.

Magazines had a place for professional wanderers and watchers, for writers at large in the world of events. By the middle of the century, a form of magazine reportage was developing that would strengthen over the years.

No magazine was more important to this tradition than *Harper's Weekly*, founded in the same year as *The Atlantic*, 1857, but in certain ways a more modern magazine, closer to the pace of events and concerned with reflecting reality. *Harper's Weekly* came into its own during the Civil War with the battlefield coverage of George Russell and the illustrations of Thomas Nast. It subsequently turned a merciless investigative eye on the corruption of Tammany Hall and during the Spanish-American War gave the world the work of Richard Harding Davis, a glamorous Roman-nosed reporter who became one of journalism's first heroes.

At the turn of the century, the muckraking magazines, notably *McClure's Magazine*, immeasurably advanced the art of reporting. The work of Ida Tarbell, Upton Sinclair, Lincoln Steffens, and Ray Stannard Baker had social effects that are well known. For a contemporary reader it is interesting to see how their work seems to foreshadow the fictionist's narrative techniques — taking note of the telling, small detail; presenting quotes in persuasively vernacular speech; and calmly weaving those elements into an argument. With a measured tone that can still be heard in modern journalism, Ida Tarbell tantalizingly opens one of the chapters of her history of the Standard Oil Company: "For several days an uneasy rumor had been running up and down the oil regions. . . ."

McClure's went to a too-early grave in 1929, but the standard was taken up by the liberal weeklies. *The Nation* (already thirty-five years old by the turn of the century) elicited social reportage from John Dos Passos and Willa Cather, for example; and *The New Republic* got first-hand accounts of the Depression from Edmund Wilson.

Twentieth-century writers learned to speak with envy,

Lincoln Steffens's 1903 portrait of Pittsburgh (top), one of a series he did on corruption in American cities for *McClure's*. Seven years later, Charles Edward Russell looked at the Iron City for *Cosmopolitan* (above).

John Reed covered the Mexican revolution for the Socialist monthly *The Masses* (opposite), before writing *Ten Days that Shook the World*, his account of the Russian revolution.

Scribner's Magazine devoted a 1919 issue to the writings and world views of a former U.S. President.

The MASSES

JUNE, 1914   10 CENTS

Drawn by John Sloan.

IN THIS ISSUE
CLASS WAR IN COLORADO—Max Eastman
WHAT ABOUT MEXICO?—John Reed

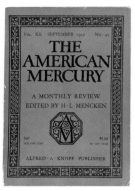

Three different styles:
McClure's Magazine, 1908;
The American Mercury,
1927; and *The Red Cross
Magazine*, 1918.

By 1938, when novelist
John Dos Passos con-
tributed this article to
Redbook, the magazine's
circulation had passed
the million mark.

ambition, or disdain of the "slicks," the big mass-market
magazines that came to dominate the industry, with — in pre-
television days — a pervasive effect on the general culture.
*Collier's, The Saturday Evening Post, Look, The Ladies' Home
Journal*, and *McCall's* offered huge audiences and budgets
to match.

Much of the nonfiction writing in these magazines was, to
be sure, formulaic, as was almost inevitable given their weekly
deadline and mass market. In the succinct description of
Theodore Peterson, a professor of journalism at the University
of Illinois and the author of *Magazines in the Twentieth Century*,
the typical piece consisted of "anecdote, generality; anecdote,
generality." And sometimes the other way around.

Yet striking pieces of journalism appeared in the slicks.
Collier's distinguished itself during the First World War with
frontline coverage by Ring Lardner, among others. During
the Second World War it published one of the first accounts
in any American magazine of a Nazi death camp. Written by
Jan Karski, a Pole who bravely masqueraded as a camp guard,
the article depicted the slaughter at Belzec, and its horror
has not been diminished by the avalanche of terrible knowledge that came later.

The women's magazines concentrated on stories that
addressed the practical and moral concerns of the reader. At
their best, "service" pieces (as the genre came to be known)
established a bond with the reader and eased the uncertainty
and isolation of domestic life. But these magazines also
felt a responsibility to cover women's issues journalistically,
as *The Ladies' Home Journal* demonstrated in 1936 with an

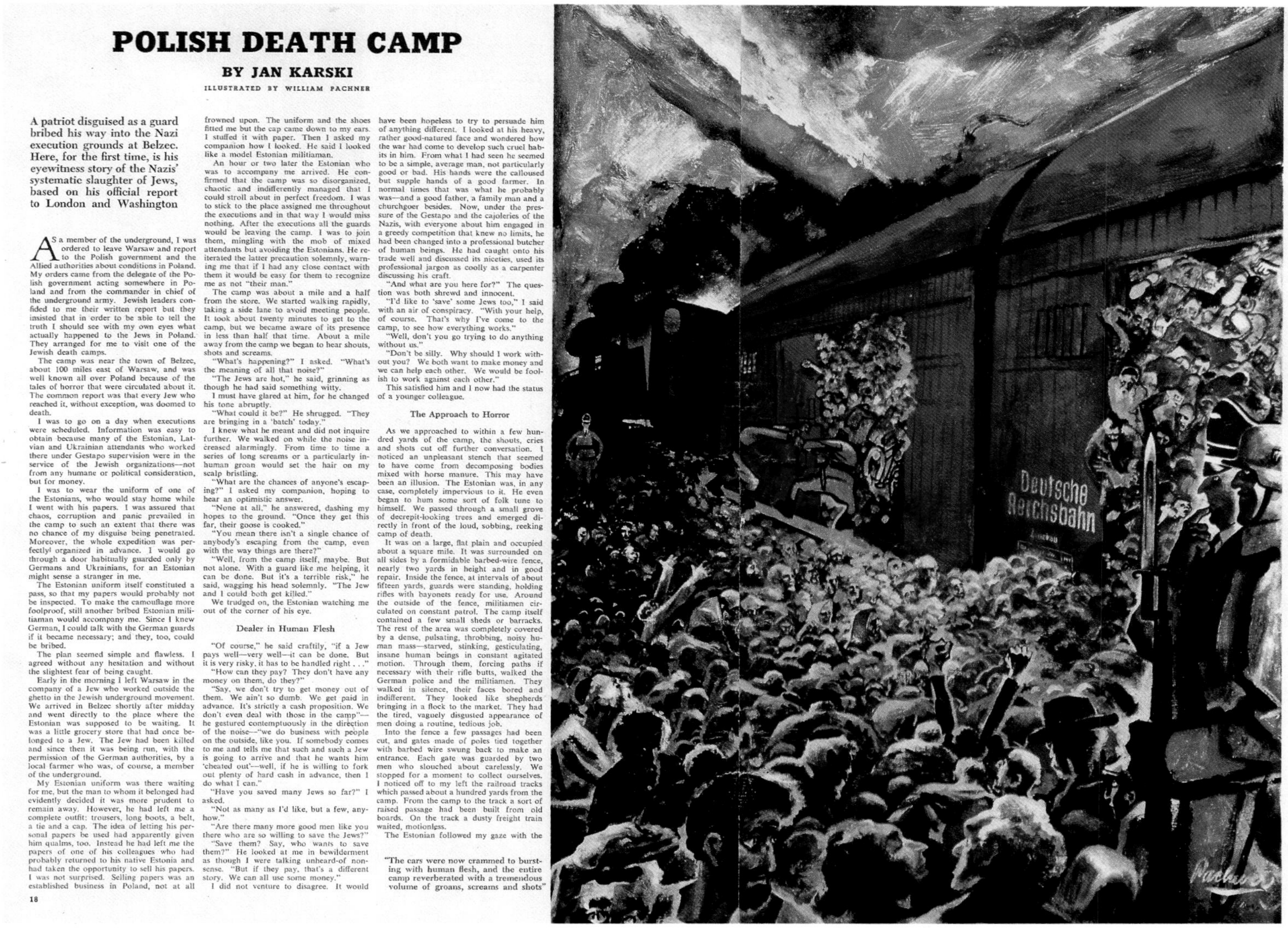

POLISH DEATH CAMP

BY JAN KARSKI

ILLUSTRATED BY WILLIAM PACHNER

A patriot disguised as a guard bribed his way into the Nazi execution grounds at Belzec. Here, for the first time, is his eyewitness story of the Nazis' systematic slaughter of Jews, based on his official report to London and Washington

As a member of the underground, I was ordered to leave Warsaw and report to the Polish government and the Allied authorities about conditions in Poland. My orders came from the delegate of the Polish government acting somewhere in Poland and from the commander in chief of the underground army. Jewish leaders confided to me their written report but they insisted that in order to be able to tell the truth I should see with my own eyes what actually happened to the Jews in Poland. They arranged for me to visit one of the Jewish death camps.

The camp was near the town of Belzec, about 100 miles east of Warsaw, and was well known all over Poland because of the tales of horror that were circulated about it. The common report was that every Jew who reached it, without exception, was doomed to death.

I was to go on a day when executions were scheduled. Information was easy to obtain because many of the Estonian, Latvian and Ukrainian attendants who worked there under Gestapo supervision were in the service of the Jewish organizations—not from any humane or political consideration, but for money.

I was to wear the uniform of one of the Estonians, who would stay home while I went with his papers. I was assured that chaos, corruption and panic prevailed in the camp to such an extent that there was no chance of my disguise being penetrated. Moreover, the whole expedition was perfectly organized in advance. I would go through a door habitually guarded only by Germans and Ukrainians, for an Estonian might sense a stranger in me.

The Estonian uniform itself constituted a pass, so that my papers would probably not be inspected. To make the camouflage more foolproof, still another bribed Estonian militiaman would accompany me. Since I knew German, I could talk with the German guards if it became necessary; and they, too, could be bribed.

The plan seemed simple and flawless. I agreed without any hesitation and without the slightest fear of being caught.

Early in the morning I left Warsaw in the company of a Jew who worked outside the ghetto in the Jewish underground movement. We arrived in Belzec shortly after midday and went directly to the place where the Estonian was supposed to be waiting. It was a little grocery store that had once belonged to a Jew. The Jew had been killed and since then it was being run, with the permission of the German authorities, by a local farmer who was, of course, a member of the underground.

My Estonian uniform was there waiting for me, but the man to whom it belonged had evidently decided it was more prudent to remain away. However, he had left me a complete outfit: trousers, long boots, a belt, a tie and a cap. The idea of letting his personal papers be used had apparently given him qualms, too. Instead he had left me the papers of one of his colleagues who had probably returned to his native Estonia and had taken the opportunity to sell his papers. I was not surprised. Selling papers was an established business in Poland, not at all frowned upon. The uniform and the shoes fitted me but the cap came down to my ears. I stuffed it with paper. Then I asked my companion how I looked. He said I looked like a model Estonian militiaman.

An hour or two later the Estonian who was to accompany me arrived. He confirmed that the camp was so disorganized, chaotic and indifferently managed that I could stroll about in perfect freedom. I was to stick to the place assigned me throughout the executions and in that way I would miss nothing. After the executions all the guards would be leaving the camp. I was to join them, mingling with the mob of mixed attendants but avoiding the Estonians. He reiterated the latter precaution solemnly, warning me that if I had any close contact with them it would be easy for them to recognize me as not "their man."

The camp was about a mile and a half from the store. We started walking rapidly, taking a side lane to avoid meeting people. It took about twenty minutes to get to the camp, but we became aware of its presence in less than half that time. About a mile away from the camp we began to hear shouts, shots and screams.

"What's happening?" I asked. "What's the meaning of all that noise?"

"The Jews are hot," he said, grinning as though he had said something witty.

I must have glared at him, for he changed his tone abruptly.

"What could it be?" He shrugged. "They are bringing in a 'batch' today."

I knew what he meant and did not inquire further. We walked on while the noise increased alarmingly. From time to time a series of long screams or a particularly inhuman groan would set the hair on my scalp bristling.

"What are the chances of anyone's escaping?" I asked my companion, hoping to hear an optimistic answer.

"None at all," he answered, dashing my hopes to the ground. "Once they get this far, their goose is cooked."

"You mean there isn't a single chance of anybody's escaping from the camp, even with the way things are there?"

"Well, from the camp itself, maybe. But not alone. With a guard like me helping, it can be done. But it's a terrible risk," he said, wagging his head solemnly. "The Jew and I could both get killed."

We trudged on, the Estonian watching me out of the corner of his eye.

Dealer in Human Flesh

"Of course," he said craftily, "if a Jew pays well—very well—it can be done. But it is very risky, it has to be handled right . . ."

"How can they pay? They don't have any money on them, do they?"

"Say, we don't try to get money out of them. We ain't so dumb. We get paid in advance. It's strictly a cash proposition. We don't even deal with those in the camp"—he gestured contemptuously in the direction of the noise—"we do business with people on the outside, like you. If somebody comes to me and tells me that such and such a Jew is going to arrive and that he wants him 'cheated out'—well, if he is willing to fork out plenty of hard cash in advance, then I do what I can."

"Have you saved many Jews so far?" I asked.

"Not as many as I'd like, but a few, anyhow."

"Are there many more good men like you there who are so willing to save the Jews?"

"Save them? Say, who wants to save them?" He looked at me in bewilderment as though I were talking unheard-of nonsense. "But if they pay, that's a different story. We can all use some money."

I did not venture to disagree. It would have been hopeless to try to persuade him of anything different. I looked at his heavy, rather good-natured face and wondered how the war had come to develop such cruel habits in him. From what I had seen he seemed to be a simple, average man, not particularly good or bad. His hands were the calloused but supple hands of a good farmer. In normal times that was what he probably was—and a good father, a family man and a churchgoer besides. Now, under the pressure of the Gestapo and the cajoleries of the Nazis, with everyone about him engaged in a greedy competition that knew no limits, he had been changed into a professional butcher of human beings. He had caught onto his trade well and discussed its niceties, used its professional jargon as coolly as a carpenter discussing his craft.

"And what are you here for?" The question was both shrewd and innocent.

"I'd like to 'save' some Jews too," I said with an air of conspiracy. "With your help, of course. That's why I've come to the camp, to see how everything works."

"Well, don't you go trying to do anything without us."

"Don't be silly. Why should I work without you? We both want to make money and we can help each other. We would be foolish to work against each other."

This satisfied him and I now had the status of a younger colleague.

The Approach to Horror

As we approached to within a few hundred yards of the camp, the shouts, cries and shots cut off further conversation. I noticed an unpleasant stench that seemed to have come from decomposing bodies mixed with horse manure. This may have been an illusion. The Estonian was, in any case, completely impervious to it. He even began to hum some sort of folk tune to himself. We passed through a small grove of decrepit-looking trees and emerged directly in front of the loud, sobbing, reeking camp of death.

It was on a large, flat plain and occupied about a square mile. It was surrounded on all sides by a formidable barbed-wire fence, nearly two yards in height and in good repair. Inside the fence, at intervals of about fifteen yards, guards were standing, holding rifles with bayonets ready for use. Around the outside of the fence, militiamen circulated on constant patrol. The camp itself contained a few small sheds or barracks. The rest of the area was completely covered by a dense, pulsating, throbbing, noisy human mass—starved, stinking, gesticulating, insane human beings in constant agitated motion. Through them, forcing paths if necessary with their rifle butts, walked the German police and the militiamen. They walked in silence, their faces bored and indifferent. They looked like shepherds bringing in a flock to the market. They had the tired, vaguely disgusted appearance of men doing a routine, tedious job.

Into the fence a few passages had been cut, and gates made of poles tied together with barbed wire swung back to make an entrance. Each gate was guarded by two men who slouched about carelessly. We stopped for a moment to collect ourselves. I noticed off to my left the railroad tracks which passed about a hundred yards from the camp. From the camp to the track a sort of raised passage had been built from old boards. On the track a dusty freight train waited, motionless.

The Estonian followed my gaze with the interest of a person seeing what kind of an impression his home made on a visitor. He proceeded eagerly to enlighten me:

"That's the train they'll load them on. You'll see it all."

We came to a gate. Two German noncoms were standing there talking. I could hear snatches of their conversation. They seemed to be talking about a night they had spent in a near-by town. I hung back a bit. The Estonian seemed to think I was losing my nerve.

"Go ahead," he whispered impatiently into my ear. "Don't be afraid. They won't even inspect your papers. They don't care about the likes of you."

We walked up to the gate and saluted the noncoms vigorously. They returned the salute indifferently and we passed through.

"Follow me," he said, quite loudly. "I'll take you to a good spot."

We passed an old Jew, a man of about sixty, sitting on the ground without a stitch of clothing on him. I was not sure whether his clothes had been torn off or whether he, himself, had thrown them away in a fit of madness. Silent, motionless, he sat on the ground, no one paying him the slightest attention. Not a muscle or fiber in his whole body moved except for his preternaturally animated eyes, which blinked rapidly and incessantly. Not far from him a small child, clad in a few rags, was lying on the ground. He was all alone and crouched quivering on the ground, staring up with the large, frightened eyes of a rabbit. No one paid any attention to him, either.

The Jewish mass vibrated, trembled and moved to and fro as if united in a single, insane rhythmic trance. They waved their hands, shouted, quarreled, cursed and spat at one another. Hunger, thirst, fear and exhaustion had driven them all insane. I had been told that they were usually left in the camp for three or four days without food or a drop of water. They were all former inhabitants of the Warsaw ghetto.

The Ultimate in Misery

There was no organization or order of any kind. None of them could possibly help or share with one another and they soon lost any self-control or any sense whatsoever except the bare instinct of self-preservation. They had become, at this stage, completely dehumanized. It was, moreover, typical autumn weather, cold, raw and rainy. The sheds could not accommodate more than two to three thousand people and every "batch" included more than five thousand. This meant that there were always two to three thousand men, women and children scattered about in the open, suffering exposure as well as everything else.

The chaos, the squalor, the hideousness of it all were simply indescribable. There was a suffocating stench of sweat, filth, decay, damp straw and excrement. To get to my post we had to squeeze our way through this mob. It was a ghastly ordeal. I had to push foot by foot through the crowd and step over the limbs of those who were lying prone. It was like forcing my way through a mass of death and decomposition made even more horrible by its agonized pulsations. My companion had the skill of long practice, evading the bodies on the ground and winding his way through the mass with the ease of a contortionist. Distracted and clumsy, I would brush against people or step on a figure that reacted like an animal; quickly, often with a moan or a yelp. Each time this occurred I would be seized by a fit of nausea and come to a stop. But my guide kept urging and hustling me along.

In this way we crossed the entire camp and finally stopped about twenty yards from the gate which opened on the passage leading to the train. It was a comparatively uncrowded spot. I felt immeasurably relieved

(Continued on page 60)

"The cars were now crammed to bursting with human flesh, and the entire camp reverberated with a tremendous volume of groans, screams and shots"

Jan Karski was a liaison officer between the political and military authorities in the Polish underground and this article is from his book Courier from Poland, the Story of a Secret State, to be published in late October, 1944, by Houghton Mifflin

18

19

Collier's alerted Americans to the existence of Nazi concentration camps with this 1944 article by a member of the Polish underground.

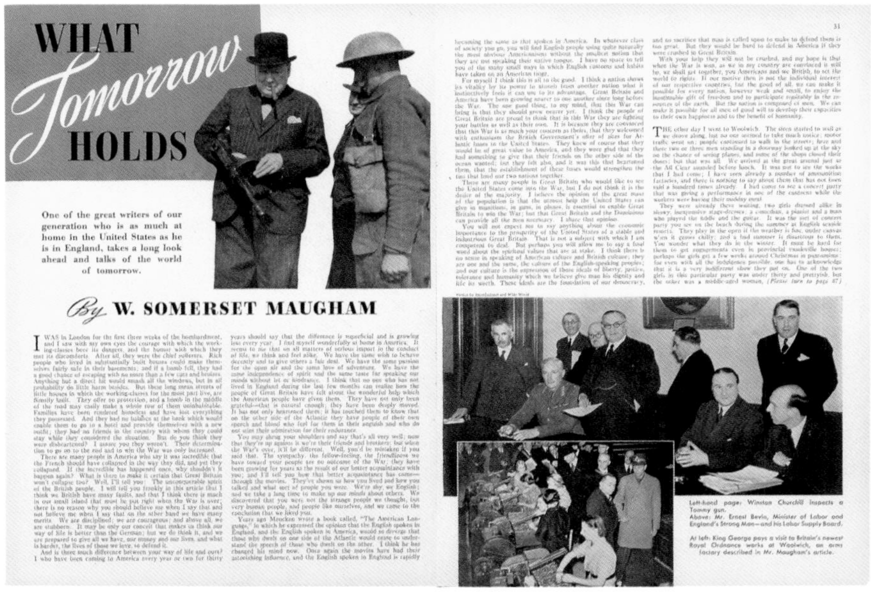

WHAT *Tomorrow* HOLDS

One of the great writers of our generation who is as much at home in the United States as he is in England, takes a long look ahead and talks of the world of tomorrow.

By **W. SOMERSET MAUGHAM**

Left-hand page: Winston Churchill inspects a Tommy gun.
Above: *Mr. Ernest Bevin, Minister of Labor and England's Strong Man—and his Labor Supply Board.*

At left: King George pays a visit to Britain's newest Royal Ordnance works at Woolwich, an arms factory described in *Mr. Maugham's article.*

In January 1941, when England stood alone against the Nazis, British author W. Somerset Maugham, writing for *Redbook*, sought to enlist U.S. support.

Holiday featured travel articles by well-known authors, including this guide to the Big Apple by *New Yorker* contributor E. B. White.

In 1964 Robert Osborn's line drawing of a lethargic humanoid set the tone for a *New Republic* cover article on the slow pace of desegregation.

The Ladies' Home Journal published Paul de Kruif's crusading article on "the preventable mortality of mothers in childbirth" in 1936. Readers were urged to "begin to protest now."

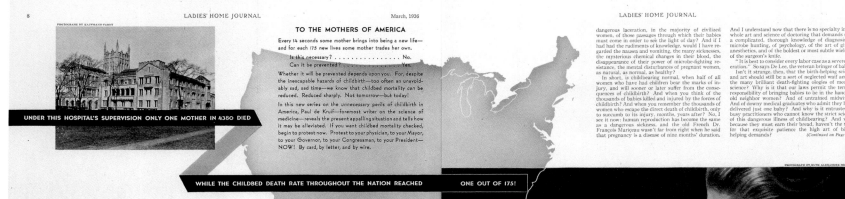

effective exposé of childbirth deaths in American hospitals.

Perhaps the best single account of the Great Depression was commissioned by Time Inc. James Agee, then on the staff of *Fortune*, was sent to report on conditions in the South. He came back with the text of *Let Us Now Praise Famous Men* — which, though not seen in the pages of the magazine, was published as a book in 1941.

Fiction dominated the slicks, but in their postwar heyday nonfiction became increasingly important. As the writer William Zinsser remarked, "Overnight, America became a fact-minded nation." Nowhere was this emphasis more pronounced than in *The Saturday Evening Post,* where charming "Tugboat Annie" stories made room for exhaustive coverage of the Cold War and — a favorite subject — crime in America. John Bartlow Martin, who came to prominence with a 1948 piece in *Harper's* called "The Blast in Centralia No. 5," became the *Post's* star reporter, even though he was a free-lancer. He was supported for as much as a year at a time to work on a single story.

"Story" was Martin's preferred term for what he wrote, for reasons that exemplify the serious magazine reporter's code. As he explained in his autobiography, "An article was a collection of facts about a given subject likely to be abstract, and almost certain to be pontifical. But a story was about people, some people in a time and a place and what happened to them."

If one magazine in this century can be said to have dominated the field of serious nonfiction it would surely be *The New Yorker,* which gave us new styles and new standards in reportage. It gave us, too, a new genre, that by now seems to have been in the language forever: the profile. As conceived by *The New Yorker,* the profile was not intended to say everything about a personality but merely to draw a provocative outline.

One of the earliest *New Yorker* profiles is also one of the best: Wolcott Gibbs's piece on Henry Luce — perhaps more aptly called a vivisection, but nonetheless a hilarious depiction of the young man who invented the concept of the news magazine. Written in a parody of "Timestyle," it contained a passage that has slipped into magazine folklore: "Backward ran sentences until reeled the mind. . . .Where it all will end, knows God!"

In 1950, *New Yorker* reporter Lillian Ross met Ernest Hemingway at Idlewild Airport, visited with him and his wife, Mary, at their hotel, and the next day went shopping and to the Metropolitan Museum of Art with them. Out of these casual encounters, Ross fashioned a perfect profile, called "How

The New Yorker is credited with inventing the profile genre. Truman Capote's memorable look at Marlon Brando ran in the magazine in 1957.

Rea Irvin's depiction of Eustace Tilley, a dandy from another era, appeared on the cover of the first *New Yorker* in 1925 and has appeared annually since.

Michael Herr's reporting on Vietnam in *Esquire* (top) in 1967; a 1961 *Holiday* containing John Steinbeck's "In Quest of America" (middle), which later became *Travels With Charley*; James Baldwin's "Fifth Avenue, Uptown," (bottom) a memoir of his Harlem birthplace, in *Esquire* in 1960.

Do You Like It Now, Gentlemen?" Although limited in time and place, it was intimate, vivid, and resonantly suggestive of its subject's strength and vulnerabilities. It was a slyly funny piece, quoting Hemingway's use of Indian talk in Abercrombie and Fitch — "Want to see coat" — and it outraged many of Hemingway's fans, but apparently not the author himself. Read today, it is a treasure, up-to-date in style and technique and yet fully evocative of the moment at which it was written.

"Civilized" was ever the word for *The New Yorker,* and it's true that the magazine succeeded in creating a dignified, unflappable tone that became a subject in itself. (No one employed it better than the gently witty E. B. White in essays and in countless unsigned "Notes and Comment" pieces). Yet the magazine over the years has been startlingly various in its subject matter, and despite — or because of — its decorum, it has been capable of a high urgency. In 1946, it gave over an entire issue to John Hersey's *Hiroshima,* which became a touchstone in the nation's understanding of the nuclear age. Similarly, James Baldwin's fervid *The Fire Next Time,* published in 1963, energized the civil rights movement.

The New Yorker also developed the art of reporting for reporting's sake. In the work of such *New Yorker* writers as Lillian Ross, A. J. Liebling, and Joseph Mitchell, the information conveyed mattered less than the sheer pleasure of watching a writer make something entertaining and occasionally beautiful out of the stuff of the commonplace world, rather like a weaver making art from the humblest of materials. John McPhee, a current practitioner who eschews statesmen and geniuses as subjects in favor of canoe-makers and sea captains, has a term for reporting that aspires to art: the literature of fact.

The sixties saw an outburst of vital magazine writing that came to be called the New Journalism. Its hallmark was the use of fictional techniques in reportage. Many protested that the form was scarcely new, and they were right, but no one could dispute the energy brought to the medium by writers like Tom Wolfe. Wolfe became the movement's spokesman, theorist, cheerleader; indeed, he sometimes seemed to *be* the movement. In his view, the New Journalist would not only employ the techniques of the novelist, he would supplant the novelist: Journalism would satisfy the society's need to understand itself. Of the New Journalists, Wolfe wrote, "They never guessed for a minute that the work they would do over the next ten years, as journalists, would wipe out literature's main event."

The Algiers Motel Incident
by John Hersey

In 1968, *Ramparts* ran
this investigative piece by
John Hersey, the author
of *Hiroshima*, about killings
that occurred at a Detroit
motel during the riots in
the summer of 1967.

Some of the best Vietnam
reporting appeared in
Esquire. John Sack's account of military training
and of the frontline
experiences of an infantry
company ran in 1966.

A pioneer of the New
Journalism of the sixties,
Gay Talese wrote this
story for *Esquire* in 1964.

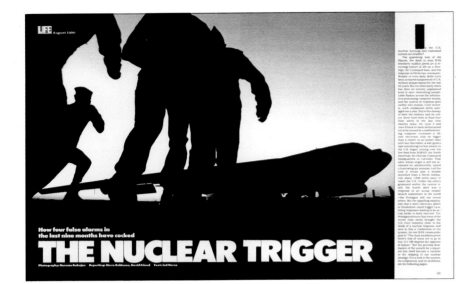

Life investigated the nation's nuclear warning system in 1980.

In 1971, *Rolling Stone* took readers on a mind-bending journey with the gonzo journalism of Raoul Duke, better known as Hunter S. Thompson.

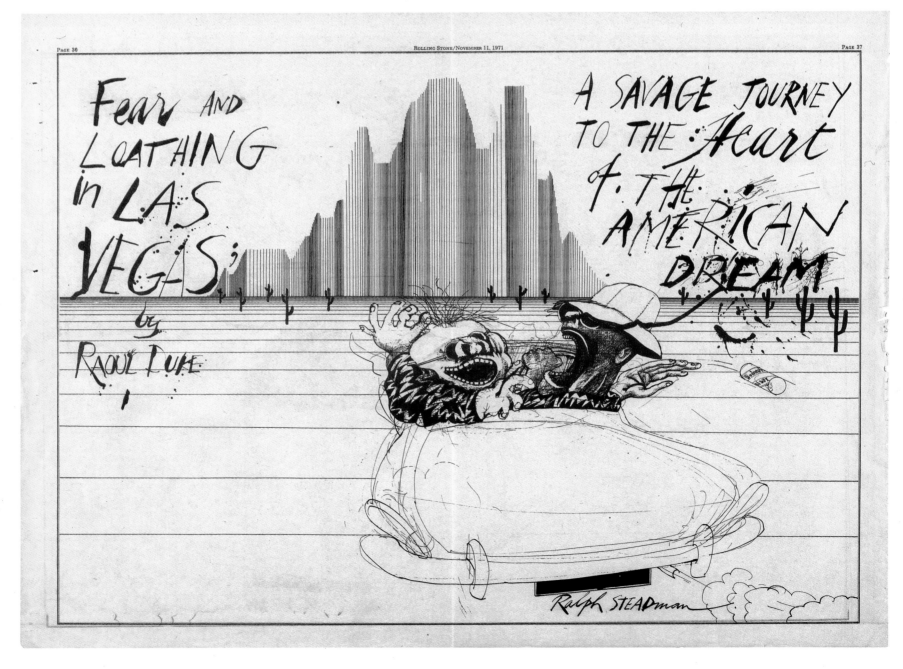

It didn't happen that way (even Wolfe turned to fiction), but the New Journalism produced some stunning pieces of magazine writing. Many could be found in *Esquire,* which published extraordinary coverage of the Vietnam War by Michael Herr and John Sack; witty profiles by Nora Ephron; Joan Didion's brooding despair over American life as represented by southern California; and Wolfe's own colorful coverage of subjects formerly thought beyond the pale: stock-car racers and rock producers.

In the "Electric Kool-Aid Acid Test" (begun for *New York* magazine's predecessor, the Sunday supplement of the New York *Herald Tribune*), Wolfe dramatized the chemically altered life of Ken Kesey and his friends. It was a time of chemical alteration. At least one journalist, Hunter S. Thompson, writing in the new magazine *Rolling Stone* ("Fear and Loathing in Las Vegas"), made drugs into a metaphor for the very act of reporting: "Gonzo Journalism."

Perhaps the best New Journalism was written by Norman Mailer, when he covered a peace march on Washington and wrote "The Steps of the Pentagon" (later the book *The Armies of the Night*) for *Harper's*.

Already the work of the New Journalists has slipped into history, and to come upon the magazines in which it appeared is to be startled by the patina of age: abandoned typefaces, quaint ads. Yet how grateful we are to the writers and editors once again for the achievement of permanence through the fervent embrace of the fleeting.

— *Richard Todd*

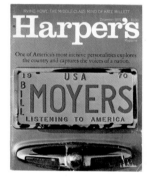

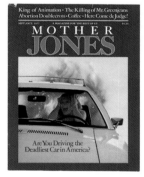

Four attention-getters (top to bottom): Tom Wolfe's 1976 take on the seventies; William Greider's 1981 account of budget management under President Reagan; Bill Moyers' 1970 attempt to catch the mood of the nation; and Mark Dowie's 1977 investigation of "Pinto Madness."

An Evolving Portrait

A first face of sorts: For almost half a century, Richard M. Nixon's face has been scowling, glowering, or smiling uneasily at the American public from the covers of scores of magazines. Presidents are natural cover boys, of course. Whether we love them or hate them, they move the reader, and that moves magazines. Even so, our thirty-seventh President is a special case. His deeds, misdeeds, and phoenix-like career have made him a favorite of magazine editors. Meanwhile, his extraordinary features — the drooping jowl, prominent nose, and trademark hairline — have ensured his popularity with art directors, illustrators, and political cartoonists, most of whom still miss his face around the Oval Office.

Staffers at the Nixon Library in Yorba Linda, California, have no idea how many times Nixon has been on magazine covers. It's just as well, because the final tally is far from complete. While former anybodies have a hard time getting their pictures *inside* magazines, Nixon continues to find his way onto their covers. Like him or not, editors will undoubtedly add to his record as one of America's most enduring cover subjects in the years ahead.

LIFE

THE YOUNG NIXON

- His career as an actor
- The steady girl he didn't marry
- Breaking into the dean's office
- Poker champ of Green Island atoll

At 14, Nixon played second violin in his high school orchestra

NOVEMBER 6 · 1970 · 50¢

The Powerful Image

THE IMPACT OF PHOTOGRAPHY

Last century's photographers, using heavy cameras like the Graflex (above), had no choice but to pose their subjects.

Steve McCurry's haunting portrait of a young Afghan woman forced to flee from her homeland (opposite) appeared on a 1985 cover of *National Geographic*.

In 1885, at the height of America's gilded age of optimism and opportunity, George Eastman, a bank clerk-turned-entrepreneur, confidently asserted that "the camera is getting to be as necessary to the newspaper correspondent as the pen." This pronouncement by the inventor of the Kodak camera was not shared by all publishers of the day, however, and it took the combined energies of several generations of entrepreneurs to make photography the vital component of American magazine publishing it is today.

Publishers had long realized that images were a potent means of conveying information, but getting photographic images on the same page as type in a timely fashion eluded them until the end of the century. The event that opened their eyes to the narrative power of imagery was a tragic one — the burning of the steamboat *Lexington* in Long Island Sound in 1840. Three days after the event, the New York *Sun* produced an "extra" with a finely wrought lithograph of the disaster (drawn by a young engraver named Nathaniel Currier), and thousands of copies were sold. Magazines co-opted pictorial journalism from newspapers, and they made it their province for much of the rest of the century. In short order, such magazines as *Harper's Weekly* and *Frank Leslie's Illustrated Newspaper* had the luxury of time in which to execute dramatic engravings.

As cameras became more portable and film more sensitive, photographers began showing up at news events, and their pictures became the basis of many of the illustrations in magazines from the 1850s onward. The journey from camera to page wasn't always easy. Some pictures that Mathew Brady and his associates took of Civil War battlefields saw print only after a negative emulsion had been transferred to a woodblock and an artist had painstakingly etched out a simplified relief image of the photographic original.

In 1880, the New York *Daily Graphic* became the first publication to experiment with a new process whereby a photographic emulsion was combined with dissolving acids to produce on a steel plate, in minute dots of ink, a faithful rendition of the subtle tones and myriad data inherent in a photographic image. Although the development of this technology may well have been as significant as the invention of the telephone a few years before, its debut was a modest affair. The first published picture — of a city slum, taken by Henry J. Newton — appeared as part of a two-page spread illustrating thirteen

In 1864, the third year of the Civil War, Mathew Brady made this albumen print of a young general. His name was George Armstrong Custer, and he was twenty-four years old.

other reproduction techniques in the graphic arts. A note stated: "On the lower left hand corner is an illustration entitled 'A Scene in Shanty Town, New York': We have dealt heretofore with pictures made with drawings or engravings. Here we have one direct from nature."

Picturesque scenes were not enough to prompt publishers to adopt a new technology. A war story was. The Spanish-American War — which some historians suggest wouldn't have happened but for the need of publishers William Randolph Hearst and Joseph Pulitzer for a circulation promotion vehicle — sent photographers scurrying off to the front to cover the action.

Leslie's, *Collier's*, and *Harper's Weekly* were among the leading magazines to respond to what had started as a newspaper war. *Collier's* was the one that, in the first decade of the new century, came to dominate the field of news photography, and James H. "Jimmy" Hare was its greatest star. Dispatched to Cuba in 1898 by *Collier's* in the company of writer Stephen Crane, the English-born Hare managed not only to fill most of the issues with his pictures, but occasionally to write the lead stories as well.

Hare's undisputed courage under fire, together with a good deal of cunning, made him a role model for later generations of news photographers. Once, he heard that a rival had secured the rights to photograph the secret launch of an America's Cup defender at night and had rigged an adjacent boat with hundreds of pounds of flash powder. Hare sneaked up on a shipyard roof, pointed his camera into the void, and managed to trip his

All is quiet in this photo of a Civil War battlefield taken by Brady's assistant Alexander Gardner. It was one of a series of powerful pictures exhibited by Brady under the title "The Dead of Antietam."

The preeminent photo-
journalist around the turn
of the century was un-
doubtedly James H. Hare,
who took this dramatic
picture of press photographers covering the site of
a 1911 explosion.

Hare, who covered five
wars between 1898 and
1918, worked principally
for *Leslie's* during the First
World War and was show-
cased in this 1917 ad.

The *best* war-pictures,
the *most* war-pictures
—*first* in

Leslie's

Two striking photos —
of New York's Flatiron
Building by Edward
Steichen, of a steam
locomotive by Alfred
Stieglitz — exemplify
the artistic force of
Camera Work, the
influential avant-garde
quarterly founded by
Stieglitz in 1903.

KOREAN CITIZENS: FUSAN, KOREA
(Group inside Municipal grounds.)

Color, which seemed an
astounding innovation,
came to the pages of *The
National Geographic* in
1910, in the form of
hand-tinted photos taken
by William W. Chapin in
Korea and China. Editor
Gilbert H. Grosvenor
called them "color paint-
ings." The experiment
was a success: Advertising
revenue soared. The age
of color photography was
off and running.

shutter at the precise instant his opponent set off the flash lights for his camera, thereby stealing his opponent's light — and exclusive photo.

Although the initial impulse of the early picture magazines was to bring sensational images into their readers' homes, sometimes the merely exotic would do. Gilbert Hovey Grosvenor, the young editor of the fledgling *National Geographic*, discovered this in 1905. By some miscalculation, just days before his January issue was to close, the printer called to tell Grosvenor that he would have to fill eleven more pages. No manuscript was available, but the morning's mail had brought an unsolicited contribution of fifty pictures of the legendary city of Lhasa, Tibet. Grosvenor chose eleven of them to fill his pages and fully expected to be fired. Instead, praise poured in, confirming his belief that a magazine should have "an abundance of pictures."

In the July 1906 *National Geographic*, Grosvenor made a leap of faith, publishing seventy-four "flashlight pictures of wild animals" in fifty pages accompanied by only four pages of text. In his remarkable half-century as editor (1899–1954), Grosvenor propelled the magazine into many firsts (the first color-tinted picture in a magazine, in 1910; the first true color photographic image, in 1914), while proving that a magazine built upon photography could provide an enthralling, and hugely popular, window to the world. In 1988, 100 years after its founding, *National Geographic* had more than 10 million readers in 170 nations.

McClure's Magazine, which addressed the working class and took up the cause of labor, put photography to work in a very different way — as a means of documenting corruption. Some of the earliest social-documentary photographs by Lewis Hine appeared in *McClure's*, *The Survey*, and *The Delineator*, in the beginning of the twentieth century.

At about the same time, Alfred Stieglitz, trained in the graphic arts in Germany, was starting a magazine called *Camera Work*. He founded the quarterly in 1903 as a vehicle for promulgating his cranky, contrary, but strikingly advanced views of modern art. Although it had a small circulation — the press run was only a thousand copies — *Camera Work* became not only the most influential journal of the avant-garde but a virtual encyclopedia of the latest styles and techniques in graphic design and reproduction. It existed until the outbreak of the First World War, and its fifty issues provided a showcase for the work of such influential photographers as Edward Steichen,

Lewis Hine was one of the first Americans to use a camera to document social problems. This portrait of a young coal miner is one of many Hine photos depicting child labor.

The Dadaist and Surrealist Man Ray photographed for *Harper's Bazaar* to support his art, but as this 1934 *Bazaar* photo reveals, his avant-garde vision was plainly evident in his fashion work.

Paul Strand, and Baron Adolf de Meyer.

Six years after Stieglitz started *Camera Work,* Condé Nast bought the society weekly *Vogue* and turned it into a fashion monthly that sent tremors throughout the field of women's magazines. *Vogue*'s stylized photographs represented not just a way for women to dress but an idealized way of addressing life. All women's magazines were touched by this editorial impulse.

Condé Nast built *Vogue* around the vision of Adolf de Meyer. A socialite with a mysterious background and a dilettante photographer with famous friends, de Meyer had fled Europe when Kaiser Wilhelm closed down the *belle époch.* He ended up in New York, short of cash but with great style and great connections. One was Nast, who promptly put de Meyer to work as chief photographer for *Vogue* and *Vanity Fair.* Furthermore, Nast instructed *Vogue*'s other photographers to copy de Meyer's soft focus and limited range of tones. De Meyer's delicate pictorial effects perfectly mimicked the prevailing photographic aesthetic of the day but also showed the clothes to their best advantage, a basic requirement in an essentially commercial enterprise.

When the world changed after the war, *Vogue* did too; de Meyer didn't. He was replaced by Edward Steichen, who

Baron de Meyer — whose title may have been self-conferred — set the tone at Condé Nast with stylish, soft-focus photography, like this 1919 image from *Vogue* (right).

Edward Steichen brought his own innovative style and theatrics to *Vogue,* including this 1926 fashion photo (opposite).

While on a 1949 Christmas vacation in Peru, Irving Penn created an innovative portfolio of photos for *Vogue*. He rented a local photographer's studio; then, taking on the man's photo assignments, he created portraits such as the one above.

W. Eugene Smith chronicled the life of a Colorado country doctor (above) for *Life* in 1948. The magazine devoted eleven pages to the photo essay.

enthusiastically embraced the modernism of the twenties with crisp lighting, sleek styling, and the use of anonymous but engaging young models who, freed of their corsets as well as their inhibitions, came to be known as flappers.

Condé Nast's early decision to cut back on society coverage in *Vogue* was aimed at carving a clearer niche for *Vanity Fair*, designed to appeal to the carriage trade. In that publication, the art of portraiture was refined by many of the same talents who were shooting fashion in *Vogue*. When high society went out of style with the Great Depression, *Vanity Fair*'s audience withered, and the magazine died in 1936, only to be revived in the roaring eighties.

Success begets competition, and for *Vogue* it came from *Harper's Bazaar*. When editor Carmel Snow left *Vogue* for *Bazaar* in 1934 and installed the relentlessly creative Alexey Brodovitch as her art director, there began a war between the two magazines to determine the world's top style-setter. That war continues to this day. Because of its more numerous international editions and spin-offs, *Vogue* has always seemed to have greater weight. As it turns out, that perception has served *Bazaar* well, forcing it to be more experimental and daring.

The meteoric Snow/Brodovitch years launched the careers of such luminaries as Hiro, Art Kane, and Irving Penn (who in the forties was lured away to *Vogue*; he remains one of the magazine's greatest assets). None of those stars, however, has had greater impact on fashion photography than Martin Munkacsi. A Hungarian who was a relatively unknown sports photographer before he began focusing on fashions, Munkacsi revolutionized the field in the thirties with his indifference to fashion's traditions and pretensions. Knowing nothing of stylized posing but accustomed to photographing life on the fly, he took his models out of the studio and into the natural light of the street. Munkacsi's models gamboled across the pages of *Harper's Bazaar* and in the process defined a new image of an American woman given to instinct and impulse. In later years marketing experts would hit upon the leaden term "active life-style" to describe the attitude that Munkacsi captured when he told his model simply to run toward the camera. Munkacsi's influence was reflected in the work of several generations of photographers — most notably Richard Avedon, who refined his master's art and who, like Penn, eventually defected from *Bazaar* to *Vogue*.

In the mid-thirties, presses were developed that could print rapidly on a large sheet of coated paper, dry the ink, and bind

Roger Bannister, the first person to break the four-minute mile, became *Sports Illustrated*'s first Sportsman of the Year, in 1954.

the magazine in one operation. Cameras had become smaller and films faster, so picture-taking became more candid and revealing. *Life*, the Time Inc. weekly launched by Henry Luce in 1936, provided the perfect format for this new abundance of photography.

Life was Luce's response to the already flourishing picture magazines of Europe and to Time Inc.'s *Fortune*, a successful business magazine that debuted in 1930 and boasted high-quality paper, fine design, and dramatic use of photographs. The photographer around whom Luce built his early *Life* was an industrial specialist from Cleveland named Margaret Bourke-White, who already had made her mark at *Fortune*.

Bourke-White's first *Life* assignment was to photograph a dam construction project in Montana, where it was assumed

Photographs for FORTUNE by Margaret Bourke-White
SCENE: ROSEBUD VALLEY, SOUTH DAKOTA   TITLE: HARVEST HOME, 1934

The Drought
by
Margaret Bourke-White
A Post-Mortem in Pictures

That this has been by all odds the most ruinous drought in U.S. history is old stuff to you by now. So are the details, as the press reported them, week by broiling week, through the summer. But all the same, the chances are strong that you have no idea what the whole thing meant; what, simply and gruesomely, it was. Really to know, you should have stood with a Dakota farmer and watched a promissory rack of cloud take the height of the sky, weltering its lightnings . . . and the piteous meager sweat on the air, and the earth baked stiff and steaming. You should have been a lot more people in a lot more places, really to know. Barring that impossibility, however, there is the clear dispassionate eye of the camera, which under honest guidance has beheld these bitter and these transient matters, and has recorded this brutal season for the memory of easier time to come. When, late or soon, it does come.

· 76 ·

"The Worst, Most Ruinous, Costliest"

. . . drought in U.S. history. Enough of the facts to explain its reputation.

ROUNDABOUT the first of May, 1933, in many parts of the Dakotas, it quit raining, and the barbecue began. Last winter's light snowfalls brought a crop of winter wheat which wrung the earth quite dry. Last spring, in those parts, was the driest on record. And with last summer's sun enlarging on the ruthless sky, the brown scorch spread swiftly, as when a cigarette is left to burn on dry paper. By the middle of last August a good third of our part of the continent was one wide crisp. The great map in the Washington office of Relief Administrator Harry Hopkins showed 1,400 scorched counties in twenty-two states, of which 1,100 were counted as harmed beyond all help, beyond loans and the purchase of livestock. Some 5,300,000 people—about 17 per cent of our farming population—and their properties and their crops and their livestock and their lean wallets were by that time for months at the mercy of the sun, the dry wind, the blown dust, the handsome rainless clouds.

The people had never known such heat as that which, in those months, stunned this continent. In the drought zone it crippled what lame growth there was, it crumpled dizzy cattle bawling into the dust. As for rain, new lows for April-through-July were set in nine western states; only New England and four other states had normal rainfall or better. It was not merely the driest growing season in U.S. history; it was the driest of three or four successive and abnormally dry years. The year's wheat crop was figured at 491,000,000 bushels (of which 400,000,000 were winter wheat) as against a 1927 to 1931 average of 886,000,000. The corn crop was estimated at 1,607,000,000 bushels; the 1927 to 1931 average was 2,516,000,000 bushels. All grain crops were the worst in thirty years. Tame hay was 46 per cent of normal, wild hay was 28, against respective percentages of 67 and 52 for 1933. Such figures, which stand for the U.S. as a whole, serve barely to suggest the wretchedness of the drought lands, where crops on the whole were hardly fit for the cattle. In fact by the middle of August, by the time rain at last began to fall—most of it far too late and most of that on the less wounded land—the season had furnished a very pretty set of illustrations of a few of the simpler ways of nature with man. And vice versa.

For the government set up relief machinery, set aside $525,000,000 for relief, made plans, made announcements. By mid-August the FCA had loaned about $4,000,-

000 for seed and feed; the FERA was carrying 800,000 with relief work; the AAA and the U.S.D.A. (United States Drought Administration) had bought, at an average of $13 a head, about 3,000,000 head of starving cattle. Of these about 400,000 were condemned and shot and perhaps a million more were shipped to better pastures in luckier states for fattening. The general plan was and is to slaughter and can or freeze them all for relief meat as quick as the processing plants can digest them. The hides may be made into relief shoes, may be held against a winter shortage. By December the government may have bought as many as 15,000,000 head of cattle—and 5,000,000 sheep. Meanwhile, feed to keep these beasts alive was a heavy problem. FERA machinery was being set up all of which the purpose was to comb the fields as they had never been combed before, and there was talk of buying Canadian hay.

Secretary Wallace made these observations last August: that the food shortage wasn't nearly so serious as the feed shortage. That the over-all food supply was only 4 per cent below average consumption levels. That animal foodstuffs were short—butter and eggs 10 per cent; beef, veal, lamb, and mutton 20 per cent; pork (recall the controlled hog-killing) 30 per cent—but that there were cereals aplenty and citrus fruits, and vegetables in general. And that thanks to the 1933 carryover (the surplus that brought the AAA into existence) there were 781,000,000 bushels of wheat on hand against a normal domestic consumption of 625,000,000. That a compensatory shift of diet would see us nicely through. That, despite the 15 per cent predictions of an assortment of agricultural economists, this winter's food prices would not outstrip the general price rise of 7 per cent. Whereto the Secretary added that the drought, while it would slightly relax plans for next year, had really done the AAA a service—had shortened by two or three years the steps required to put agriculture on a "normal" basis, under full control. He also said something about food chiselers and how the government would get after them.

The President backed him up on these statements. But he said nothing further about his great forest-belt project. Nevertheless, purchase of land toward that end, and persuasion of the farmers, do proceed—steadily if very slowly, as does erosion-control work in general. Slowly too, and quietly (for Reclamation Commissioner Elwood Mead had broken the idea abruptly

· 77 ·

and caused alarm) goes the delicate work of persuading the Dakota farmers, the sons of the very farmers whom the government had persuaded to take homesteads there, to move to land from which they can hope to wring a reliable living. The idea is that the Dakotas may once more be what nature meant them for—the finest grazing lands on the continent.

When we know what causes droughts, we may know better how to predict and how to battle them. About the best we know to date is: that the earth turns before its sun like a hog on a spit. That, subject of course to the infinite syncopations that are the forms of earth and air, the weather *seems* to work on the world in cycles of thirty-five and of eleven years. That the clockwork of the heavens was so geared this season that not merely the U.S. but Mexico and Middle Europe and Russia and Australia and—most hideously—the Yangtze Valley of China have helplessly suffered burns. That this is not the first but really the fourth year of an American drought. And that next year may easily be as bad, or worse. But if better, not likely much better; for the swings of the weather seem as a rule to be gradual. As yet, in short, we are neither very wise nor very capable against the sun.

"The clear dispassionate eye" of Margaret Bourke-White's camera provides a record of a "brutal season" for posterity. Bourke-White joined *Fortune*, in which this "post-mortem in pictures" appeared, in 1930. When *Life* started in 1936, she moved there.

The greatest campaign picture ever made, *Life*'s editors said of John D. Collins's 1940 photo. It shows Republican Presidential candidate Wendell Willkie arriving in his Indiana hometown to make his acceptance speech.

her proven skills would yield some monumental studies of industry. She performed as expected, delivering an architectonic cover image for the first issue, but the supplemental pictures she took of the daily lives of the workers and their families were a surprise to all. The editors created a nine-page lead story from these pictures, showing a Wild West boom town in the making. It marked the beginning of a narrative form new to America — the photographic essay.

The public would have tired of a weekly pastiche of pictures had there not been something compelling to say in them. Fortunately for publishers, if for no one else, war broke out in Europe and Asia, providing the impetus for picture magazines to develop their techniques and broaden their audience. (It appears to be axiomatic that the public's fascination with death and destruction stimulates innovation in the picture press.) After 1945, such photographers as W. Eugene Smith and Leonard McCombe, to name but two, elevated photojournalism to a level of elegance that would last until television captured a good part of its audience in the mid-sixties.

Changes in the booming postwar American society soon found their reflection in magazines. One such change was a desire to see the world — an interest that could be satisfied thanks to the then-almighty dollar. In *Holiday*, art director and editor Frank Zachary upgraded travel-minded readers from

Life documented the horrors of Nazi concentration camps — here in Margaret Bourke-White's eloquent photo of the liberation of prisoners at Buchenwald (top) — and showed war close up — as in Robert Capa's photo of the Normandy invasion, in June 1944 (above).

Nurses at London's Westminster Hospital sing to wounded soldiers on Christmas Eve 1940. *Life*'s editors titled it "Hark the Herald Angels Sing."

In 1964 *Look* let its readers enter the lives of some of America's poor with this photographic essay by John Vachon and commentary by Michael Harrington.

the comfy parlor atmosphere of *National Geographic* to first-class-cabin style. He sent unlikely pairs of celebrated writers and photographers — many of whom had never worked for travel magazines — to improbable destinations. The results were often inspired, as when Arnold Newman, portraitist of artists and statesmen, was shipped off to Africa to photograph tribal chiefs.

For men who preferred living it up without necessarily leaving the country, Hugh Hefner created *Playboy*, which included first-rate fiction, articles, and interviews but really focused on nude women. The magazine's first issue, in 1953, featured Marilyn Monroe as cover girl and centerfold. Its hallmark has been sculpting fantasy playmates for several generations of American males.

The increasing use of photographs raised the visual literacy of readers, which, in turn, pushed magazines to become more sophisticated. Nowhere was this effect more evident than in *Look*. For the first two decades of its existence, the fortnightly relied heavily on agency pictures. In the late fifties, however, art director Allen Hurlburt, and later his assistant Will Hopkins, transformed *Look* into a gallery for photographers whose work was not usually found in general-interest magazines. Avedon photographed the Beatles, Penn shot the Hell's Angels, and Hiro treated the chariots of Detroit as if they were diamonds from Tiffany's.

Another example of inspired assigning came from *Esquire*, which frequently tapped the talents of documentary expressionists like Robert Frank, Bruce Davidson, and the enigmatic Diane Arbus. Arbus was a photographer thoroughly familiar with photography's willingness to be an accomplice to artifice. She used her camera (and frequently a penetrating flash) to peel back her sitter's persona, revealing the psyche beneath as well as the photographer's own obsessions. The images were often too haunting or harrowing for the magazines for which she worked (they included *Harper's Bazaar* and the Sunday magazine of *The Times* of London).

In 1967, Arbus, Garry Winogrand, and Lee Friedlander were given an exhibition at New York's Museum of Modern Art. The three represented a new generation of documentary photographers for whom the picture magazine held little promise. Nonetheless, Arbus continued to work for magazines all her life while Winogrand and Friedlander left the field when their visions developed in ways the magazines found hard to accept.

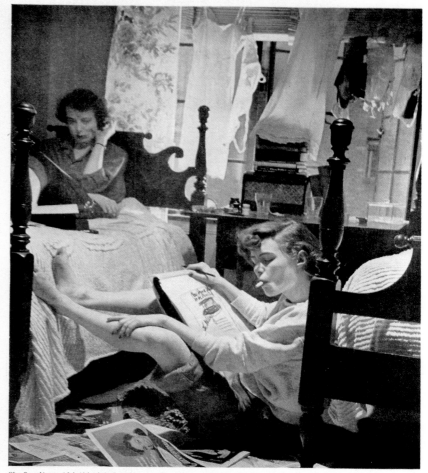

A spread from a 1948 *Life* essay by Leonard McCombe reveals the private life of a career girl. The photo essay, which the magazine introduced to America's readers in 1936, became a staple of *Life* and its competitors.

A Stanley Tretick photo taken for *Look* in 1961 catches President John F. Kennedy relaxing "in a golf cart aswarm with the clan's small fry."

Life's Paul Schutzer — later killed while covering the Israeli Six-Day War — took this photo of Vietnamese villagers fenced in by cactuses (above).

Week after week, photographs brought the pathos and horrors of the Vietnam War home to the American public. *Life*'s John Olson photographed soldiers being transported by an armored personnel carrier, as medics try to save a life.

Photographer Robert Ellison's *Newsweek* cover caught the intensity of a key battle in the Vietnam War. *Newsweek* called for U.S. de-escalation of the war and ultimate withdrawal in this 1968 issue.

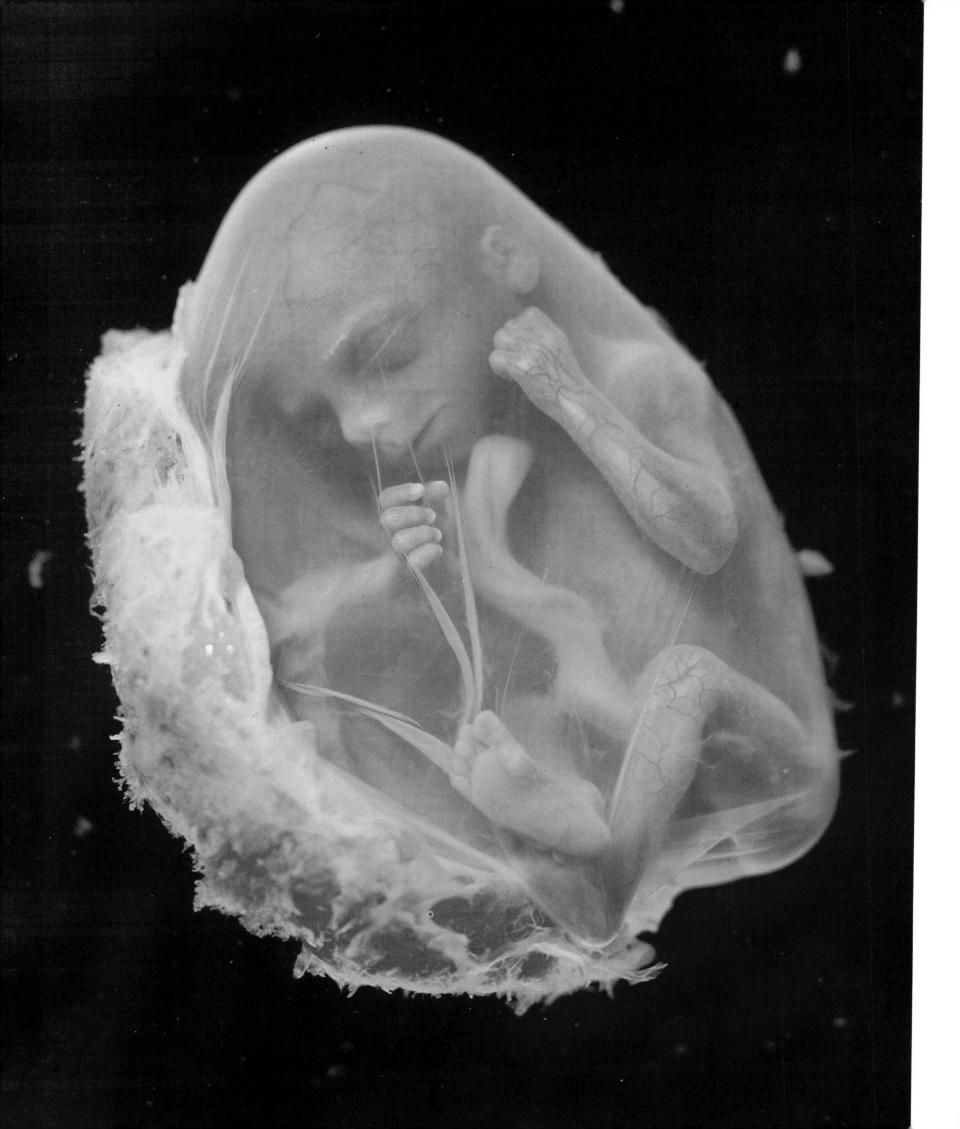

Rolling Stone (above) — "sort of a magazine and sort of a newspaper" — was launched in 1967 and nurtured a new generation of photographers.

"Drama of Life Before Birth" (opposite), an astonishing series of photos by Lennart Nilsson, appeared in *Life* in 1965.

The seventies saw the end of *Look* — it folded in 1971 — and the weekly *Life*, which folded the following year. The big picture magazines died, in part, because they were unable to adapt to changes in the way the public perceived images, especially after a generation of television. The photograph arranged in storyboard fashion no longer had the narrative power it once held for readers. On the other hand, single pictures, artfully conceived and stunning in their execution, could tell entire stories. The conceptual portrait, one that bore evidence of the strong hand of the photographer, became the currency of a new photojournalism, and magazines as diverse as *Rolling Stone* and *People* began to discover a new generation of photographers influenced by Arbus and her peers.

Rolling Stone, a product of the youth movement of the sixties, matured in the seventies but still had an attitude. Photographically, that attitude was best expressed by Annie Leibovitz (who was lured away to the revived *Vanity Fair* a decade later). As towering as Arbus was diminutive, Leibovitz stalked her subjects — often within the confines of a small room — until at last they yielded a revealing stance or glance. *People*'s brand of imagery, reflecting its heritage of former *Life* editors and photographers, was less cerebral but no less manipulative.

Diane Arbus's unsparing portrait of the king and queen of a senior citizens' ball appeared in *Esquire* in 1971.

Within two hours of the acquittal, the victory celebration started for the defendants and their lawyers. Stans soon went home to be with his ailing wife. But John Mitchell hung on; it was the kind of celebration he liked. There were drinks and self-congratulations all around, plenty of hugs and horseplay, even a medley of Irish and Scottish drinking songs. Telegrams poured in from Mitchell's former White House colleagues and from strangers. For defense lawyers Walter Bonner and Peter Fleming (who left the party early, pleading exhaustion), their skillful courtroom victory assured professional fame—and the high fees which accompany it. But John Mitchell was celebrating more than legal acquittal: for him the evening was the end of months of private anguish and public disgrace. Earlier that morning, leaving his own suite, Mitchell had been granite-faced. Since the trial began he had been a shadowy and furtive figure at the Essex House, where he had moved after leaving his wife Martha last September (PEOPLE, March 11). Fearful of being recognized in public, Mitchell had rarely used the hotel's front door; instead, he came and went through the back entrance, often shielding his face.

Now Mitchell, relaxed and smiling, took a few phone calls in his own room before joining the other lawyers and a few close friends in Bonner's suite. Slowly, as the evening wore on, the impassive mask Mitchell had worn for so long began to disappear. His face and manner again began to take on the assurance of authority and vindication.

After several hours of toasting one another, the group decided to end the evening with dinner in Manhattan's Little Italy. This time, on reaching the main lobby, Mitchell deliberately led his entourage toward the hotel's main entrance. Several well-wishers recognized him. A woman holding a camera grabbed his hand. "I want to wish you luck, Mr. Mitchell," she said. Mitchell laughed heartily. "I don't need luck," he said. "Haven't you heard? I've just been acquitted." SALLY MOORE

At celebration, defense counsels (from left) Edward O'Connell, Bonner and John Sprizzo offer Mitchell congratulations.

11

People, launched by Time Inc. in 1974, gave photojournalists a new market and readers a weekly glimpse of lively news and celebrity photographs. Here, Harry Benson catches the mood of a celebration that followed the acquittal of former U.S. Attorney General John Mitchell. Mitchell, charged with conspiring to block a federal investigation of fugitive financier Robert L. Vesco, is flanked by his lawyers.

More than fifty years after its inception, the photo essay remains a compelling vehicle for documenting social conditions and everyday life, as in this 1990 *Life* spread photographed by Eugene Richards.

CHILDREN OF THE DAMNED

The lady and the serpent — artfully photographed by Richard Avedon — formed a sinuous combination in the pages of *Vogue* in 1981. The photo was part of an essay devoted to actress Nastassia Kinski.

The runaway publishing success of the eighties, *People* created a genre of personality journalism that influenced not only other magazines but also newspapers and television. The sudden competition for celebrity subjects forced photographers to get more intimate or outrageous, whatever was necessary to obtain a striking picture. It was no coincidence that the photographers who stage-managed *People*'s early images were former Fleet Street veterans Harry Benson and Mark Sennet and newspaper-trained free-lancers Jill Krementz and Raeanne Rubinstein. Even *Life*, when it reappeared as a monthly in 1978, had learned during its hiatus that a single portrait today could be worth ten spreads of yesteryear — if the photographer's "signature" was bold enough.

A little more than 150 years ago, when photography first appeared in America in the form of shimmering likenesses on silvered daguerreotype plates, Oliver Wendell Holmes described the new medium as "a mirror with a memory." Great magazine photographs mirror our world, and are memorable because of an elusive quality that invites us to look again, to see again, and to make new discoveries about the world they contain.

— *Sean Callahan*

In Every Issue

Drawing cards: *New York Woman*'s "Loose Lips," *Woman's Day*'s "How To," and *Reader's Digest*'s "Humor in Uniform" (below).

A key ingredient in most successful magazines is the enduring feature — the regular section, column, or page that breeds loyalty and invites the reader back again and again. It could be a prosaic how-to column or an irreverent gossip page; it might offer a quick update on the state of the world or a breathless tour of the hip and the unhip.

Prior to the Revolutionary War, readers of Thomas Paine's *Pennsylvania Magazine* turned to "Monthly Intelligence," a regular section, for political news and missives from George Washington. At the end of the nineteenth century, *The Ladies' Home Journal* under Edward Bok invented the modern advice column with "Side-Talks with Girls." More recently, *Harper's* monthly "Index" has discovered life and even humor in statistics on everything from the number of potholes in U.S. roads to the life span of an adult mayfly.

Such features may inform, inspire, and excite. At their best, they're like a good friend, leaving the reader eager for the next encounter.

LOOSE LIPS

BY HELEN ROGAN

THE GALS OF D.C.

NYW recently received a mailing from a Washington, D.C., fundraising group for Democratic women called "EMILY's List." This coy-sounding name serves to illustrate the, well, *dowdiness* of Washington women. Called to account, a spokesperson said that EMILY stands for "Early money is like yeast." Adding, "It makes the dough rise." Asked whether she didn't find this a bit precious, the spokesperson said, "Well, we think it's kind of cute. And as a marketing tool it...

Margaret Tutwiler

the how to

HOW TO MAKE IT—HOW TO DO IT—HO

AND NOT A PIECE OF NEW FURNITURE

See pages 68 and 69

GENERAL DIRECTIONS

Diagrams 1 and 2 give exact dimensions and directions for building lamps and coffee tables. Diagrams 3 and 4 give general methods for building end table and wall unit with bookshelves; Diagram 5 gives procedure for altering sofa bed. Exact dimensions for these changes and others on pages 68 and 69 depend on size

When glue has dried, apply 2 coats of clear varnish.

If you cannot find abacá cloth in your local handicrafts store, write to:

H. G. Lubo
400 Fourth Ave.
New York 16, N. Y.

Two yards of 24" abacá cloth (minimum order), including postage, cost $1.50.

LAMP

Follow Diagram 1. Cut wire mesh 16¼" x 20"; bend 20" length to form tube

SEPARATED AT BIRTH?

Steely political footnote Geraldine Ferraro . . . | and once-important pop star David Bowie? | Tetchy actor of his generation Robert De Niro . . . | and tetchy actor of his generation Laurence Olivier?

Spy's popular "Separated at Birth?" pairs personalities with similar features.

...OM HELL

...unting New Yorker found
...at a place in a rambling
...pper West Side building. The
...ng it (by flashlight, as
...electricity in the apartment)
...about her "boss," the land-
...rned out to be Jay Weiss. "You
...said, "I was the person who
...out the Happy Land fire. I'd
...the radio." Asked if there were
...eautify the ...ilding's public
...e said, "Pro...here's only
...who takes
...ontaining f...
...be availab...
...ow, fire

Your ow...

THE C...
OU...

The Man with the Net

QUEER FACTS

In the early thirties, *Popular Science*'s "The Man with the Net" column (right) entertained and informed the magazine's readers with a mixed catch of "queer facts."

BEETLES *compose the largest family in the world.*

A SCHOOL *for inventors has been opened at Stockholm, Sweden. The tuition for the course is twenty dollars.*

BLUE WHALES *have stomachs large enough to hold several full-grown men, but their throats permit them to swallow nothing larger than small fish.*

SAY AH!

SARGASSO SEA *water is the clearest found anywhere in the Atlantic Ocean.*

PHOTOGRAPHIC PLATES *are now made twice as sensitive as the human eye.*

ELECTRIC *smell meters are used by British sportsmen to determine the best days for trailing with fox hounds.*

WHAT D'YA MEAN, SPORT?

OYSTERS *were cultivated by man before the birth of Christ.*

AMERICA *uses twice as much petroleum as drinking water in a given period.*

GIRAFFES *sometimes have hides an inch thick. Tanned, they outlast the hide of the rhinoceros.*

THAT'S WHY YOU'RE SO HIGH 'N MIGHTY!

GOLD *is so ductile that a 900-mile wire, it is estimated, could be drawn from a single pound of the metal.*

GRAVESTONES *from cemeteries in Moscow, Russia, were cut into blocks and used to face a new embankment built along the Moskva River.*

ELECTRIC NETS *to catch fish more easily and cheaply are a recent invention of Soviet scientists detailed to advise fishermen in the Barents Sea.*

DOWN WITH SCIENCE

Humor in Uniform

THERE were 165 of us, mostly Army and Air Force personnel, scheduled to depart for Vietnam by plane, a commercially contracted carrier. As we boarded, a stewardess stood by the loading door passing out the usual magazines. An old sergeant ahead of me asked her, "Don't you have any *Playboys* on this airplane?"
"You bet we do," replied the stewardess, "165 of them."
—SSgt. MICHAEL D. JONES, USAF *(Tacoma, Wash.)*

WHEN my brother joined the Marine Corps, the whole family was curious about his view of boot camp. This is what he wrote us: "The camp is pretty much what I expected, only rougher, and they don't leave you feeling much like yourself when they're through. The first day I was yelled at, issued fatigues and shaved bald.
"When I was showering that night, I noticed a bald, scared-looking kid next to me and I asked, 'How's it going?' He just looked scared and kept lathering up. I tried again, but he still wouldn't talk to me. Finally, I looked straight at him, and got the shock of my life. I was looking at myself in the mirror!"
—RENAMARY PARNELL *(Missoula, Mont.)*

SO THAT Polaris submarines may re...
...main at sea continuously...
marine has tw...

asked one of the veteran crewmen how he liked this system.
"Fine," he said. "Whether you get on with your wife or not, you get six months of happiness every year."
—VICE ADM. HARRY SANDERS, USN (Ret.) *(Coronado, Calif.)*

WHILE in the Army, I had a short assignment as chauffeur to an officer who was known for his impatience and quick temper. One day, as we were entering a high-speed turnpike, we found ourselves behind a woman who had come to a complete stop at the yield sign. She sat and sat and sat, waiting until she thought it was safe to merge with the speeding cars.
Finally, my officer could hold his tongue no longer. He rolled down his window, stuck out his head and boomed, "Hell, lady, the sign says yield, not surrender!"
Unruffled, the woman shouted back, "I'm driving a Ford, not a tank."
—JOSEPH F. MANN *(Williamstown, N.J.)*

MY HUSBAND's nephew was an Army chaplain serving a tour of duty in Vietnam, where one of his daily duties wa... attending wounded GI... pital. Earl...

PLAYMATE DATA SHEET

NAME: FAWNA MacLAREN
BUST: 35 WAIST: 24 HIPS: 35
HEIGHT: 5'10" WEIGHT: 122 lbs.
BIRTH DATE: 12-18-65 BIRTHPLACE: SANTA MONICA, CA.
AMBITIONS: TO REPRESENT PLAYBOY AS WELL AS I CAN,
TO DEVELOP MY CRAFT AS AN ACTRESS & WIN AN ACADEMY AWARD!
TURN-ONS: A GREAT DINNER - CHAMPAGNE, CAVIAR, OYSTERS -
HOME FOR SOME TV & LOVEMAKING THAT LASTS ALL NIGHT !!
TURN-OFFS: HOUSEWORK, MEN WHO THINK THEIR MONEY IS SEXY,
RUNNING LATE, STANDING IN LINE, TAXIS.
APHRODISIACS: OYSTERS, MORE OYSTERS & CRISTAL CHAMPAGNE.
MY LINGERIE DRAWER: BLACK LACE PANTIES, PINK GARTER BELTS,
SHEER STOCKINGS, DIOR BRAS & LOVE LETTERS.
ROLE MODELS: CHER, FOR HER COOLS; MARILYN MONROE, FOR HER
SENSUOUSNESS; DR. RUTH, FOR HER HEIGHT.
FAVORITE SPORTS: SKIING, AEROBICS, DANCING, BACHANIA
& LOVE.
FREUDIAN DREAM: IN PARADISE, WHERE WAITERS ATTEND MY EVERY NEED,
I ORDER A TALL, HANDSOME MAN & . . . WE WAKE UP TOGETHER.

Each month, *Playboy*'s centerfold girl provides facts, figures, and fantasies (above). *The New Yorker* (below) speaks its editorial mind in a section overseen by Eustace Tilley.

The Lower case

Carl's Jr. story in this spot right in here if don says
The Phoenix Gazette 4/13/90

Hafen is an enthusiastic reader and claims "Lame is Rob" by Victor Hugo as her favorite book.
The Scroll (Rexburg, Idaho) 4/22/90

Run-away boy found walking
The Reporter (Fond du Lac, Wis.) 3/19/85

Dog collars drug suspects
Columbus (Ohio) Dispatch 5/11/90

Carol Hendrix of York produces about 960 eggs per year, more than three times that of the average chicken.
York (Pa.) Daily Record 4/13/90

Program gears up to enhance compentence
The Retainer (Philadelphia Bar Association) 3/21/90

Black rhinos to benefit artists with dance at the art museum
The Aspen (Colo.) Times 4/12/90

Topless club owner donated to official
The Commercial Appeal (Memphis, Tenn.) 5/10/90

Permanent ban on jewish asked by U.S. agency

States News Service
WASHINGTON — The National Marine Fisheries Service, alarmed by the dwindling population of jew-fish in the Gulf of Mexico, has proposed a ban on fishing for the friendly undersea giant.
The Miami Herald 4/11/90

Not running
AP
Telegram & Gazette (Worcester, Mass.) 4/4/90

Police arrest 59 disabled in protest
Peninsula Times Tribune (Palo Alto, Calif.) 3/16/90

CJR will pay $25 for items published in The Lower case. Please send only original clippings suitable for reproduction, together with name and date of publication.

Editorial bloopers — typos and embarrassing juxtapositions of photos and text — are found in "The Lower case," the inside back cover feature of the *Columbia Journalism Review* (above).

THE NEW YORKER
THE TALK OF THE TOWN

Notes and Comment

WE have been thinking about a church that opened for services recently in Alexandria, Virginia. Called the Little Country Church, it was built with money received by the television program of the Hand to Heaven Evangelistic Association, Inc., and it boasts an artificial graveyard. It is the graveyard, chiefly, that we have been thinking about. The Reverend Joe Uhrig, who conducts services at the new church, was quoted in the papers as saying, "No one will ever be buried in the graveyard, and it is the only one of its kind in America." Now, the . . . add to the charm of the Church by sc . . .

stroke, provide an unfortunate Egyptian with a decent burial in Alexandria (whose name, at least, would be familiar), furnish his new graveyard with a respectable tenant, and establish his church as the only one in America to have both television facilities and a mummy more than sixteen hundred years old.

Lovers

OUR old friend Ju . . . Jr., on . . .

faces, before some ancient and dingy loft building, plainly assumed that we had lost our marbles, but we weren't abashed; devotion has the look of eccentricity in any weather, and if the building was ancient and dingy, it was al . . . us, precious.
In the cast-iron . . .
Mr. Reed . . .

The Delineator came with a special treat each month — The Little Delineator, a two-page children's section that when cut and folded made eight smaller pages of informative and amusing reading.

The Ladies' Home Journal's "Side-Talks" column in 1896: Editor Edward Bok was the first "Ruth Ashmore." In the course of sixteen years, the column brought in nearly 160,000 letters.

SIDE-TALKS WITH GIRLS

BY RUTH ASHMORE

I would ask of my girls that, when they write to me desiring an answer by mail, they will be careful to write clearly, not only their own names and the name of the town in which they live, but the name of the State as well. Also, before their signatures, when they do not send addressed envelopes, will they please put in brackets either "Miss" or "Mrs." to prevent me from seeming rude? I want to thank my girls for all their kindness to me, and especially for the appreciation they have shown the little book which I consider belongs to them.

MAY—It is not considered in good taste for a girl of eighteen to drive out alone with a young man.

LILIAN—In sending wedding invitations or announcements the outer envelope should be sealed.

GRACE—In addressing a letter to a young unmarried lady, "Miss" should always precede her name.

A SUBSCRIBER—It would be in very bad taste to appear at an informal afternoon card-party in full dress.

E. C. R.—A lady should always thank a gentleman for showing her any courtesy, no matter how slight it may be.

COUNTRY GIRL—The gentleman usually chooses the engagement ring that he presents to his betrothed.

RETLAW—In making an introduction the gentleman is presented to the lady, and not the lady to the gentleman.

ALICE E. D.—I do not think it wise, even if you are teaching these young men, to give them your photograph.

INDIANA GIRL—A gentleman walking with two ladies should take the outer side and not walk between them.

VIOLET—Finger-bowls and the tiny doilies under them are removed from the small plates on which they are placed.

FAWN—In signing your name to a letter written to a man friend let it be "Yours very cordially, Mary Stuart Calvert."

MAY W.—When a man friend has taken you to a concert thank him for his kindness in giving you a pleasant evening.

GRAY ROCK—"The Misses Smith" includes as many daughters of Mrs. John Livingston Smith as are out in society.

HOPE—Rub vaseline on your nails every night before going to bed. The white spots are said to come from bruises.

BEATRICE—I think it very proper for young girls to read good novels, but care should be taken that the right kind are selected.

BESS—If the lady to whom you are introduced is elderly while you are young, is a matron while you are unmarried, then you should rise to bow, but if she is of your own age and position take your bow without rising is sufficient.

M. C. H.—"Father" and "mother" are the best and sweetest names to give to one's parents. (2) It is never in good taste to take a lady's arm unless she is an invalid, very old, or needs assistance in crossing a crowded street.

BOY—I do not think it in good taste to ask permission of the young lady to whom you are not engaged for the privilege of calling her by her Christian name. (2) A letter should not commence "Dear Miss Nellie," but "Dear Miss Smith."

B. G. R.—Most writers are overwhelmed with requests for autographs; at the same time, there would be no impropriety in writing to that one whose works you enjoy, and asking this favor. Inclose in your letter a stamped and addressed envelope.

SAN ANTONIO—I cannot advise the use of peroxide of hydrogen on the hair. It certainly does it no good, and the color obtained by it gives a woman a very undesirable appearance. (2) A girl of seventeen should be thinking of more important things than corresponding with a young man.

WILHELMINA—It is not necessary, because your table is dressed in green and white, to have your own costume show the same colors, although it would be wise to have it harmonize with the color scheme of the room. (2) The best authority on cooking, to my way of thinking, is an experienced cook.

I. M. B.—Knives are placed on the right and forks on the left of each place, while a small piece of bread or French roll is folded in the napkin and laid between the knife and fork. (2) When tea or coffee is served a spoon is in the saucer of each cup. Spoons are no longer put on the table either in dishes or holders.

BON—If you wish to see a good play or hear some fine music, and cannot arrange for a companion, there would be no impropriety whatever in your going alone to a matinée. (2) The reading of the newspapers and magazines of the day and talking about them will tend to make you versatile in conversation.

Glamour introduced its "Dos & Don'ts" column — a "must read" for avoiding fashion faux pas — in the mid-sixties.

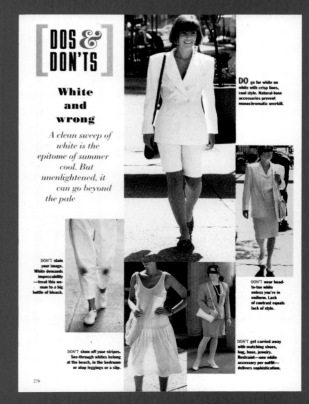

Outdoor Life's readers tell their own tales of adventure in this popular feature, which lures contributors with a cash incentive.

In a crunch, however, some progress might be welcome

Life, like many magazines, likes to leave its readers smiling. Although the title of the closing page has changed over the years, the editorial purpose has remained the same.

This sheaf of special sections includes (from top to bottom) samples from Consumer Reports, The Saturday Evening Post, Mechanix Illustrated (note the 1957 prediction of a removable car radio), and National Lampoon.

Under various titles, *Sports Illustrated* has taken note of those "faces in the crowd" — including a seventeen-year-old golfer named Jack Nicklaus (center).

SCOREBOARD

these faces in the crowd . . .

Angel Macias, pint-sized, ambidextrous *niño* from Monterrey, Mexico, turned right-hander to pitch perfect 4–0 no-hitter against bigger La Mesa, Calif. in final game, giving his Cinderella team Little League World Series title at Williamsport, Pa.

Jack Nicklaus, husky 17-year-old homebred, made up two-stroke deficit soon after start of final round but had to hang on grimly in face of determined challenge by John Konsek to win (294–296) international jaycee junior golf title at Columbus.

Bob Robbins, 21, speed-loving daredevil from West Suffield, Conn., bounced his Class D utility outboard around calm Lake Quinsigamond at average speed of 51.65 mph to win 100-mile Mennen Grand National at Worcester, Mass.

GOOFUS and GALLANT

BY GARRY CLEVELAND MYERS

PICTURES BY MARION E. HULL

Goofus rushes into the street after his ball and never looks for cars.

Gallant watches the rolling ball from the curb and then looks for cars.

Goofus and Gallant, who live up to their names, have been teaching manners and ethics to readers of *Highlights for Children* (above) for several decades.

BEST BETS

Recommendations of events, places, and phenomena of particular interest this week

By Nancy McKeon

Peking Man

Come to the Cabaret

Breaking Up Is Hard to Do

As You Like It

Snow Business

For more than twenty years, *New York*'s "Best Bets" (above) has tipped off upscale readers to hot consumer items and to the latest in fashion and entertainment.

Overheard

PERSPECTIVES

"I'm Dan Quayle. I'm Dan Quayle. I'm Dan Quayle. I am Dan Quayle. I'm Dan Quayle. The real Dan Quayle. The real Dan Quayle stand up. I'm Dan Quayle. I'm Dan Quayle."
DAN QUAYLE, in a transcript of an eloquence-training lesson soon after George Bush selected him as his running mate

"What do you do if you're in a room with Muammar Kaddafi, Saddam Hussein and John Sununu and you have a gun that has only two bullets? Shoot Sununu twice."
Massachusetts Gov. MICHAEL DUKAKIS, telling a joke about White House chief of staff John Sununu, who was Dukakis's nemesis in the 1988 presidential campaign

"If it'll make you feel better, I promise not to drop you from the ticket in '92...."

© 1990 MIKE LUCKOVICH — ATLANTA CONSTITUTION

COMRADE, WHAT DO YOU THINK OF MY NOBEL PEACE PRIZE?

NEEDS SALT.

© 1990 CAMUSO — SYRACUSE HERALD-JOURNAL

"I want to say to the family of Mr. Truesdale, 'I'm dead. You don't have to hate me anymore'."
Convicted murderer WILBERT LEE EVANS, just before he was executed last week in Virginia for killing sheriff's deputy William Truesdale

"Satan, you demonic spirit, I bind you in Jesus' name. Loose those finances. Mountain of bills, be thou removed. Be cast into the sea. Go. Go. Go. La-ba-sue."
ROBERT TILTON, the new ratings favorite among televangelists, speaking in tongues during a recent broadcast in which he asked viewers to each pledge $1,000

"Give him a couple million. He should second job to support himself. Oakland Athletics...

"Vote for Mestrinho. He could be your father."
A campaign slogan circulated by enemies of Brazilian gubernatorial... Mestrinho, who has f...

Newsweek's "Perspectives" page gives the reader a sampling of the week's best political cartoons and "Overheard" comments from the famous and the obscure.

HARPER'S INDEX

Number of American universities that have instituted restrictions on public speech since 1988 : 137
Number of personal-computer disks seized from American homes by Secret Service agents last May : 23,000
Total number of documents classified as "secret" or "top secret" by the federal government last year : 5,506,720
Number of times the phrase "read my lips" has appeared in the *Washington Post* since George Bush's inauguration : 140
Average portion of their tax dollars Americans estimate are wasted : 1/2
Number of El Salvador's 15 highest-ranking officers whose troops have committed "brutal human rights abuses" : 14
Number of these officers who have received U.S. training : 12
Average number of South African police officers who have resigned each day this year : 23
Percentage change, since last fall, in the number of riot-control troops on duty in the Soviet Union : +250
Ratio of the average office rent in Moscow's business district to the rent in midtown Manhattan, per square foot : 2:1
Percentage change, since the first quarter of 1989, in the total capital raised by new junk bond issues : −94
Percentage of all outstanding junk bonds that are owned by U.S. life insurance companies : 17
Number of U.S. life insurance companies that have gone bankrupt since 1985 : 68
Percentage of all savings and loan associations that failed during the Depression : 5
Percentage that the government expects will fail in the next five years : 25
Percentage of Americans who say that, given the choice, they would rather hear the bad news first : 63
Number of international terrorist organizations in 1969 : 13
Number today : 74
Incidents of international terrorism since 1977 that involved a BMW : 33
Incidents that involved a Chevrolet Camaro : 1
Rank of Hong Kong, among localities with the most Rolls-Royces per capita : 1
Number of automobiles that have been discarded in the United States since 1946 : 288,324,898
Months after Exxon hired Veco International to clean up the *Valdez* spill that Veco bought the *Anchorage Times* : 9
Chances that the level of pollution in a U.S. river has gotten worse or not improved since 1970 : 9 in 10
Number of families who have applied to purchase homes at Love Canal this year : 225
Number of people who still live in areas contaminated by the Chernobyl accident : 2,200,000
Federal funds to be spent this year on lead-lined trucks to house the administration during nuclear attack : $58,000,000
Amount the President proposes to spend on this program next year : $85,000,000
Federal funds spent on drug-rehabilitation programs for state and local prison inmates last year : $2,000,000
Federal funds budgeted for these programs this year : 0
Ratio of reported rape victims with incomes of less than $3,000 to those with incomes of more than $15,000 : 6:1
Chances that the death of a 10- to 14-year-old American in 1968 was a suicide : 1 in 69
Chances today : 1 in 17
Number of Colombians killed by death squads last year because they were believed to be homosexuals or prostitutes : 364
Estimated percentage of AIDS carriers, worldwide, who contracted the virus through heterosexual sex : 60
Amount the U.S. Air Force spent this year to study the effects of jet noise on pregnant horses : $100,000
Percentage of veterinarians who say they have felt depressed after putting an animal to sleep : 67 (see page 25)
Percentage of men between the ages of 40 and 64 who snore heavily : 60
Percentage of rural Chinese couples who say they usually spend less than a minute on foreplay : 34

Figures cited are the latest available as of June 1990. Sources are listed on page 78.
"Harper's Index" is a registered trademark.

Its editors describe the always interesting and often-imitated "Harper's Index" as "a single page of numbers that measure the drifting tide of events."

Esquire's "Dubious Achievement Awards" poke fun at the foibles of many of the year's headliners. In its twenty-ninth year, the section has become a tradition.

One column of *Metropolitan Home*'s "Metro" section on interesting life-style tidbits is devoted to "Icon," which picks a product — like this inexpensive "precursor of the video game" — and provides a pocket history.

ICON

ETCH A SKETCH

DATE OF BIRTH: Late 1950s, Paris

CREATOR: Toy designer Arthur Grandjean

ORIGIN: Grandjean invented L'Ecran Magique in his garage and sold it at the 1959 Nuremberg Toy Fair to the Ohio Art Company toy makers. They rechristened it Etch a Sketch Magic Screen and introduced it in 1960. Since then more than 50 million have been sold worldwide. The Etch A Sketch Club has some 10,000 members, from age two to 74.

HOW IT WORKS: The screen's reverse side is coated with a mixture of aluminum powder and plastic beads. The left knob operates the horizontal stylus; the right, a vertical one; turn them simultaneously and they etch a curve. Shake the screen and the powder recoats the glass, erasing all.

APPEAL: Etch A Sketch is part puzzle, part artistic medium. It's an engaging hand-eye exercise with the creative challenge of drawing a continuous line. The toy offers the elemental satisfaction of drawing in sand. As a precursor of the video game, it's much less expensive (about $10), and almost indestructible.

EVOLUTION: The magic screen has changed little since its introduction. (The company briefly offered hot-pink and bright-blue frames during the rainbow-happy Seventies.) A new microchip-driven model has just been introduced, the Etch A Sketch Animator 2000. Purists might argue that the Animator (at around $50) isn't as much fun or as demanding as the original: You can erase lines and move the image around at will.

RELEVANCE: Etch A Sketch makes artists out of children and adults alike. Professional artists have adopted it as a portable sketchpad with the soothing quality of worry beads. Some have even sold their Etch A Sketch pictures (after removing the powder and spraying a fixative on the back of the glass). The toy's wonderfully forgiving message is that a fresh start and a brand-new canvas are always just a shake away. —*Diane di Costanzo*

VOGUE

INCORPORATING VANITY FAIR

FIFTY
BATHING
SUITS

V ★ O   COPYRIGHT 1940. THE CONDÉ NAST PUBLICATIONS, INC.

BEACH FASHIONS · BEAUTY · SUMMER TRAVEL · JUNE 1, 1940 · PRICE 35 CENTS

Visual Dynamics

THE MAGIC OF GRAPHIC DESIGN

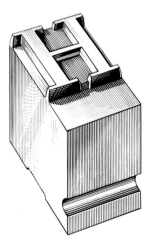

One of the building blocks of a powerful layout: letters shaped to the designer's unique vision (above).

Lisa Fonssagrives posed six ways for photographer Erwin Blumenfeld to create this 1940 *Vogue* cover designed by Mehemed Fehmy Agha (opposite).

In the dusty attic of a house in a small New York State town a few years ago, I came upon a stack of pristine *Fortune* magazines dating from before the Second World War. Dignified and rather somber-looking, so large as to seem almost ponderous, they lay there in an old trunk, miraculously preserved, like ancient mammoths trapped in glacial ice. The owner of the house, an old man with only a shred of memory left, had been a graphic designer at a New York advertising agency decades ago and kept these issues of *Fortune*, with their powerful, pioneering layouts, just as armchair travelers hoarded copies of *The National Geographic*. As I opened one, I instantly understood why. The first two-page spread I came upon carried an article about President Franklin Roosevelt's fiscal policies — a difficult subject to bring to life visually. But the art director of the magazine had found a way.

Across the top and bottom of both pages ran continuous bands of small, informal portraits of FDR, very likely made with one of the new, small cameras that were revolutionizing photography at the time. Seeing the President's face repeated perhaps twenty times, with slight changes of expression from one picture to the next, was as dramatic and riveting as a Pathé newsreel. The style has been employed often since that time (most familiarly to illustrate interviews in *Playboy*), but this use in a long-ago *Fortune* may have been the first, at least in America. Even half a century later, the effect was unforgettable.

In its early years, as a new magazine at a still-new company — and a business magazine during the worst period for business in this country's history — *Fortune* established its identity through such memorable visual coups. The extraordinary work of photographers like Walker Evans and illustrators like Reginald Marsh was laid out imaginatively on page after page, issue after issue.

As astonishing as the graphic design of *Fortune* was, it is even more astonishing that the magazine was just one of many periodicals in the mid-thirties that exerted a visual influence on Americans no less potent and persuasive than that of Hollywood. In the brilliantly choreographed pages of *Harper's Bazaar*, *Vanity Fair*, *Town & Country*, *Vogue*, *Life*, *Film Fun*, *Esquire*, and other showcases of visionary design, readers encountered wonders that taught them to see in the same way Fred Astaire's films taught them to dream or Frank Capra's encouraged them to hope. The men and women at the drawing boards of great magazines — and some that were less

Caslon — the predominant typeface in Colonial times — was invented by British type-founder William Caslon in the 1720s. Ben Franklin used it; it was used for the first printing of the Declaration of Independence; and it is still in use.

than great — were the set designers of the American mind.

In the art history of magazines on this side of the Atlantic, this period of experimentation, novelty, and bravado was the early flowering of a Renaissance that has continued with extraordinary energy until today. (If the passionate magazine lover feels that the greatest days of that flowering are past, it may be because so much of the design work during the past half-century has been so innovative, and because the graphic creativity of magazines has spilled over into so many other media — the pyrotechnics of MTV being a case in point. In the new age of hypergraphics, the revolution in magazine design has been obscured by its own success.)

To call the middle third (approximately) of the twentieth century a Renaissance is not to say that everything that went before was the Dark Ages. Magazines have always been designed, however haphazard the process, but the key elements in their look have necessarily been limited by the technology of printing. In a sense, the patron saint of American magazine publishing was Benjamin Franklin. Long before he became famous as a diplomat and politician, Franklin succeeded as a publisher of periodicals, printer, and purveyor of ink and paper. He showed considerable concern for the look of a page as well as its content, and was quick to use new type designs when they became available.

The look of early magazines depended almost entirely on typography, and the compulsive urge to decorate pages often resulted in typeface combinations that were the visual equivalent of a raucous crowd. Newspapers, then as now stuck with the task of attracting readers on a daily or weekly basis, were more likely to edge toward this typographic hysteria, but magazines were far from restrained. Perhaps the most significant graphic advance of this primal time was English typemaker William Caslon's introduction of Caslon type, a handsome design used for the first printed version of the Declaration of Independence and still in use. At around the same time, Giambattista Bodoni, a typemaker in Parma, created an elegant face that would become the progenitor of modern type.

Pictorial illustration found its way into magazines at first through the use of printed decoration. Because paper was scarce and white space an unaffordable luxury, magazine type was confined to narrow columns in a tight, vertical format. Leaf designs, elaborate scrollwork, and that well-known attention-getter the pointing hand were sprinkled through pages more or less randomly to combine with type variations

New York Weekly filled its top front page with dramatic illustration, such as this 1872 shipwreck that introduced the week's romantic story.

Several technical journals devoted to the art of printing sprang up after the Civil War. The *Inland Printer* covered all aspects of illustration, design, and production.

The first manifestations of pictorial illustration often appeared as an element of printed decoration, as in this splendidly detailed 1890 *Ladies' World* masthead.

GODEY'S FASHIONS FOR OCTOBER.
1866

Godey's Lady's Book employed 150 women to hand-color its cover engravings and fashion plates. This plate shows "costumes for a fancy ball." Most fanciful of all is the camera-like hat and photo-bordered skirt combination worn by one salon figure.

and break up the close ranks of text. The goal of this ad hoc art direction was not much different from that of magazine designers today — to provide relief to the eye and keep a reader's interest.

Among the first true illustrations were portraits in the form of silhouettes (named after Etienne de Silhouette, a French government official), the simple and elegant black-on-white progenitors of the celebrity pictures that have proved addictive to so many magazine editors and art directors. Silhouettes were followed, around the beginning of the nineteenth century, by far more elaborate line drawings printed from woodcuts. In the arduous process of making woodcuts much of the subtlety of the original art could be lost, yet the inclusion of illustrations was one of the most significant steps toward making magazines the home companions they eventually became. A case in point is a magazine called *The Port Folio*, published in Philadelphia from 1801 to 1827 and cited by Clarence Hornung and Fridolf Johnson in *200 Years of American Art*. It managed to survive without advertising, in part by including landscape scenes that readers could cut out and frame.

Illustration as pure buyer's incentive continues (how else can the fabled *Sports Illustrated* swimsuit issue or the *Playboy* centerfold be perceived?). Yet illustration alone, one suspects, would not have been enough to make magazines required reading. The breakthrough into the modern concept of magazine graphics was made by a couple of prototypical women's fashion publications, *Godey's Lady's Book* and *Peterson's Magazine*, both of which appeared before the middle of the nineteenth century and lasted almost to its end. *Godey's* used steel engravings on copper for its covers and fashion plates inside, hand-colored by a staff of 150 women. A circulation of 150,000 was proof that *something* was working. In 1840, a new periodical called *Graham's Magazine* began publishing stories and poems by some of America's best writers — such contemporary glitterati as Longfellow, Cooper, and Poe — and hired artists and engravers to illustrate their work. The golden age of illustration was launched, and along with it the notion of the magazine as a muse for the eye and the imagination.

As it became apparent that illustrations enhanced sales, the technology of printing images improved. Such innovations as lithography and, eventually, photoengraving let artists break free of their dependence on the skills (or clumsiness) of hand engravers. As the work on the page increasingly resembled the original art, the importance of illustration — and illustrators —

An 1882 *Harper's Weekly* cover — "The Trout Display at Fulton Market" in New York City — reveals the remarkable level of artistry attained by engravers of the period. The drawing for this engraving was by Daniel Beard.

Silhouettes lent classical simplicity to the hodge-podge of early magazine design. They often depicted famous figures, such as George Washington, shown here.

In this 1907 *Sports Afield*,
illustration is used to create
a bucolic world for hunters
and anglers, the magazine's
main subscribers.

grew. And when the Civil War stimulated a public hunger for
pictorial journalism, magazines like *Harper's Weekly* and *Leslie's*
got the chance to *show* dramatically what newspapers could
only report, more or less matter-of-factly. *Harper's Weekly* sent
Winslow Homer into the field as a "picture correspondent"
to draw the encampments and battlefields firsthand. Other
artists carried their sketchpads to hell and back to give form to
journalistic fact (and myth), and woodblock makers translated
the momentous pictures taken by Mathew Brady and his
small brigade of war photographers.

Homer, though far from the first American artist to reach
an audience through magazines, was the most famous. He set
the stage (and the standard) for the illustrator-heroes who
would dominate graphic arts in this country well into the
twentieth century. The fame of these artists was so resonant
that the names of most of them remain immediately recogniz-
able: Charles Dana Gibson, Maxfield Parrish, John Held, Jr.,
J. C. Leyendecker, Howard Pyle, Will Bradley, N. C. Wyeth,
Howard Chandler Christy, Frederic Remington, and Norman
Rockwell were some who reached the summit of the profession.
With their highly individual styles and their gift for bringing
dramatic or wry shape to words or ideas, they created the
special excitement of magazines at the same time magazines
were enthroning them. Because their work was instantly accessible, crafted to reach out to the reader the moment a page was

At the turn of the century,
when artwork was enjoying
great popularity, many magazines gave their illustrations double-page spreads,
as *Harper's Weekly* did here
for E. W. Kemble's drawing
of William Jennings Bryan.

THEIR MASTER'S VOICE

"OLD DR. BRYAN HAS INAUGURATED A CAMPAIGN OF PHONOGRAPH RECORDS OF HIS SPEECHES. HE IS NOW TESTING THEM AT HIS NEBRASKA FARM."—*Daily Paper*

DRAWN BY E. W. KEMBLE

Frederic Remington, best
known for his paintings
of life in the Wild West,
worked as an illustrator
for *Harper's Weekly* in
the early 1890s (opposite).
Later, he served as a
reporter-artist and, during
the Spanish-American War,
as a war correspondent.

A GOOD TACKLE.

THE COCK CROWS.

AFTER THE SNAP-BACK.

FOOTBALL ARMOR.

BLOCKING.

RUBBING DOWN IN THE GYMNASIUM.

A BIT OF ADVICE.

A DAY WITH THE YALE TEAM.—Drawn by Frederic Remington.—[See Page 1110.]

Paintings for FORTUNE by Robert Riggs

BEHIND THE GREEN LIGHTS

Here you see the famed West Forty-seventh Street police station, serving the febrile Times Square precinct. The scene happens to be New Year's Eve; but, except for the horn held by the wavering souse at the left, it could be approximately duplicated almost any busy Saturday night. Typical are the fighting drunk at the rail of the lieutenant's desk; the prisoner being frisked; the battered belligerents (extreme left) continuing their brawl verbally before the bored patrolman; the solicitous cops with the lost boy; the ambulance interne; the plain-clothes man surveying the scene with interest over his coffee cup. Unusual is the presence of the body box (left foreground) consigned to the morgue. It contains the remains of a female who jumped out of a hotel window.

Nineteen Thousand Cops

A dishonored police department is regenerated by a hardboiled Commissioner. These days they've got to be good, and they've got to be straight. They are.

12 Midnight. At midnight the watch over New York changes, the new day for the police department begins. From the 1st Precinct at Old Slip, down near South Street below the Fulton Fish Market, to the 123rd Precinct far across the harbor in Tottenville, Staten Island, platoons of patrolmen and squads of detectives begin their tour, to keep watch until 8:00 A.M. Some go to lonely posts—in Bayside or Flatbush or Wall Street or Forest Hills—where the city is asleep. Others to spots that are still bright, like Chinatown and Fourteenth Street and Times Square—one of the busiest police precincts in the world. And still others go to the city within a city that literally never sleeps: Harlem.

12:04 A.M. The high-pitched "beep" of the police radio, prelude to every call, brought to attention 100 pairs of the cruising patrolmen in the city. In a moment all but two crews relaxed as the calm voice spoke: "In the 13th Precinct. Cars 950 and 524. Address 73 Fifth Avenue, between Thirteenth and Fourteenth streets, in bar and grill. Signal 32." Signal 32 meant "Investigate." The two cars were each within eight blocks of 73 Fifth (at the precinct's farthest limit, they would have been nineteen blocks distant). They swung around, headed for the spot, and pulled up at almost the same moment fifty seconds later. Three of the four patrolmen piled into the grill. They found a noisy drunk, who calmed down instantly at sight of blue uniforms. Three or four minutes of talk, then one of the policemen asked the barkeep, "Well, what do you say? Want to make a complaint?" "No, I just want him to get the hell out." To the drunk: "Go along home, Jack, and stay there." As the man

NIGHT COURT: THE EVENING'S HAUL

Culprits arrested after 4:00 P.M. when day courts adjourn, and charged with misdemeanors are taken to night court in West Fifty-fourth Street. Here a magistrate sits from 8:30 P.M. until as long after midnight as necessary to clear the docket. The prisoners, typically beggars, peddlers, petty hoodlums, can be tried on the spot, fined, jailed, or dismissed. Prisoners picked up on felony charges are always held overnight by police for day courts.

meekly slipped out, one of the patrolmen went to the telephone booth. He dropped a nickel, which the operator returned when he recited his shield number, told the police Radio Dispatcher that cars 950 and 524 were resuming patrol. It was 12:10 A.M.

12:10 A.M. Patrolman McCabe,* sitting at the announcer's desk in the Radio Control Room at Police Headquarters, glanced at the clock and droned into his microphone: "All cars. Special attention to fire-alarm boxes within your sectors will prevent an increase in the number of false alarms." He didn't even have to read it; he recited it every night at this hour, just as the operators on the other shifts recited it at 8:50 A.M., noon, and 5:00 P.M. But the midnight reminder is important because many of the false alarms—34 per cent of all fire calls in New York City—are pulled by drunks in the early morning.

1:10 A.M. On Rockaway Boulevard, Queens, a patrolman on post exchanged

All names in this log are fictitious.

salutes with his sergeant cruising slowly by in a radio car, then walked into a nearby lunch wagon and said to the counterman: "Well, I just got my see. I'm due for a cup of coffee." Five minutes later an inspector's lieutenant walked in, found the patrolman lounging with his gloves off, smoking a cigarette. Probable penalty: a one day's "rip" (fine of a day's pay).

1:25 A.M. Patrolman Dunnigan, walking his post near Columbus Avenue and West One Hundred and Tenth Street, heard shots. He ran down Columbus with his revolver in hand, saw a knot of people in front of an apartment house and went in. He stepped nimbly over a revolver in the inside hallway and entered the open doorway of the nearest apartment. Just inside lay a woman with blood all over her dress front. A man knelt over her, whimpering, and a woman in a wrapper stood by with her hands over her mouth. Patrolman Dunnigan stood where he could eye the doorway and said to the kneeling man: "You—

In 1939, *Fortune*'s editors relied entirely on paintings to illustrate a long article about New York City's police department. The artist was Robert Riggs. Interestingly, while *Fortune* denied bylines to its writers, it gave a credit line to Riggs.

turned, they had tremendous celebrity and attracted large followings. In *America's Great Illustrators*, Susan E. Meyer notes that the Arrow Collar Man created by Leyendecker was said to have received 17,000 love letters in one month.

Propelled by the increasing importance of advertising to the success of their magazines, editors and publishers competed for the top illustrators using the classic blandishments — money and prestige — plus the promise of fame. For the first rank of illustrators, the money was phenomenal. Not long after the turn of the century, when a dollar still had the power to impress, *Collier's* paid Gibson $100,000 for 100 pen-and-ink drawings. That determined and adventurous weekly paid Remington and Parrish even more than $1,000 per picture, and other illustrators did almost as well at competing magazines. It was not unusual for a popular illustrator to earn an annual salary of between $60,000 and $100,000 — and this was at a time when a shave and a haircut was still two bits. The prestige afforded by appearing regularly in a good illustrated magazine was enormous. James Montgomery Flagg, one of the stars of the period, wrote: "To be reproduced in *Scribner's* in 1904 was the same thing to an illustrator as being hung in the Paris Salon was to a painter."

In the days before Hollywood worked its magic, the great illustrators were the creators of the most consistently exciting visual experience available to the public, and their fame has no parallel in today's graphic arts. If there is a modern equivalent for "the beloved illustrators" (Susan E. Meyer's apt description), it may be the pop stardom — based largely on canny visual presentation — of such rock video performers as Michael Jackson and Madonna. Illustrated magazines like *Scribner's*, *McClure's Magazine*, *The Century*, *Harper's Weekly* and *Harper's Bazar* (the extra "a" was added later), and *The Saturday Evening Post* were the dominant form of home entertainment, and the men who made the pictures reigned supreme.

In the early 1900s, with magazines having attained circulations in the hundreds of thousands and illustrators clearly crucial to their success, a symbiotic creature known as the art editor rose to power. His task was to attract talented individuals and then see to the business of tender care and sumptuous feeding. The skills required for this work, aside from an eye for effective art, seem to have been much the same as those of acquiring editors in book publishing. Joseph Hawley Chapin, art editor of *Scribner's*, was described by one of the magazine's famous contributors as friendly, naturally dignified, and thoroughly knowledgeable: "the beau ideal of art editors to us artists." At *Harper's Weekly*, art editor Charles Parsons was similarly described as kind and encouraging, "a gentleman of refined tastes."

Magazines depended heavily on such refined tastes to establish their look and reputation. However diverse the illustrations might be in any given issue, a signature style was essential, and the art editor was often as important as the editor in establishing that style. Although art editors did not always need to know how to design pages early in this century (that job was often done by the printer) their position prefigured in many ways the prominence of the art director in the great graphic revolution that reached a peak after the First World War.

The beginning of that revolution actually came before the war, and if one event can be seen as its spark, it would have to

W. T. Benda's cover illustration (top) for a 1923 *Life* depicts an extraordinary metamorphosis, rendered in graphic splendor. *Judge*, "the World's Wittiest Weekly," by its own reckoning (above), devoted an issue to outlandish inventions and illustrated the cover with one of the most whimsical.

Art director Mehemed
Fehmy Agha put this
Miguel Covarrubias
illustration of Franklin
Roosevelt manipu-
lating capital and labor
on the cover of a 1935
Vanity Fair.

be publisher Condé Nast's hiring of Frank Crowninshield to
edit a recently purchased magazine called *Dress & Vanity Fair*.
The witty, worldly Crowninshield had been the art editor of
The Century; when he took the job, he shortened the name
of the magazine to *Vanity Fair* and dropped women's fashion in
favor of coverage of the arts. With his keen eye and sense
of design, Crowninshield brought to his magazine a distinctive,
innovative appearance that provided a showcase for the
period's great artists and photographers (the young Edward
Steichen was one of the in-house geniuses) and balanced beau-
tifully the brittle élan of its prose. By recognizing the importance of this balance, Crowninshield set the standard for verve
and intelligence that guided magazine men and women for
years. The list of artists and photographers featured in the
magazine — often for the first time in this country — is endless, and endlessly astonishing.

Crowninshield conceived of his magazine as a graphic
entity from cover to cover. Not incidentally, *Vanity Fair* was a
tremendous hit with advertisers from the start, and by the end
of 1915 was a leader in ad linage. Thus was established the
value of art direction as an essential part of a magazine's success.

In 1929, Nast brought to New York Mehemed Fehmy Agha,
a young Ukrainian-born Turk who had been working at the
German edition of *Vogue*. Agha was to serve as art director of
Vogue, *House & Garden*, and *Vanity Fair*. Called "Doctor"
because he had an advanced degree in political science, Agha
was energetic, imperial, fanatically involved with details. He
was a template for the star art directors the next forty years
would produce. As Crowninshield the editor had taken naturally to art direction, Agha the art director had a distinct effect
on editorial content. Once, he produced an entire issue of
Vanity Fair without using a capital letter, and he invented
photo essays for which he produced impeccable layouts. Not
the least dramatic of Agha's design breakthroughs was the
splendid use of the two-page spread, an elegant presentation
that gave magazines a far greater sense of unity and continuity
than they had possessed previously. As someone involved
with every aspect of the magazine, Agha — who reigned at
Condé Nast until the early forties — was the very model of a
modern art director. He described his job as being "first cousin
of the movie director," and it was with a De Mille-like combination of autocratic drive, perfectionism, and collaborative
generosity that he built an aesthetic machine still running
with formidable effect.

LT. COL. T. B. LARKIN IS BOSS

THE TIN CITY RODEOS . . .

COMPETITION between hot spots in the shanty towns of the 1936 Wild West is as keen as it is in New York. Ruby Smith's place (*below*) is an old favorite which has held up. Ed's Place (*opposite*) is slipping. Some say the customers are turning against Ed's murals. But Ed is faithful to them. He boasts that the painter, one Joe Breckinridge, averaged only twenty minutes a panel. Bar X (*below*) is almost as popular as Ruby's. Bar X is more dance hall than bar but that doesn't prevent the customers from drinking, or the taxi-dancers either.

BAR X

RUBY'S PLACE

This is the beer bar. The only drink you can legally sell by the glass in Montana is beer and you mustn't sell that to Indians. For the heavy liquor the customers go to another bar behind. It's merely a formality. The back bar is just as open.

ONE-FOURTH OF THE MISSOURI RIVER WILL RUN THROUGH THIS STEEL "LINER"

This apparatus goes into one of the four diversion tunnels which will carry the river around Fort Peck dam during construction, will later control release of water. With sections in place, the steel spider web will be removed. Theoretically

THE NEW FRONTIER TOWNS AROUND THE FORT PECK DAM PROJECT ARE 275 MILES BY ROAD FROM BILLINGS, MONTANA

. . . RUN ALL NIGHT

LIFE in Montana's No. 1 relief project is one long jamboree slightly joggled by pay day. One of its shanty towns has 16 all night whooperies. The workers are on night shift as well as day with the result that there is always someone yelling for a whiskey or calling on the little ladies of Happy Hollow. College boys mingle with bums in the crowds. Bill Stender, at the bottom of the page, is a Texas U. footballer who bounces for Ruby Smith. He hopes to get to be a football coach when he graduates but he is studying history and engineering just in case.

MAJOR CLARK KITTRELL IS No. 2

ED'S PLACE

RUBY HERSELF

Ruby, second from the left is the founder of the town of Wheeler—and its rich woman. What she learned in the Klondike she has turned to good account. Bill Stender of Texas U. (the big fellow above) is keeping in condition as her bouncer.

Life's first issue, dated November 23, 1936, contained its first photo essay — by Margaret Bourke-White — one spread of which is shown here.

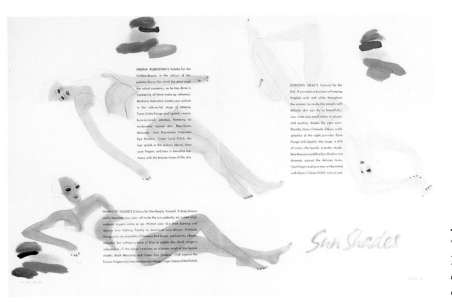

Sun Shades

With typical panache, Mehemed Fehmy Agha designed a *Vogue* spread on cosmetic palettes in 1935.

"MARGUERITES"
WITH DANIELIAN
AS MEPHISTO

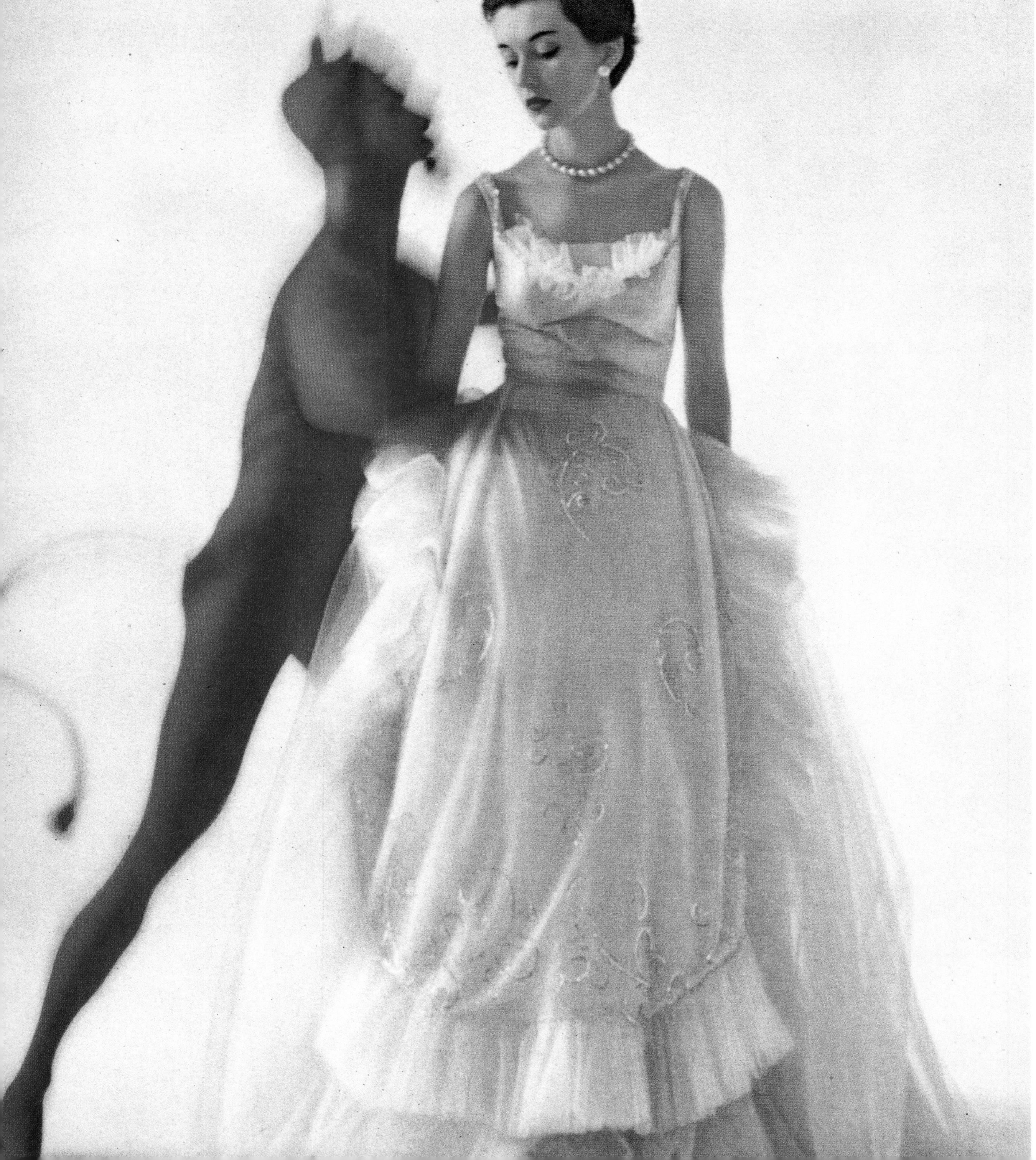

Not long after Agha established himself at Condé Nast, another influential immigrant added cachet to the image of the art director, and brought along the energy and eye-opening innovation of the avant-garde art and graphic movements on the Continent. If Agha gathered unprecedented power to the art director's office, Alexey Brodovitch — a Russian expatriate who began working for *Harper's Bazaar* in 1934 — added a fervor to the job that changed forever the expectation of what could be done with the magazine page.

Although Brodovitch never demonstrated much interest in women's fashion, he had a willing patron in *Bazaar* editor Carmel Snow, and a license to astonish from Hearst Publishing, which was determined to steal the spotlight from venerable *Vogue*. Therefore, he was able to use the magazine almost as an experimental laboratory, employing artists and photographers from the first rank of European talent to make *Bazaar* vivid and unpredictable. The magazine became the preferred reading matter of many who, like Brodovitch, didn't have much interest in fashion, as well as fashionable women whom he converted to a new way of looking at the world. For twenty-four years, Brodovitch invented and re-invented the magazine, invigorating American graphic design as he went along and inspiring a phenomenal group of artists and art directors in the process. Richard Avedon and Hiro and Art Kane worked — or rather, slaved — for him, or studied at a series of now-famous classes he taught in New York. So did many others who are now near-legendary figures themselves. Even men and women who worked exclusively for the competition fell under his gravitational pull. Irving Penn, perhaps the greatest photographer at Condé Nast since Steichen, put it this way in 1972: "There isn't a designer or photographer in our time who hasn't felt the influence of Brodovitch. The waves that went out

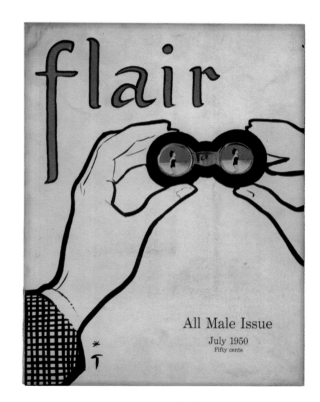

Every cover of *Flair* had striking features, like these "peepholes" (above).

Irving Penn's *Vogue* fashion photography (opposite) is marked by a sense of drama and classic elegance.

Haute cuisine: Just as the commercial jet was shrinking the world, art director and photographer Otto Storch borrowed a wing to showcase a transnational mix of breakfast delights for a 1965 *McCall's*.

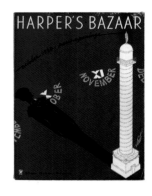

Erté's 1934 cover for *Harper's Bazaar* let readers know that the Paris fashion season was opening.

from *Harper's Bazaar* since his first issue are still rippling."

In 1950, Brodovitch teamed up with editor Frank Zachary to produce *Portfolio*, a paradigm of dramatic graphic design and a high point in the history of American magazines. Zachary, who is now the editor-in-chief of *Town & Country*, is a modern incarnation of Frank Crowninshield, an elegant, energetic man with a rare mix of editorial and design talents. He wanted to create a magazine devoted to graphic arts that would be an American equivalent of certain European publications, and hired Brodovitch to moonlight as art director during the evenings and weekends when he wasn't doing *Bazaar*. Zachary and his partner, George Rosenthal, decided that *Portfolio* shouldn't accept advertising, a noble policy that had two effects: The magazine lasted only three issues, and those issues were near-perfect designs from front cover to back. Hans Namuth's famed pictures of Jackson Pollock at work first appeared in *Portfolio*, as did the first artistic experiments in a curious new process called Xerography and the first article on 3-D photography (complete with special glasses). The relationship between editor and art director was ideal: Brodovitch gave Zachary the magazine of his dreams, and Zachary (who calls the legendary Russian "my friend and master") gave Brodovitch a chance to dream up a magazine of sublime vision.

Agha and Brodovitch, each from a European tradition of discipline and discipleship, had a lasting effect not only on the way magazines looked but on how that look was achieved. Although Agha was a masterful office politician and Brodovitch was prickly and not particularly charming, both used a similar method when it came to working with photographers, artists, and subordinates. When somewhat sub-par pictures or layouts were presented to them, they would say, "These are interesting, but could you try something else?" Or words to that effect. And people would try, and try again and again until they came up with things they never imagined they could do. Irving Penn, who studied with Brodovitch at the Philadelphia College of Art, had this to say about the art director's method: "He was rarely supportive, had little human concern, showed only minor pleasure in a student's burst of growth and achievement. The climate around him was never warm and easy. . . .But within these austere and forbidding circumstances, when the student did somehow manage to push forward into new ground, Brodovitch glumly, even grudgingly, left no doubt that something remarkable had been done. And it seemed that the very sparseness of his recognition lent

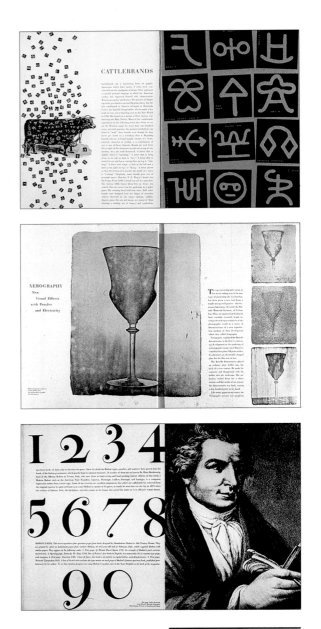

In 1950 Alexey Brodovitch, the dean of designers, and editor Frank Zachary brought out *Portfolio*, a magazine devoted to the graphic arts. Only three issues appeared; the spreads above suggest the remarkable quality of this noble experiment.

A master choreographer
of type and the photo-
graphic image, Bradbury
Thompson created this
spread of fashion designer
show-and-tell for a 1952
Mademoiselle.

At *Harper's Bazaar*,
Brodovitch inspired such
photographers as Hiro,
Richard Avedon, and
Derujinsky, who composed
this harmonious duet.

New Arrangements for Dinner

● Left: A dinner and dancing dress
designed to look particularly
alluring across a table top.
Its top, a blaze of pearls
and gold embroidery; the bodice, white;
the cummerbund, a saffron color;
the skirt, a dark chocolate —
all in Celanese slipper satin.
By J. L. F. Originals. About $70.
Saks Fifth Avenue; Julius Garfinckel.
● Above: A short evening duster of vanilla moire (the white
coat for night is new and delicious). This flows
from a high waistline into a circumference huge enough to
cover the hugest crinoline. By J. L. F. Originals in Enka moire.
About $50. Saks Fifth Avenue; William H. Block.
Capezio shoes. The harp, from Lyon and Healy; the bass viol, from G. Schirmer.

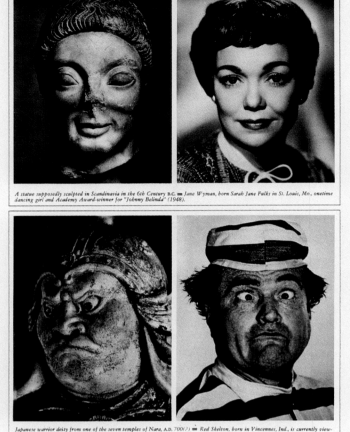

Art director Henry Wolf matched ancient sculptures with contemporary stars for this 1963 *Show* spread.

Seventeen's famous art director Cipe Pineles opened the magazine to artists "who were not confined by the clichés of illustration." Here, she avoids clichés in wishing readers a Merry Christmas.

it an intensity of meaning and importance hard to explain to someone who did not actually experience it." By all accounts, this austerity never softened.

It's tempting to see Agha and Brodovitch as giants on the earth and their era as a kind of genesis after which everyone, and everything, has been smaller and less significant. But their power was so persuasive that, intentionally or not, they spawned a generation of art directors who made dazzling magazines for years. Brodovitch and Agha were the advance guard of a movement that transfigured the printed page. The movement had been building before they appeared on the scene, and it continued, enlivened, after they were gone.

The network of talent was formidable. Cipe Pineles, who worked for Agha, became art director of *Seventeen*, and during her years there she gave an adventurous and sophisticated look to what might have been a safe and plodding magazine. Marvin Israel, an extraordinarily talented disciple of Brodovitch, followed him at *Bazaar*, and was followed in turn by Henry Wolf (now a successful and influential photographer). William Golden worked for Agha before going to CBS and establishing that company's preeminence in graphic design (as exemplified, for years, in the quality of Columbia's LP album covers). James Bradbury Thompson came to New York from Kansas, drawn by *Vanity Fair*, *Vogue*, and *Bazaar*. For twenty-four years he served as art director for *Westvaco Inspirations*, an intriguing company publication too few people ever saw. Thompson also worked his magic on *Mademoiselle*, *Smithsonian*, and *Art News*. And Alexander Liberman, who followed Agha at Condé Nast and has directed all of the company's magazines for almost fifty years, has had — and continues to have — an incalculable effect on the taste and the visual temper of our times.

The rise of the art director produced so many virtuoso performers that one chapter of one book cannot do them justice, or even accommodate all their names. Otto Storch at *McCall's* set a standard for women's service magazines that made no concession to coziness and domesticity, and invariably saluted the reader's intelligence. Allen Hurlburt at *Look* gave picture magazines a singularly new appearance. Then, there was Leo Lionni, whose years at *Fortune* produced magazines so handsome that people couldn't bear to throw them out.

Given the imperative for magazines to evolve, adapt, and remain emphatically contemporary (an imperative made all the more urgent by the visual competition of television and

A portfolio of covers shows the creative style of four top art directors (top to bottom): Leo Lionni, 1960; Alexander Liberman, 1949; Henry Wolf, 1963; and Samuel N. Antupit, 1967.

In its two-year existence, *Smart* was a showcase for designer Roger Black's intelligent and stylish computer-generated typography.

In 1977, Walter Bernard took up the challenge of redesigning *Time*, giving it a new graphic cohesion. This spread is from 1979.

Melissa Tardiff was the art director, Skrebneski the photographer, and Anthony Clavet the body painter for this composition used to illustrate a 1982 *Town & Country* article titled "The Artful Body."

In the world of Surrealism, the female form becomes part of a dreamlike landscape, a further piece of a further puzzle. In this landscape, a muscular arm reaching through a wall, floating sculpture, diamonds turning into liquid and nudes bound by a diagonal of gauze seem perfectly in place. Bracelets by Van Cleef & Arpels. Sculptures by Lynda Benglis, Dart Gallery, Chicago. The polished, toned and sleek bodies here are the result of Méthode Jeanne Piaubert, three individual programs for complete body care.

videocassettes), graphic design has undergone almost continuous regeneration and revival. There have been recurrent upheavals during which art directors have taken it upon themselves to fix what did not always seem broken. When Milton Glaser, one of the most universally talented artists and art directors ever to work in magazines, joined editor Clay Felker in creating *New York* magazine in the late sixties, he injected new life into illustration, which had declined during the previous decades as photographers' celebrity increased. When J. C. Suarès helped design *7 Days*, the energetic (if short-lived) New York "tabloid magazine," he keyed the content of pages with recurring illustrated elements that harked back to Deco style yet seemed utterly fresh. Similarly, Walter Bernard, successor to Glaser at *New York*, gave new visual life to *Time* (and continues to redesign magazines in partnership with Glaser). Mary Shanahan took *Cuisine* above and beyond popular expectations for food magazines, once shocking gourmets — and *Gourmet* — with a beautiful but lurid photograph of a very dead Peking duck. And in an effort of noble significance, Roger Black has tackled the unglamorous but crucial job of civilizing the wild kingdom of computer type.

And so magazine graphic design seems to have come full circle. Today's designers are trying to make the best use of new type and new technologies just as Benjamin Franklin did a quarter of a millennium ago. But the circle is only an illusion: We're not back where we started but in a place magazines have never been before, and on the way to something completely new. Look carefully and you'll see that the circle is actually a spiral. An upward spiral, if what's past is prologue.

— *Owen Edwards*

The distinctively wild and crazy style of *Spy* art director B. W. Honeycutt is exemplified in this opening page of a 1989 article.

7 Days designer J. C. Suarès puts some personality in his type for a 1989 cover on Atlantic City (right). Creative director Tibor Kalman fills *Interview* with offbeat portraits of celebrities, as with this 1990 cover of actress Winona Ryder (far right).

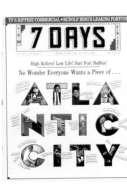

The Art of Illustration

The first magazine illustrations in the early nineteenth century were "blackies" — small black silhouettes of profiles and vignettes. As technological advances made possible the reproduction of various mediums, illustration took on all the formal attributes of easel painting while offering a greater range of subject matter. In fact, it was the democratic art — the most accessible medium for representation, expression, and imagination. During the mid-nineteenth century, before photographic reproduction was perfected, and up until moving pictures captured public attention, illustration provided news, commentary, and entertainment. No wonder the leading illustrators were celebrities.

Reporter-illustrators like Winslow Homer, Frederic Remington, and Joseph Pennell introduced readers to unknown

Paul Revere a magazine illustrator? Yes. He produced many satirical engravings, some based on British originals, such as this one for *Royal American Magazine* in 1775 (above).

In this lithograph for *The Masses*, artist George Bellows comments eloquently on racism in the United States in 1917.

This Frank Bellew cartoon was published in *Harper's Weekly* on the occasion of Lincoln's re-election in 1864. The caption read: "Long Abraham Lincoln a Little Longer."

A GROUP OF VULTURES WAITING FOR THE STORM TO "BLOW OVER."—"LET US *PREY.*"

A series of Thomas Nast cartoons in *Harper's Weekly* helped bring down "Boss" Tweed and his "ring of vultures."

One of the most popular magazine artists of the century was N. C. Wyeth, who contributed more than 2,000 illustrations. This 1908 *McClure's* picture depicts a preacher shouting, "I hereby pronounce yuh man and wife."

Frederic Remington, who became the preeminent artist of the Wild West, drew this for *The Century* in 1888.

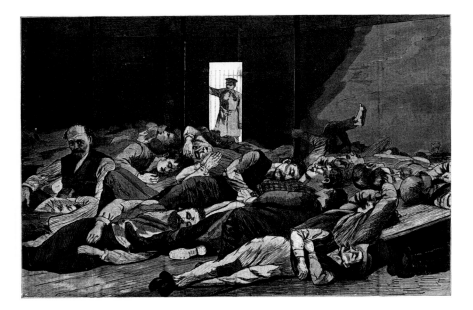

B. Cory Kilvert was the illustrator of this lighthearted look at street-gang life for a 1903 *Collier's* cover.

Winslow Homer began his career as a magazine illustrator in 1858. For *Harper's Weekly* he depicted this police station full of men who had lost everything in the panic of 1873.

James Montgomery Flagg, creator of the Uncle Sam who superseded all others, here has fun depicting a manic Enrico Caruso for a 1914 cover of *Harper's Weekly*.

The caption of this timeless spoof of the military — done by Robert Minor for the back cover of a 1916 issue of *The Masses* — is "At last a perfect soldier!"

Army Medical Examiner: "At last a perfect soldier!"

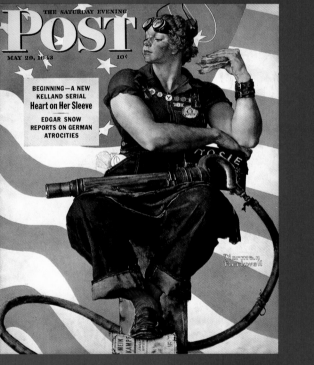

Coles Phillips specialized in creating elegant women. This illustration for a 1909 *Life* cover (left) is titled "Which?" Norman Rockwell's "Rosie the Riveter," on the cover of this 1943 *Saturday Evening Post*, personified the powerful contribution American women were making to the war effort (below left).

cultures through "on-the-spot" pictorial essays. Other illustrators, working in the dominant realistic style of the late-nineteenth and early-twentieth centuries, invented and perpetuated some of America's lasting myths. Among the most prestigious magazine illustrators of this so-called Golden Age were Charles Dana Gibson and Harrison Fisher, renowned for their paradigms of American womanhood; James Montgomery Flagg, creator of the emblematic Uncle Sam; J. C. Leyendecker, famed for his iconic Arrow Collar Man; and, of course, Norman Rockwell.

In the beginning, illustration was used as a lure for readers, and consequently advertisers. It quickly became the visual mainstay of most American magazines and remained so until well after the Second World War, despite the success of such photo magazines as *Life*. One reason is that the public related to

Ladies in Waiting

Among the most popular illustrators at the turn of the century was Charles Dana Gibson, creator of "the Gibson girl." This cartoon ran in *Life* in 1921.

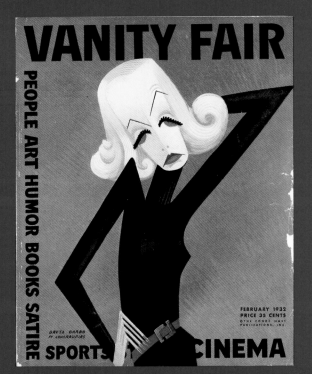

William Henry Cotton
catches the thrill of a
Coney Island roller coaster
ride in this 1933 *New Yorker*
cover (left). Mexican artist
Miguel Covarrubias was
in his early twenties when
he started doing covers
for *Vanity Fair*. This one
(below left), showing Greta
Garbo, dates from 1932.

illustrations in much the same way viewers
today do to television series. Illustrations
were lifelike but not real; entertaining but not
threatening. They provided a buffer between
fantasy and fact.

They also contributed significantly to a
magazine's overall personality. The great
magazines of the thirties — *Vanity Fair*, *The
New Yorker*, *Fortune*, *Vogue*, and *Harper's
Bazaar* — were defined by the coterie of
highly gifted illustrators whose work regularly
appeared on their covers. Many of them
(notably Paolo Garretto, Miguel Covarrubias,
William Cotton, Erté, Benito, and A. M.
Cassandre) developed public followings equal
to those of the magazine's literary contributors. Moreover, they influenced the look
of American advertising, which hired many
of the same artists to do ads.

A wealth of talent is show-
cased in three covers by
(from left to right) A. M.
Cassandre (1939), Carl
"Eric" Erickson (1932), and
Maxfield Parrish (1922).

J. C. Leyendecker began painting covers for *The Saturday Evening Post* in 1899; he was still at work — and worrying about war — at the end of 1939.

The All-Year-Round Girl

Droll satirist of the flapper age, John Held, Jr., here pokes fun at "The All-Year-Round Girl." Held's illustrations appeared in *Life*, *Collier's*, and *Vanity Fair*, among others.

In 1937, *Fortune*'s editors saw the new Wayne pump (above right) as a "mechanical monster." Artist Stevan Dohanos made it loom ominously. "Home Life in Europe Today" was the title of this sardonic 1935 *Vanity Fair* illustration by Paolo Garretto (right).

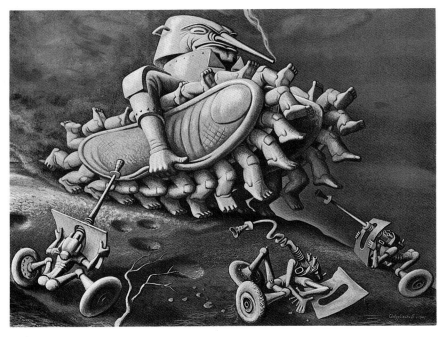

For a 1942 *Esquire* (top)
Arthur Szyk depicted Axis
leaders Hermann Göring,
Benito Mussolini, and
Hideki Tojo in a chain
gang of comic terror. Boris
Artzybasheff, who painted
more than 200 covers for
Time, made an art out of
giving human dimensions
to modern machinery, as
in this 1941 *Life* illustration
entitled "Imperturbable
tank and anti-tank guns"
(above).

Starting in the twenties,
Alberto Vargas depicted
a new kind of American
beauty. For years, "Varga
girls" were a staple of
Esquire.

Magazine illustration, though never totally abandoned, fell on hard times during the late fifties, when photography was recognized as a more effective documentary tool and cutting-edge artistic medium. With few exceptions, the veteran representational illustrators were relegated to the fiction or humor pages of general-interest magazines. Yet even this had a positive effect, for it encouraged younger artists to develop new, more expressive methods. In the mid-fifties, Robert Weaver pioneered an expressive form of illustration that combined abstract and representational forms with a freer, more painterly gesture than that of his predecessors. At the same time, Milton Glaser and Seymour Chwast, co-founders of Push Pin

Anthony Russo illustrated a 1989 *Mother Jones* story about a teenager with AIDS and the community's fear and hostility (right). Saul Steinberg's Manhattan mindscape (below right) appeared in *Flair* in 1950.

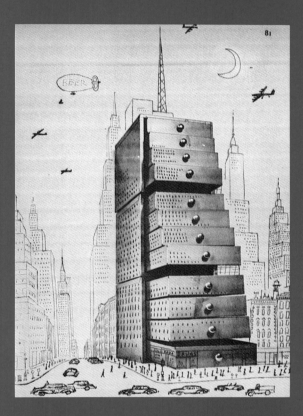

Salvador Dali produced a vision for *Vogue* in 1939.

In 1958, *Esquire* devoted seven full pages to coverage of a three-day war imagined and created by artist Robert Andrew Parker.

Studios, returned eccentricity to illustration through revivals of historical and vernacular styles — a mixture of Art Deco and the comics. In the work of these and other innovative artists, economy replaced detail, and wit replaced sentimentalism. More important, conceptual thinking rooted in metaphor and symbolism replaced the convention of illustrating a phrase or detail from a manuscript. This conceptual approach has been extended into realms of personal (and at times political) expression by Brad Holland, Marshall Arisman, Sue Coe, Alan Cober, and Edward Sorel, all of whose images supplement a text rather than merely restate it.

— Steven Heller

Ronald Searle, who did this *Holiday* cover (right) in 1964, is a master satirist who can be both droll and sharp. *Mother Jones* takes a stab at reporter and novelist Tom Wolfe in a 1983 cover by Robert Grossman (below right).

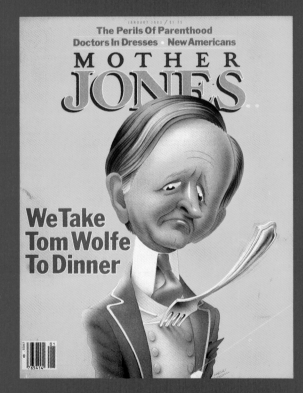

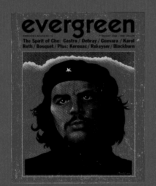

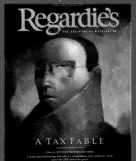

The magazine cover provides both panel and frame for portraits, as demonstrated by (clockwise) Ben Shahn's 1965 drawing of Martin Luther King, Jr.; Paul Davis's 1968 painting of Che Guevara; Edward Sorel's 1966 Frank Sinatra; and Brad Holland's 1989 masked tax cheater.

Illustrator and designer
Milton Glaser provided this
stylish cover for *Holiday* in
1967.

Ralph Steadman of
England, whose early
work appeared in *Punch*,
found ample scope for
outrage in America, as
in this 1979 illustration
for *Penthouse*.

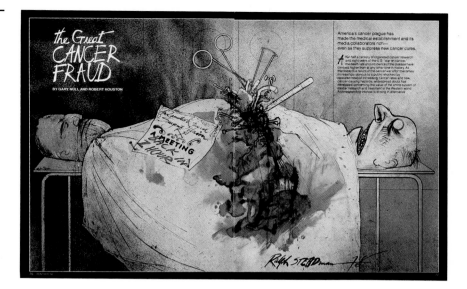

Master of the clear and
sharply critical line, David
Levine portrayed "Lyndon
Johnson at Sea" for *Look*
in March 1969.

Sue Coe's nightmare image,
published in *Entertainment
Weekly* in early 1991, was
inspired by the prospect
of chemical warfare in the
Persian Gulf.

The violence of modern life
is a recurrent subject in the
work of Marshall Arisman.
This painting accompanied
a *Penthouse* piece about TV
news shows.

Creative Persuasion

THE INFLUENCE OF ADVERTISING

As a nation takes to wheels, advertising for auto-related goods gets rolling as well, like this 1913 tire ad (above).

Starting in 1931, Coca-Cola popularized the image of a jolly, roly-poly Santa (opposite) dressed in red and white — Coke's colors.

In *A Visit from St. Nicholas*, published in 1823, Clement Clarke Moore evoked a "jolly old elf" who, plump as he was, managed to slip down the chimney. Some forty years later, when Thomas Nast sketched Christmas scenes for *Harper's Weekly*, he followed Moore's lead and showed Santa Claus as elfin in stature if not in girth. In the depictions of other artists, Santa was lean. Or he was beardless. Or he wore a crown of holly, like England's Old Father Christmas. Sometimes his costume was red, sometimes blue or green or white. One constant was that he seemed to mingle with mortals only while they slumbered. Santa Claus was, in short, a concept in search of a single, satisfying image. Then, in 1931, Haddon Sundblom painted a portrait of him for a Coca-Cola Company advertisement. Santa, in the parlance of advertising, was branded.

There was nothing elfin about Sundblom's Santa except, perhaps, the twinkle in his eye. He was a ruddy-faced fellow, with a hearty smile and a lap ample enough to accommodate a child or two. Not incidentally, his suit and cap were red and white — the colors of the soft drink's logo.

This image of Santa, reinforced year after year in magazines read by millions of people, became etched in our collective psyche. It epitomizes the power of magazine advertising, a power summed up by the Crowell Publishing Company in a 1938 trade magazine ad: "In time, magazine advertising makes a product part of our national life: part of our national eyes, palate, fingertip feel, sensory habit, rooted in the popular flesh and nervous system as well as in the popular mind." Crowell, which published *Collier's* and *Woman's Home Companion*, went on to claim that "virtually every product that has national identity, universal acceptance, has a background of magazine advertising — whatever other media were used."

This claim could not have been made a half-century earlier. In the 1880s, magazines were just emerging as a major force in the American economy. The first magazine advertisement appeared in the May 1741 issue of Benjamin Franklin's *General Magazine*. The copywriter could hardly be accused of indulging in hyperbole:

THERE IS A FERRY KEPT OVER POTOMACK (BY THE SUBSCRIBER), BEING THE POST ROAD, AND MUCH THE NIGHEST WAY FROM ANNAPOLIS TO WILLIAMSBURG, WHERE ALL GENTLEMEN MAY DEPEND UPON A READY PASSAGE IN A GOOD NEW BOAT AND ABLE HANDS. BY RICHARD BRETT, DEPUTY-POST-MASTER AT POTOMACK.

The frame in this 1894 advertisement is the product itself — a band to keep cuff and sleeve free from ink stains.

In the 1880s — when this Bradley ad ran in several magazines — surreys, buckboards, and two-wheelers could be ordered "direct from the manufacturer."

Advertising boosted the popularity of brand-name products; the increasing use of color in the 1890s furthered the allure, as in this 1896 ad from *The Ladies' Home Journal*.

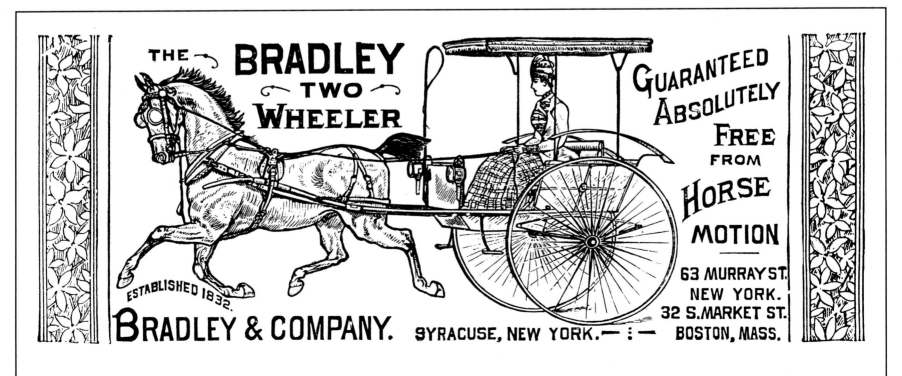

Until well into the next century, most magazine advertisements were similarly terse. Their function was to inform readers of an available product or service. Some were accompanied by a stock illustration. Most were only an inch or two long, and they generally were grouped in a few back pages. Some magazines were exceedingly picky about the kind of ads they would accept. For fourteen years after its launch in 1850, *Harper's New Monthly Magazine*, for example, refused to publicize any product except Harper & Brothers' books. Magazines depended on the goodwill of their subscribers, who, being refined or aspiring to be so, regarded publicity as vulgar and dismissed most product advertising as mendacious. Which, by and large, it was.

Patent-medicine manufacturers were the leading advertisers in the mid-nineteenth century. Their wares were particularly evident in religious journals, the first publications to depend on advertising revenue. Pious Americans were repeatedly confronted with ads for such nostrums as Dr. H. T. Helmbold's Extract of Buchu and Lydia E. Pinkham's Vegetable Compound. Teetotalers swigged the stuff with a good conscience, blissfully unaware that most of the extracts and compounds and elixirs relied on the numbing effects of alcohol or opiates to treat "the demons of catarrh," "female complaints," "weak manhood," and a host of other ailments, real or imagined. For all its shortcomings and silliness, patent-medicine advertising demonstrated the value of having a proprietary name; also, by trial and error, it taught a basic lesson: If you want to sell a product, you had better make clear what it can do for the buyer that similar products can't. Brands thrived when they were widely promoted; they foundered when they weren't.

P. T. Barnum was one of the era's ubiquitous advertisers. A caricature of Barnum on the cover of an 1862 issue of *Vanity Fair* depicts the showman tooting a horn at the portal of his American Museum in Manhattan, which is pasted over with posters for such exhibits as "The Singing Lobsters" and "The Educated Clam." Barnum's rousing posters and newspaper advertising lured the public to such other curiosities as Mlle. Fanny, an orangutan ballyhooed as the link between man and beast. "I owe all my success," Barnum confessed in his autobiography, "to printer's ink." In fact, he owed his success to his ability to excite the common man's desires — desires that became the driving force behind an economy based on consumer goods.

The American system of manufacturing — machines

WOLCOTT'S INSTANT PAIN ANNIHILATOR.

The makers of patent medicines — some of which were 20 to 40 percent alcohol — claimed they cured headaches, hangovers, and most anything else that ailed the unsuspecting.

ALLCOCK'S POROUS PLASTERS,
THE
STANDARD PLASTERS OF THE WORLD
ARE
USED AND PREFERRED BY ALL.

A child's best friend: Advertising that pulled at the heartstrings was alive and well even in 1888 (above).

Domino Sugar (opposite) goes global in this 1909 ad in *Collier's*.

He won't be happy till he gets it!

Better than a pacifier: Pears' used this 1888 ad of an anguished infant to convince parents that a bar of its soap would make for a clean and happy baby.

producing uniform products in large quantities for mass consumption — was just taking hold as the nation celebrated its centennial. Goods that had been made locally and sold from barrels at the general store would soon be packaged and shipped from coast to coast. A major centennial event, the Philadelphia International Exhibition of 1876, served as a giant showcase for the sort of goods that would come on the market before too long (and would be advertised in national magazines). There, for the first time, Americans saw Bissell carpet sweepers, Remington typewriters, and Alexander Graham Bell's telephone. Charles E. Hires offered a temperance drink called root beer. A 700-ton steam engine shook Machinery Hall, driving hundreds of sewing machines and other mechanical devices that pumped out products ranging from newspapers to straight pins. It was a wondrous demonstration of American ingenuity to most of the ten million visitors. But British biologist Thomas Huxley was bemused. "What are you going to do with all these things?" he asked.

We were, of course, going to sell them.

By the 1890s, products that previously had no distinct identity were being branded with such names as Heinz Pickles,

MUTUAL ADMIRATION.

BARNUM TO JUMBO. "You are a *humbug* after my own heart. You have even beat me in advertising."

Thomas Nast lampoons P. T. Barnum, a master of self-advertising, in *Harper's Weekly* in 1882.

Francis Barraud's painting of his terrier listening to an early phonograph became the trademark of the Victor Talking Machine Company in 1901.

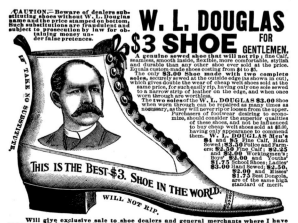

W. L. Douglas used ads like this to reach wholesale buyers as well as individual consumers nationwide.

Royal Baking Powder, Pillsbury Flour. And the competing brands were battling each other for consumer acceptance in quarter-page, half-page, and full-page magazine advertisements. Housewives could choose between Ivory soap (which was 99 and 44/100 percent pure, and floated), Pear's (which actress Lillie Langtry recommended for improving the complexion), and several other products. Manufacturers hoped that their brands would build a loyal following; consumers looked to the brand names as a warrant of consistency. Defining the nature of that consistency, and persuading consumers of its particular merits, became the new function of the advertising message.

Advertising agents were essentially brokers who purchased space in periodicals and then sold it to advertisers, taking a liberal commission. Their job wasn't easy; the marketplace was hostile. Many office buildings displayed signs that warned: "No beggars, peddlers, or advertising solicitors." *Harper's* was "horrified," as one account put it, when in the 1870s J. Walter Thompson offered $18,000 for its back page on behalf of the Elias Howe Sewing Machine Company. Thompson kept chipping away at the resistance, guaranteeing payment to publishers whether or not he collected from advertisers. He promised advertisers that he would spice up dull ad copy, making it as memorable as biting into a red pepper in a bowl of soup.

Thompson's ads for Mennen in the 1890s convinced the public to buy talcum powder that was packaged in a tin can — "the box that lox" — instead of the traditional cloth bag. During the same decade, he appropriated the Rock of Gibraltar as a symbol for the Prudential Insurance Company and made Pabst beer famous not only in Milwaukee but nationwide. Most significantly, Thompson preached that consumer magazines — which enjoyed a wider distribution than newspapers and were kept around the house a lot longer — were "the cream of advertising mediums." He assured "legitimate advertisers of the better class" that magazine readers had "both *taste* for their goods and the *means* to satisfy it." By the late 1880s, Thompson had become the exclusive agent for more than a hundred titles, each of which vied for a place on the annually updated list of thirty magazines that graced the agency's letterhead and that the agency pushed the hardest with advertisers.

The Century, which began publication as *Scribner's Monthly* in 1870 with the claim that advertising would "render the magazine readable and attractive," was a perennial on Thompson's list. Able to attract top writers, the magazine

Advertising quality: Judson Pin Co. guaranteed that its Capsheaf Safety Pins were "absolutely superior to all others" in this 1904 ad in *The Burr McIntosh Monthly*.

Baker's used the company's trademark, the cocoa-carrying maid (bottom left corner of ad), to foster customer identification and loyalty.

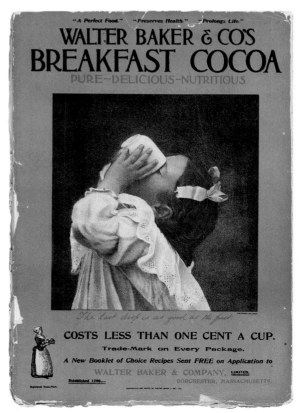

When you "Feel like Flying" from the load of housework

Be Calm ~ and use

SAPOLIO

WORKS WITHOUT WASTE   CLEANS SCOURS POLISHES

When writing to advertisers please mention THE AMERICAN MAGAZINE.

Even back in 1910, ads were claiming that a simple bar of soap could work wonders in easing the life of a housewife.

(my mama used Wool Soap)   (I wish mine had)
WOOLENS will not shrink if
WOOL SOAP
is used in the laundry

Making their debut in the 1890s, the Wool Soap kids demonstrated children's power to sell in print advertising.

was also the first serious periodical to welcome full-page ads.

Harper's responded to *The Century's* innovations by slashing its own ad rates. Other magazines went further. *Youth's Companion*, for example, formed a department that created eye-catching display advertising. The lithograph of a popular painting of Cupid that it prepared for Mellin's Foods in 1893 was the first full-color advertisement in an American periodical. As advertising became more graphic, it influenced the look and feel of magazines. A black-and-white illustration of two little girls dressed only in their woolen undershirts ran in many publications in the 1890s. "My Mama used Wool Soap," says one girl. "I wish mine had," replies the other, whose buttocks are bared because her garment has shrunk so much.

The ad is notable not only because it appeals to parental guilt (a style of advertising that breakfast foods and insurance companies would soon latch on to), but also because it shows the power of the image to transmit a sales message. Editors, who had been watching advertising creep onto their covers (or those of their competitors) and into the editorial well, began to vary their typography and to dress up their own pages with artwork. Publishers increased the size of pages to provide advertisers with a larger canvas. But what advertisers needed most was a larger audience.

The population of the United States in 1890 was about 63 million; the combined circulation of the 140 magazines listed in *Ayer's Directory* (including farm, trade, and religious journals) was only 7.1 million. Frank Munsey — a short-tempered, mercurial man who was continually merging, reformulating, and shutting down publications — reasoned that the more readers he could attract to the lowbrow, general-interest magazine he had named after himself, the easier it would be to attract advertisers. In 1893, he cut the cover price of *Munsey's Magazine* from a quarter — a standard price — to a dime. Circulation soared, and ad pages rolled in.

Cyrus H. K. Curtis was another of the early innovators. He started *The Ladies' Home Journal* in 1883 as a spin-off to a farm journal. By charging a low subscription rate, by advertising aggressively, and by energetically wooing potential advertisers, he built the monthly's circulation to 700,000 within six years. When he doubled the *Journal's* subscription price to a dollar in 1889, the N. W. Ayer advertising agency faithfully extended a $200,000 line of credit and guaranteed Curtis's note at his paper supplier. Curtis's genius in promotion (he once said that it was the only task too important for him to delegate) was

Aromints used the image of a well-heeled life-style to sell its breath sweetener in this 1919 ad in *Scribner's*.

At the moment—the fun of picture taking—afterward the joy of possession. There's all this for those who keep the personal story of their outings with a

KODAK

George Eastman relied heavily on ads like this one (above right) to sell Kodak camera and film. Ads showing the brutality of the Hun (right) helped convince Americans to buy $24 billion worth of Liberty Bonds during the First World War.

SOMEBODY'S LITTLE GIRL
Suppose She Were Yours
Buy Liberty Bonds To Save Her

Infection Can't Dent the Lysol Line

WAVE upon wave of unaccountable billions of disease germs constantly assail your life and health. The germ's business is disease and death, and it attends strictly to business.

Mental stress—loss of sleep—anything that sends your vitality below par, makes you an easy victim to disease.

But infection can't dent the Lysol line.

In every home there are germ-breeding, disease-breeding places that must be disinfected systematically, if you would make a better fight against disease than it can make against you.

Lysol Disinfectant totally annihilates all germ life at the instant of contact. No germ, no matter how great its strength or how powerful its virulence, can live a moment in the presence of Lysol solution.

Big hospitals everywhere rely upon it to keep contagion from running riot within their precincts.

A reduction of sickness in the homes of thousands of families might be definitely traced from the time they began to disinfect regularly with Lysol.

Begin today to make your home germ-proof. Use Lysol regularly to disinfect toilets, sinks, drains, garbage cans, cuspidors, and dark, damp, sunless corners.

The regular use of Lysol is easy and economical. A 50c bottle makes 5 gallons of powerful disinfectant; a 25c bottle makes 2 gallons. Get a bottle today—disinfect the danger spots mentioned above. You will then make a better fight against disease than disease can make against you.

Lysol is also invaluable for Personal Hygiene.

There is but One, True Lysol—the product made, bottled, signed and sealed by Lehn & Fink, Inc. Don't trust a counterfeit. Accept only the genuine article, sold in all drug stores, in our original yellow packages, for 25c, 50c and $1.00.

Lysol Toilet Soap Contains Lysol, and therefore protects the skin from germ infection. It is refreshingly soothing and healing and helpful for improving the skin. Ask your dealer. If he hasn't it, ask him to order it for you.

• OUR SIGN IS OUR BOND •
Lehn & Fink
New York
Inc.

Lysol Shaving Cream Contains Lysol, and kills germs on razor and shaving brush (where germs abound), guards the tiny cuts from infection, and gives the antiseptic shave. If your dealer hasn't it, ask him to order a supply for you.

Samples Mailed Free. Send us your name and address, and we will gladly send you samples of Lysol Toilet Soap and also of Lysol Shaving Cream for the men of your family.

LEHN & FINK, Inc., Manufacturing Chemists   *Makers of Pebeco Tooth Paste*   101 William St., New York

matched by his ability to select editors who were in touch with middle-class values.

Edward Bok, who became editor of the *Journal* in 1889, infused the magazine with his own combative personality. Curtis banned patent-medicine advertising from the *Journal*'s pages in 1893; Bok attacked the elixirs editorially. Subsequent exposés in several magazines effectively destroyed the industry, which had remained a major advertiser. By this time, popular magazines were setting the social agenda for the nation, and the agenda was based on the needs and wants of the masses. Bok once editorialized that the reason the *Journal* didn't devote more attention to "the servant-girl problem" was that 82 percent of American families didn't have one. What women did have, competitor *McCall's* told advertisers, was the power to spend 90 percent of the family income.

In his autobiography, published in 1923, Bok wrote that contemporary editors had become preoccupied with what today would be called the bottom line. If editors and publishers were to concentrate on bringing out a magazine that appealed to a wide readership, he argued, advertisers would be drawn like bees to honey, for the advertiser "must go where his largest market is." By that time, the largest market by far was reading Curtis's other publication, *The Saturday Evening Post*.

Curtis bought the *Post* in 1897, when its circulation stood at about 2,000 and ad revenue was $7,000. He charged only a nickel for the weekly, then set out to find an editor who, like Bok, had a knack for attracting readers — and the advertisers that inevitably followed them. In 1899, as Bok was urging Curtis to close down the money-losing *Post* before it sank the *Journal*, George Horace Lorimer became the *Post*'s editor.

Lorimer wanted a magazine that would appeal to everyone. The *Post*, as much as any magazine ever has, did just that. As Warren Harding lay dying, his wife sat at his bedside reading aloud a *Post* article about the President. His last words were "Read some more." Advertisers flocked to the *Post* as circulation grew into the millions. Lorimer handed out $20 gold pieces to his staff in 1927, after ad revenue topped $50 million. When *Post* representatives visited cities in which the Curtis Publishing Company did not maintain an office, they placed an ad in the local papers advising advertisers to call for an appointment.

Time's obituary for Curtis, who died in 1933, said that he "developed advertising as a sort of hydro-electric system to drive the wheels of the publishing business" and went on to

"Lasting satisfaction is a Perrin Glove attraction," boasts an elegant 1927 ad in *Vogue* (top). Heinz assures its *Vogue* readers (above) that only the best of the "tomato class of 1935" made it into its juice.

The 1919 Lysol ad (opposite) presents consumers with a simple choice: "Annihilate all germ life" or face "disease and death."

Even Santa enlisted in the propaganda effort in this 1944 *Life* ad for Interwoven socks (top). Westinghouse offers all the appliances postwar homemakers could want in a 1947 ad in *Time* (above).

claim that Curtis had done for magazines what Henry Ford had done for automobiles. In fact, the two industries spurred each other's growth, and automobile manufacturers have long headed the list of magazine advertisers. At first, ads for the motorcar concentrated on trying to dispel the popular notion that the newfangled product was "an expensive luxury for the man who does not need one," as *The New York World* put it. That effort was of course a tremendous success, and it proved, advertising historian Frank Presbrey has observed, "the ability of the average American to acquire an article of luxury when the pleasure of possession is clearly pictured to him."

Magazine advertising spurred the phenomenal growth of cameras, phonographs, and safety razors (and the film and records and blades they required) in the first quarter of this century. Devices that ran on electricity — many promising to eliminate the "drudgery of housework" — were introduced. Cigarette consumption skyrocketed as celebrities like Ty Cobb and Charlie Chaplin endorsed their favorite brand in full-page ads. Cosmetics sales jumped sevenfold. Magazines took in 28 percent of the nearly $1 billion spent for print advertising in 1925, a dollar increase of more than 1,000 percent in twenty-five years.

The Great Depression of the thirties and the wartime restrictions of the early forties pinched manufacturers' promotion budgets; at the same time, magazines, struggling to hold down their cover prices during the lean years, became increasingly dependent on ad revenues. The launching and near-foundering of *Life*, Henry Luce's weekly picture magazine, in 1936 is a case in point. Even before the first issue appeared, it became clear that a lot more than 250,000 copies — the number on which Luce had based advertising contracts — would be sold. It cost Luce substantially more to produce those thousands of extra copies than he took in from *Life*'s readers. Luce was forced to absorb $6 million in losses before he could adjust his ad rates.

By the mid-twentieth century, Luce's various magazines — notably *Time*, *Life*, and *Fortune* — had become enormously influential in setting and explaining the national agenda. That influence was evident when John F. Kennedy took office in 1961. He granted *Time*'s White House correspondent, Hugh Sidey, almost unlimited access. It was similarly revealing that as television reached into more and more homes and played a greater role in politics, Sidey saw less and less of the President. Early in 1963, David Halberstam notes in *The Powers That Be*,

New heights in fashion

Soaring into the heady realms of fashion, this year's collection replaces

fashion-past with boldness, assurance, verve. Here is more generosity in

proportions, more daring in effect than any millinery in a generation. The new

Lincoln motorcar shares those ineffable qualities

of originality and daring and unerring taste that transport a

true creation far above the commonplace. You will not see these spring and

summer hats on everybody's head . . . and you

will not see Lincoln—the one fresh, new personality

among fine cars—in everybody's driveway.

MR. ARNOLD lifts the wide-brimmed picture hat to a new height by
draping geranium-printed silk into a tall crown, garnished with gay blossoms.

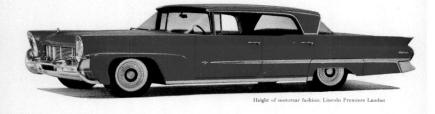

Height of motorcar fashion: Lincoln Premiere Landau

Selling fashion *and* transportation: The new lines of spring hats and Lincoln luxury cars were both advertised in this 1958 *Harper's Bazaar*. The full ad ran six pages.

Since the late nineteenth century, the tobacco companies have been major magazine advertisers. This ad ran in *Life* in 1946.

Thrilling Beauty News *for users of* Liquid Shampoos!

LUSTRE-CREME is the favorite beauty shampoo of 4 out of 5 top Hollywood stars... and you'll love it in its new Lotion Form, too!

Marilyn Monroe
starring in
"GENTLEMEN PREFER BLONDES"
A 20th Century-Fox Production
Color by Technicolor

MARILYN MONROE says, "Yes, I use Lustre-Creme Shampoo." When America's most glamorous women use Lustre-Creme Shampoo, shouldn't it be *your* choice above all others, too?

Now! Lustre-Creme Shampoo *also* in New Lotion Form!

Yes! Now take your choice:
Famous Cream Form...or new Lotion Form

Famous Cream Form in jars or tubes, 27¢ to $1. *(Big economy size, $2.)*

New Lotion Form in handy bottles, 30¢ to $1.

NEVER BEFORE—a liquid shampoo like this! Lustre-Creme Shampoo in new Lotion Form is much more than just another shampoo that pours. It's a *new* creamy lotion, a fragrant, satiny, easier-to-use lotion, that brings *Lustre-Creme glamour* to your hair with every heavenly shampoo!

VOTED "BEST" IN DRAMATIC USE-TESTS!
Lustre-Creme Shampoo in new Lotion Form was tested against 4 leading liquid and lotion shampoos . . . all unlabeled. And *3 out of every 5 women preferred Lustre-Creme* in new Lotion Form over each competing shampoo tested—for these important reasons:

★ Lather foams more quickly!
★ Easier to rinse away!
★ Cleans hair and scalp better!
★ Leaves hair more shining!
★ Does not dry or dull the hair!
★ Leaves hair easier to manage!
★ Hair has better fragrance!
★ More economical to use!

POUR IT ON—OR CREAM IT ON! In famous Cream Form, Lustre-Creme is America's favorite cream shampoo. And all its beauty-bringing qualities are in the new Lotion Form. Whichever form *you* prefer, lanolin-blessed Lustre-Creme will leave your hair shining clean, eager to wave, never dull or dry.

Prove it to Yourself...
Lustre-Creme in new Lotion Form is the **best liquid** shampoo yet!

Shortly before appearing on the cover of the first issue of *Playboy*, Marilyn Monroe pitched shampoo in *Ladies' Home Journal*.

I dreamed I stopped them in their tracks in my *maidenform* bra

New Sweet Music® bra by Maidenform...spoke-stitched cups for gently rounded contours—the new, naturally *you* way to look! Snug-fitting, all-elastic band keeps you *comfortable*, laminated undercups *never* let you down! This and 6 *other* styles, from 2.50.

TAN...don't burn...use COPPERTONE

Get a faster, <u>deeper</u> tan plus GUARANTEED sunburn protection!

Sunbalanced Screening does it! With Coppertone, you get a faster, smoother, *deeper* tan, with maximum sunburn protection—than with any other leading product! That's because Coppertone's special screening agent, homomenthyl salicylate, lets in the ultraviolet tanning rays that activate coloring matter deep within your skin... as it shuts out rays that burn and coarsen your skin.

Conditions Skin, too! The extra lanolin and other protectives in Coppertone keep it on the skin longer, protect you even after swimming. Coppertone prevents ugly drying and peeling, too.

America's Favorite! Originated in sunny Florida, Coppertone now far outsells all other suntan products. Use it whenever you're out in the sun—at beach, pool, fishing, or right in your own backyard. Available in Lotion, Oil, Cream, Spray, and new Coppertone Shade for children and those with sensitive skin. Also Noskote. Get a rich, long-lasting Coppertone tan! Get Coppertone in large size to save most.

COPPERTONE Suntan Lotion

Don't be a paleface!

AUGUST 1959   63

The Maidenform Woman (above right) has been showing up in all sorts of places since 1949. Coppertone's unforgettable scene of innocent play at the beach (right) manages to burn a slogan or two into the reader's mind as well.

Kennedy solicitously asked Sidey about rumored problems at *Life*. "The ads are off; it must be television," Sidey replied.

For some time, in fact, network television had been making inroads in attracting the kind of large national audience traditionally captured only by the mass-circulation magazines. Although *Collier's* and *Woman's Home Companion* were each being bought by more than four million readers when they folded in the mid-fifties, advertising revenues were no longer sufficient to subsidize the rising costs of printing and distribution. In 1963, *Life* and its two remaining competitors in the weekly general-interest field, *Look* and *The Saturday Evening Post*, could boast of having paid circulations ranging from 6.5 to 7.5 million. Despite rising production costs, they offered cut-rate subscriptions to maintain those numbers, which allowed them to charge advertisers a higher rate. The competition was fierce, and the casualties mounted. The *Post* folded as a weekly in 1969, *Look* in 1971, *Life* in 1972.

As these giants tumbled, however, magazine advertising was gaining a footing on other levels. Publishers were delivering well-defined audiences to marketers through *Playboy*, *Sports Illustrated*, *TV Guide*, *Bride's*, *Rolling Stone*, and hundreds of other magazines. At roughly the same time, the advertising industry was undergoing a "creative revolution." The results were print ads with a fresh and sometimes irreverent vitality, like those for Hathaway shirts, or Schweppes quinine water, or that odd little German import, the Volkswagen Beetle.

Now, as new products proliferate — many of them developed for a specific age or interest group — and as advertisers try to reach a specific niche in the marketplace, magazines that can offer precise targeting are flourishing. The computer magazine *PC Sources* was launched in October 1990 with 418 pages of advertising. Compare that to *The Saturday Evening Post's* largest issue, published on December 6, 1929. It contained 168 ad pages.

As the marketplace continues to fragment, magazines seem to be positioned to survive and thrive as a choice medium for advertisers. John O'Toole, president of the American Association of Advertising Agencies, offers two reasons for optimism. First, magazines have shown "a better understanding" of how to reach a segmented audience than have other media. Second, as network television becomes more clotted with commercials, even as its audience declines, advertisers will turn away from the medium that killed off the big general-interest magazines.

In 1989, readers paid more than $7 billion for the top 300

How to make a '54 look like a '64.

Hathaway announces a totally new stripe: rather costly and very discreet

Volkswagen sold America on its "Beetle" (top) in the sixties with a Doyle Dane Bernbach ad campaign that many consider the best in history. David Ogilvy bought an eyepatch on the way to the office for his Hathaway model (above) — and made him a nationally recognized figure.

Calvin Klein Underwear

Bruce Weber's 1980 photograph for Calvin Klein gave men's underwear and the male body itself new status in magazine advertising.

ABSOLUT WARHOL.

FOR GIFT DELIVERY ANYWHERE CALL 1-800-CHEER-UP (EXCEPT WHERE PROHIBITED BY LAW) 80 AND 100 PROOF/100% GRAIN NEUTRAL SPIRITS (ABSOLUT COUNTRY OF SWEDEN) © 1985 CARILLON IMPORTERS LTD. TEANECK, NJ

Years after Andy Warhol parodied ads with his painting of a Campbell's Soup can, he was commissioned to create ads for Absolut Vodka.

Annie Leibovitz's photos for the American Express ad campaign featured celebrity "cardmembers" ranging from Ella Fitzgerald to Tip O'Neill, shown here.

American magazines, according to *Advertising Age*, and advertisers bought close to $10 billion worth of space in them. (A few magazines do without advertising altogether, and some of them — such as *Consumer Reports*, with a circulation of almost five million — enjoy considerable success.) Collectively, then, advertisers sponsor one of the most important sectors of the nation's marketplace of ideas. On occasion, the commercial message may intrude on editorial integrity; when that happens, other magazines can be counted on to cry foul. Meanwhile, as intrusive as the message sometimes is, the alternative would seem to be a much-diminished field of magazines, representing a narrowed range of opinions — and even, conceivably, a nation without a clear idea of what Santa Claus looks like.

— *Thomas Forbes*

The famous — including Dizzy Gillespie, photographed by Herb Ritts — and the not-so-famous posed for a series of black-and-white ads for the Gap.

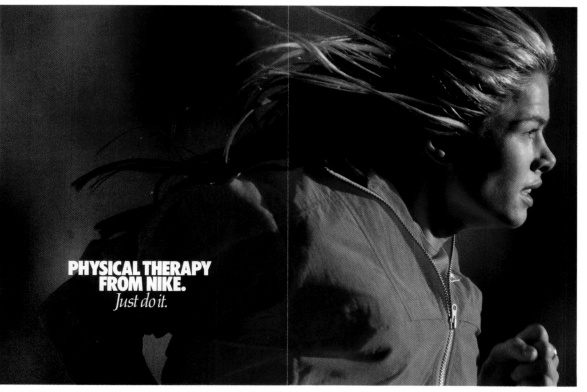

Ads for Nike footwear and apparel were tailored to the late-eighties health and fitness craze.

An Insider's View

To those involved in the process, putting out a magazine — be it slick, fat, and four-color or slim and black-and-white — calls for blood, sweat, and often a lot of shouting. The process begins anew each production cycle and inexorably forges a group of people with disparate interests into an extended family. The members of this unlikely team work together with one goal in mind — to create the most attractive and compelling issue possible and to do it on schedule.

On the following pages, nine talented photojournalists document aspects of the editorial process at a diverse group of magazines; along the way they capture some of the people who make magazines succeed. If some of the scenes convey a sense of chaos, that's because a certain amount of this basic element of the creative process is an integral part of the high-pressure world of magazine publishing.

The newsweeklies gear up for war. In week one of the Gulf conflict, *Newsweek* art director Patricia Bradbury (above) shows final layout for a special issue on the war to (seated, left to right) editor Maynard Parker, editor-in-chief Richard M. Smith, executive editor Stephen Smith and other staff. (Opposite) Electronically transmitted news photos arriving from the Middle East are received into computers and formatted; detailed maps are readied; and several *Newsweek* staff members await a strategy meeting. Photo editors make their selects; and a mock-up of the cover is finalized (right).

Photographs by Mark S. Wexler

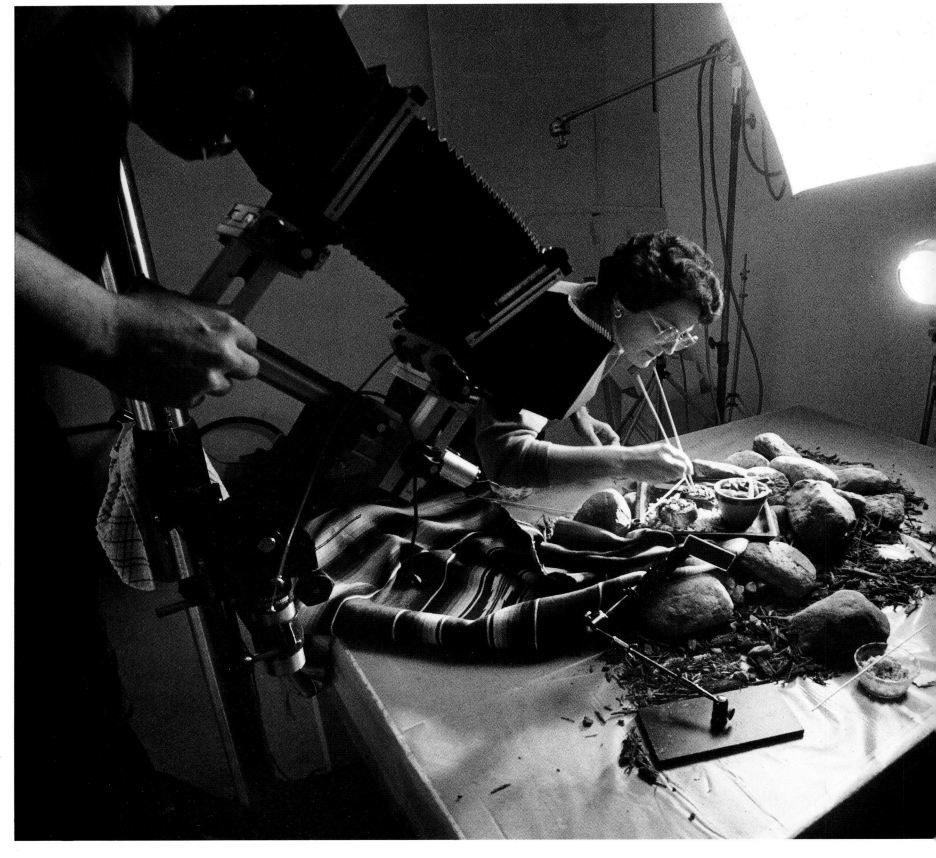

Putting the house and home in focus: Magazines like *Better Homes and Gardens* profile everything from furniture to food, all to enhance the living environments of their readers. Janet Herwig "styles" an al fresco trail meal in the midst of the photo shoot (left, below). Art director Brad Hong, layout artist Nancy Kluender, and editors David Jordan and Lamont Olson make cover choices (far left); a room takes shape in the photo studio; graphic designers Kelly Barton and Susan Vedelhofen check transparencies for an upcoming issue; and designer Sandra Soria oversees the photo shoot of a lamp with a disproportionately small shade — a combination *Better Homes and Gardens* does not advocate for its readers. Murray Baskin keeps an eye on the end product — finished magazines coming off the press (below).

Photographs by Nicole Bengiveno

E*bony* has given its black readership informed news and entertainment for more than forty-five years. An editorial meeting is attended by (opposite, left to right) Robert Johnson, editor of *Ebony*'s younger sibling *Jet*, Linda Johnson Rice, president of the magazine, John H. Johnson, founder and publisher, executive editor Lerone Bennett, Jr., and — seen from the rear — Sylvia P. Flanagan, senior editor of *Jet*. John Johnson in the exercise room and barber shop that adjoin his office (opposite below). Linda Johnson Rice in her office with her father (right). M. Eunice W. Johnson, director of *Ebony* Fashion Fair, oversees a fashion shoot (below); *Jet* editors Robert Johnson and Sylvia Flanagan assess the month's editorial package; Lerone Bennett fields a call in the art department.

Photographs by Eli Reed

The editor's life: Victor Navasky, editor of *The Nation*, a weekly journal of opinion, starts a new day in New York, breakfasts with his wife, Anne, before boarding a bus, and later stops to chat with subscribers (opposite). In his office, Navasky puts assistant editor Micah Sifry on hold (right), while down the hall, the magazine's literary editors, Art Winslow and Elsa Dixler, confer. Navasky has a working lunch with author and contributor E. L. Doctorow (below).

Photographs by Eugene Richards

On one of a number of trips they take into far-flung fields each year, Jeff Cox, contributing editor of *Organic Gardening,* and Mike McGrath, the magazine's editor-in-chief (below), inspect the effects of a hard freeze on an organically grown vineyard in Mendocino County, California. McGrath photographs peas grown within the vineyard (left) and captures Linda Dawson harvesting mustard greens (lower left); Cox and McGrath inspect fresh-picked, yard-long, oriental green beans.

Photographs by George Steinmetz

The tables are turned: This time *Vanity Fair* is the *subject* of the photo shoot as *The Times* of London sets up (above). The group waiting with editor-in-chief Tina Brown (center) includes (from right to left) special correspondent Marie Brenner, contributing editors Jesse Kornbluth and Anthony Haden-Guest, managing editor Pamela McCarthy, and a *Times* technician. Brown gets a message (right), and McCarthy has a meeting at her desk with production manager Ellen Kiell, United Kingdom edition coordinator Tanya Lenkow, and art and design director Charles Churchward.

Photographs by David Burnett

The consummate Cosmo girl: Helen Gurley Brown, editor-in-chief of *Cosmopolitan* (right), lets her pillows do the talking. (Below, left to right) She travels to New York's 21 Club with publisher Seth Hoyt and beauty and health director Mallen DeSantis for a luncheon meeting with advertisers. Later, another provocative *Cosmopolitan* page gets laid out, and fashion editor Sandy de Nicolais plays model to costume jewelry used in a fashion shoot at the magazine's offices.

Photographs by Misha Erwitt

John Iacono readies his camera equipment (left) to shoot a New York Giants–Chicago Bears playoff game for *Sports Illustrated*. S.I. photographer John Biever (below) has his hands — and mouth — full tracking the action; Iacono works the sideline with his assistant; and, at half-time, breaks into the open to hand off exposed film to a courier for the run to the magazine's film processing lab. Director of photography Karen Mullarkey exercises the picture editor's fifth limb, the telephone, while Michael Jordan does some exercising of his own (opposite). In the art department, color is proofed (opposite below); photo editor Bob Mitchell stretches between tasks; and with the deadline to close the magazine looming, photo editors Jeff Weig, Mitchell, Margaret Hastings, and Don Mann get briefed.

Photographs by Andy Levin

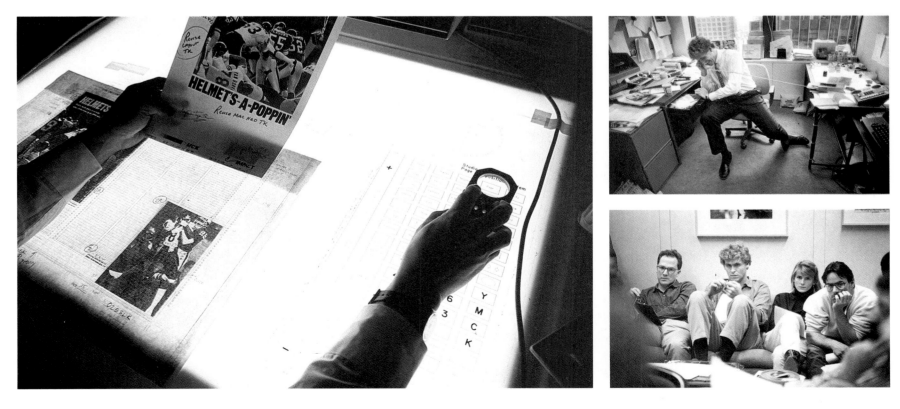

Taking work to the beach: A large expanse of sand and a black "seamless" create an open-air studio (left) for an *L.A. Style* fashion shoot. Waris Dirie (above) hunts for the perfect pose as a high-tech beachcomber uses a metal detector to search for lost valuables. In the trailer, Tara Abate gets a hairstyle (opposite above) while *L.A. Style*'s editor and publisher, Joie Davidow, gets business done; John Caruso gives Tara Abate another style-up; and Waris Dirie makes a quick change during the shoot. Tara Abate (opposite below), flanked by the magazine's fashion photography editor Jodi Nakatsuka and make-up artist Bethany Karlyn, holds a pose.

Photographs by Jeff Jacobson

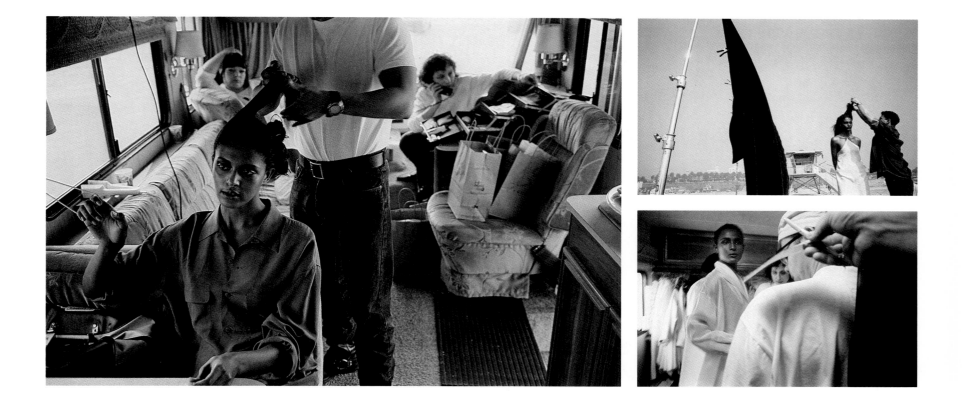

The Magazine and the Future

The year is 2020. For Alycia Logan, a chemical engineer in Los Angeles, the day has been a long one. She spent hours reprogramming the computer to detect new chemical compounds. Then the pneumatic rail system stalled on her commute home. It is 9:00 P.M. before the children have been put to bed and Alycia has some time to herself. It will be hours before her husband, Kerrick, returns. Alycia flicks on a remote control and scans through a list of magazine titles projected on the screen that dominates her home-entertainment unit: People, McCall's, The Left Bank, The Saturday Evening Post, The New Yorker, Organic Gardening, Thrasher, Macramé Monthly, The Flautist, Vogue. . . . Hundreds of titles roll by.

Tonight The Left Bank, a clever look at the latest fashion and art trends coming out of Paris, catches her eye. Alycia clicks the remote once again. Words begin to flash on the screen: "Transmission begun." Then: "Document printing." In less than ten minutes the words "Delivery complete" flash. Alycia walks over to a small, square machine no bigger than a videocassette recorder, raises a panel, and lifts out the magazine.

The pages, as she flips through, are glossy. The artwork that accompanies the stories is dramatic, the colors wonderfully vibrant. The ads are personalized: Many use her name; virtually all reflect her taste and buying habits. The magazine is not a series of loose pages, but bound. The small mechanical box, by this time a common household fixture, is an in-home publishing facility, able to access and process information via its satellite link, then produce a finished magazine within minutes. Despite the high-tech surroundings and the complex series of communications codes it took to print and deliver it, the magazine itself looks uncannily like those that populated the newsstands of the nineties. And Alycia, curled up on her couch as she peruses the pages, looks like a typical, circa-1990 magazine reader as well.

●

"If you look at the future, you have to look at historical patterns first to find the constants," says Roger Selbert, a real-life futurist who edits and publishes *FutureScan*, a newsletter that analyzes marketplace trends. "The constants are the only things you can be sure about in the future. And the magazine format is one of those constants. The electronic word is not going to replace the printed word. It will add to it, it will be another option, it may even displace some percentage of the market, but it's not going to replace the written word."

For the most part, those in the business of giving a framework to the world of 100 or 200 years from now believe that although technology will probably have reshaped the world in ways we cannot envision today, there will still be a glossy magazine or two on what looks remarkably like a coffee table, a well-thumbed newsweekly in the bathroom, a recipe ripped out and attached to the door of a refrigerator or its high-tech equivalent. This magazine will, however, have other elements that will let the reader turn what was once a rather narrowly focused experience into one that has a multitude of dimensions. We are already seeing the antecedents of this, as advertisers use magazines as a testing ground for new technologies that help them engage consumers and stand apart from their competitors. The Ford Motor Company has experimented with binding a floppy disc into magazines; pop the disc into your p.c. and a high-tech driving simulation unfolds on the screen. Absolut Vodka has brought sound to the printed page by implanting a computer chip into some of its magazine ads. Forced by a competitive marketplace to attract attention, advertisers will probably take the lead in sorting out the technological possibilities, discarding those that are too costly or simply bore the reader, refining those that are affordable and effective.

Fundamentally, the magazine will remain the same — a blend of words and pictures that entertains and enlightens — but there is much debate over whether those words and pictures will continue to exist on a printed page, as futurist Selbert suggests, or be transformed into a completely electronic medium, one that is not hand-held but viewed on a screen.

Jerry Borrell, editor-in-chief of *Macworld*, is experimenting with producing a magazine completely on a compact disc; the text is displayed on a computer screen. The cost of producing a single disc that can be mailed to subscribers is, Borrell says, "a dollar and some change." Because "video is omnipresent," he adds, "we magazine editors and designers need to use the future tools, to learn to design with them effectively. We know almost nothing about video, animation, sound, music." Borrell's magazine-disc *does* use animation and sound, but in its present form, storage space is minimal: The disc can hold only five feature articles. That will change as more people acquire the systems that will allow them to see or read or experience such a publication. Borrell is bullish: "There's every indication that this will catch on."

Reginald K. Brack, Jr., president of Time Inc. Magazines, agrees, up to a point. In the future, he says, "there will be magazines, including ours, that instead of twelve monthly issues will have several issues on videocassette or compact disc. They will certainly have color, they will have to be portable, and they will have to cost a nominal amount so that they can be bought by virtually everyone." Cost and portability are the remaining hurdles.

John Mack Carter, editor-in-chief of *Good Housekeeping* and director of new magazine development for the Hearst Corporation, puts himself in the camp of those who believe that technology will enhance, but not radically alter, the form of the magazine. That fundamental form, says Carter, did not come about by happenstance. "It evolved and was developed by the reader, by selection and rejection," he points out. "I don't pretend to be a futurist, but I've paused long enough to think about whether there will or will not be magazines, and I've come to the conclusion that there will be and that the form will not be that different, just as I really believe people will not be that different."

That is not to say that Carter and others in the industry see magazines as static or resistant to change in the twenty-first century. The one factor that will remain unchanged is the *need* for a magazine — an eminently portable means of deepening one's knowledge of an area of interest, of expanding one's understanding of at least a piece of the world, and yes, even of warding off loneliness. The components that make up a single magazine, on the other hand, will be transfigured by time.

Using broad strokes, Jagdish Sheth describes a number of ways in which magazines are likely to evolve in the next century. Sheth is a Robert E. Brooker distinguished professor of marketing and research at the University of Southern California and founder and director of USC's Center for Telecommunications Management. He suggests that special-interest magazines, which now number in the hundreds, will proliferate — and that their focus will narrow considerably. Titles like *Car and Driver*, for example, will give way to ones like *Nissan Novice* or *Mercedes Mechanic*. Today, such tightly focused fare tends to be produced and published by the maker of the product, but the new magazines, Sheth predicts, will be independent, driven by reader interest, and funded by both subscriptions and the handful of advertisers most interested in those readers.

Sheth is hardly alone in his belief that the future will belong to highly specialized publications. Richard B. Stolley, editorial director of Time Inc. Magazines, says his company is already in the process of redefining the whole concept of special-interest publishing. He cites *Money* as an example of a special-interest magazine that attracts a national audience even though it sees everything from the viewpoint of personal finance. "The day when a magazine can be all things to all men and women has been ending for a long time," Stolley says.

However one defines it, specialization is becoming far more feasible as advances in technology drive down costs and tighten the loop between idea and execution. Doris Walsh, former publisher of *American Demographics*, has written that "growth will come not from volume, but from targeting customers more efficiently." Thomas O. Ryder, president of American Express Publishing, is already targeting. "At *Travel & Leisure* we can determine which of our subscribers read more for business travel and which read for pleasure or leisure travel," he says. "We are beginning to have the ability to create a customized product for those with special business interest." To do that, *Travel & Leisure* taps into an extensive database on American Express credit-card holders, analyzing everything from brand preferences to buying habits. "With that knowledge, we will be able to tailor the editorial and advertising messages to those readers," says Ryder. "We are at the edge of it. Within five years, it will be the norm. Readers probably won't know clearly that it's happening unless they sit down with their next-door neighbor and compare."

Large publishing concerns are just beginning to move toward extreme targeting, but it is already the lifeblood of the minuscule publishing ventures known as "zines," a cross between a magazine and a newsletter. Zines, which claim circulation bases that range from twenty-five subscribers to 100,000, communicate a specific vision. *AFRAID,* for example, is a horror-fiction monthly. *Abiolysist Macroscope* deals with cryonics and other life-extension technologies. *A Taste of Latex* is devoted to the exploration of gender issues, role reversals, and behavior generally outside the mainstream.

"There have been a couple of technological drivers that have helped the explosion of zines," says Mike Gunderloy, co-editor of *Factsheet Five*, a catalogue that reviews the estimated 10,000 zines currently in existence. "The first was ready accessibility to photocopiers, and the second was personal computer programs that could do even rudimentary corrections." Desk-top publishing has only expanded the possibilities, enabling one or two people to produce a remarkably sophisticated publication. As a result, a growing number of people who would like to have a certain kind of magazine can create it themselves.

While publishers are zeroing in on audiences, some magazines are moving in what might seem a very different direction: They are seeking to expand their circulation base around the globe. Jagdish Sheth, who predicts that American magazines "will increasingly find their market all over the world," points out that globalization and specialization are not necessarily incompatible: "The more specialized the magazine becomes, the wider will be its global scope." No nation, he explains, has a monopoly on interest in food; a magazine addressed to gourmets will find an audience all over the world. Technology simply becomes a tool to facilitate change.

Big-league players in the American magazine industry are already jockeying for position on newsstands around the globe. "Every major publishing company is making agreements that range from something as simple as licensing titles and materials to acquisition and 100-percent ownership," says John Mack Carter. Although such partnerships — even the fifty-fifty kind that Carter believes will be the norm — are relatively uncommon, more and more U.S. magazines are succeeding internationally. Editions of *Time* and *Newsweek* are sold worldwide. *Cosmopolitan* is distributed in seventy countries. *Vogue* has had an international following for years. Publications as different as *Business Week* and *Omni* offer the international reader a perspective on events and information, but they don't refashion their message for individual cultures or countries. "The world really is getting smaller and more cosmopolitan, both economically and culturally," says Donald D. Kummerfeld, president of the

Magazine Publishers of America. "Linguistic and cultural barriers will still exist, but we will find better ways to overcome them."

Richard B. Stolley cautions that "there are a limited number of American magazines that are translatable" and that trying to transplant an American product to foreign soil is risky. Yet there are publications that have taken on the risk and succeeded, among them *Reader's Digest*, which pioneered in the internationalization of print media. After introducing its first foreign edition, in the United Kingdom in 1938, it quickly followed with foreign-language editions in South America and Central America. Last year, *Reader's Digest* published thirty-nine editions in sixteen languages, and it is now gearing up to produce a Russian edition, scheduled to be on sale at newsstands in several cities in the U.S.S.R. by August 1991. At the start of the last decade of the twentieth century, more than 12 million of its 29 million subscribers live outside the United States. The *Digest* attributes its international success to its policy of leaving editorial decisions in the hands of local managers and editors who understand the nuances of the culture; they don't simply take the American magazine and translate it into different languages.

In 1990, Myrna Blyth, publishing director and editor-in-chief of *Ladies' Home Journal*, made a successful foray abroad, bringing out a Soviet-American edition. The 10,000 copies of the special issue, with a thirty-two-page, Russian-language insert, were snapped up off Moscow newsstands and passed along to relatives and friends throughout the country. The most popular *Journal* feature among the Soviet women was one that has drawn American readers to the magazine for years: "Can This Marriage Be Saved?" (The wife's complaint — "He doesn't help around the house" — was something Soviet women said they understood, according to Blyth.)

Just as some U.S. magazine publishers see the rest of the world as their marketplace, publishers from "over there" and "down under" view the United States as a good place to do business. Notable examples are Australian-born Rupert Murdoch, whose substantial holdings include *TV Guide* and *New York*; the German firm Gruner + Jahr, which owns *Parents Magazine* and *YM*; the British company Reed International, which produces *Modern Bride*; and the French firm Hachette, publisher of *Elle* and *Woman's Day*.

Along with further globalization and specialization, the future will bring far more personal magazines than those we have today. Media historian John Tebbel believes that as we move toward the twenty-first century, readers will demand a more intimate connection between themselves and the magazines they buy. "There are approximately 22,000 magazines in this country, and they cover every field of human activity," Tebbel says. "But the closer magazines can get to their reader, the better off they'll be."

In late 1990, *Time* made a big step in that direction, personalizing its cover four million times, so that each subscriber's name appeared in the cover lines of his or her copy. "That technology will ultimately enable us to personalize the content," says Time Inc.'s Reginald Brack. For magazine advertisers, the technology serves a practical purpose. Currently, advertisers identify areas (typically by zip code) in which the people most likely to buy their product live, then run ads only in those areas. In the not-too-distant future, advertisers will be able to target not just areas, but individuals.

Magazines of the future will also be judged on their ability to offer a depth of experience, according to Myrna Blyth. Although she doesn't envision a complete conversion to an electronic magazine, Blyth does believe that magazines will have to incorporate elements that stimulate all the senses. "In the past 250 years we've gone from magazines that were more word intensive to ones that are more visually intensive," she notes. "In the future, you may not just sit there and read. People will expect it to be more of an experience." Just as perfume-makers have changed the smell of magazines, other vendors will use technology to find innovative ways of putting product samples within the pages of a magazine.

Paul Saffo, an information technology expert at the Institute for the Future in Menlo Park, California, likens the technological possibilities in publishing to "a huge electronic piñata: There is a thin paper crust around a huge electronic core. The core is expanding and the crust is getting thinner. The new won't replace the old directly; instead, it will allow us to do new and engaging things." Already there are all sorts of what he refers to as "electronic exotica" — digital paper, for one, that feels like oilcloth and can store and display data. "We are today at a moment between two revolutions," says Saffo. "One is print, which is four centuries old; the other is electronics, which is only three decades old. A new order is not going to appear for another thirty years. For now, everything is up for grabs."

It's nearly midnight when Kerrick Logan gets home. He finds Alycia asleep on the couch, The Left Bank still open beside her. He puts the magazine on the coffee table, pulls the generations-old quilt from the back of the couch to cover Alycia, and looks in on the children — members of a generation whose magazines will take a shape we can only begin to imagine.

— Betsy Sharkey

A Magazine Timeline

Look back at America's vital magazine history and it is a story of surprises. Magazines of every name and purpose have come and gone — with more than a few coming once again. Over the period, the American magazine has most resembled a living organism — dividing and proliferating, existing in anything but sterile isolation. A particular magazine might attract readers for a score of years or so, and then perish. But its creative ideas were often taken up and adapted by succeeding magazine generations.

While this selected timeline appears as a simple chronology with start-up dates, it does not simply celebrate individual birthdays; it honors a most durable species — one with such vitality, in fact, that in the very depths of the Great Depression some of this nation's hardiest magazines sprang up.

1741

American Magazine, or Monthly View
1741–1741

The General Magazine, and Historical Chronicle
1741–1741

American Magazine and Historical Chronical
1743–1746

Boston Weekly Magazine
1743–1743

Christian History
1743–1745

THE

American Magazine:

JANUARY, 1740-1.

This firſt Number begins with an Abſtract of the Proceedings of the Aſſemblies of New-Jerſey, Pennſylvania, *and* Maryland, *in Relation to the King's Inſtructions recommending to them the* [illegible] *and tranſporting* [illegible] *that were afterwards ſent from thence againſt the* Spaniſh Weſt-Indies; *and firſt of*

NEW-JERSEY.

June 26, 1740.

HIS Excellency the Governor having commanded the Attendance of the Houſe, being then ſitting, made them a Speech, wherein he acquainted them with his Majeſty's Intentions to attack the *Spaniſh Weſt-Indies*; and then proceeded in the following Manner. "His Majeſty therefore truſts and expects, that his loyal Aſſembly "of *New-Jerſey* will provide "Victuals, Tranſports, and all "other Neceſſaries for the "Troops to be raiſed in this "Province, except their Cloaths, "Tents, Arms, Ammunition "and Pay, 'till their Arrival at "the General Rendezvous in the "Weſt-Indies; from which "Time the ſaid Tranſports "ſhall enter into his Majeſty's "Pay.

"This I am commanded to "let you know, and in his Majeſty's Name to recommend "to you the making of ſuch "Proviſion, that the Expedition be not retarded for "Want thereof.

"This I now do, and doubt "not you will in this Caſe act "as becomes a loyal Houſe of "Repreſentatives, for his Majeſty's Service, and your own "immortal Honour."

The Houſe immediately took his Excellency's Speech into Conſideration, and the next Day ſent a Meſſage to his Excellency acquainting him, that they were inclinable to comply with his Majeſty's Expectation; but humbly conceiving a ſhort Adjournment would not retard the Deſign, prayed Leave to adjourn for a Fortnight, in order

A

1745

1750

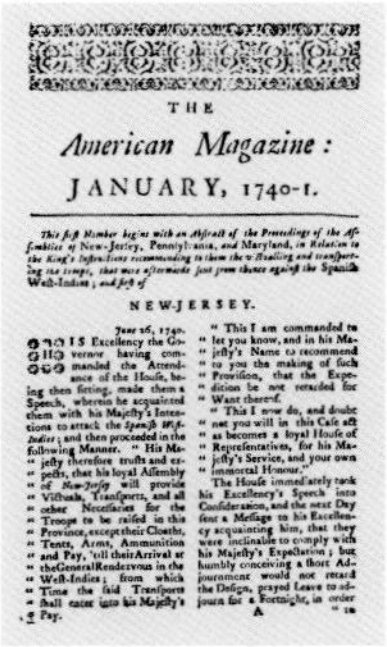

Independent Reflector
1752–1753

Occasional Reverberator
1753–1753

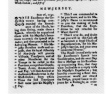

1755	1760	1765	1770	1775	1780	1785	1790

Instructor
1755–1755

John Englishman
1755–1755

American Magazine and Monthly Chronicle
1757–1758

New American Magazine
1758–1760

American Magazine or General Repository
1769–1769

Censor
1771–1772

Royal Spiritual Magazine
1771–1771

Royal American Magazine
1774–1775

Pennsylvania Magazine
1775–1776

United States Magazine
1779–1779

Boston Magazine
1783–1786

Gentleman and Lady's Town and Country Magazine
1784–1784

American Monitor
1785–1785

American Musical Magazine
1786–1786

Columbian Magazine
1786–1792

New-Haven Gazette and the Connecticut Magazine
1786–1789

New Jersey Magazine
1786–1787

Worcester Magazine
1786–1788

American Magazine
1787–1788

American Museum
1787–1792

New York Weekly Museum
1788–1817

Arminian Magazine
1789–1790

Children's Magazine
1789–1789

Christian's, Scholar's, and Farmer's Magazine
1789–1791

Gentlemen and Ladies Town and Country Magazine
1789–1790

Massachusetts Magazine
1789–1796

New–York Magazine
1790–1797

American Apollo
1792–1792

Lady's Magazine
1792–1793

The Old Farmer's Almanac
1792–

American Minerva
1793–1797

Columbian Museum
1793–1793

Free Universal Magazine
1793–1794

New-Hampshire Journal: or Farmer's Weekly Museum
1793–1810

New Hampshire Magazine
1793–1793

Monthly Miscellany and Vermont Magazine
1794–1794

United States Magazine
1794–1794

THE
Royal *American* Magazine,

OR UNIVERSAL
Repository of Instruction and Amusement.

For JANUARY, 1774.

CONTAINING,

1795 **1800** 1805 1810 1815 1820 1825 1830

American Monthly Review
1795–1795

New-York Weekly Magazine,
later Sentimental and
Literary Magazine
1795–1797

Philadelphia Minerva
1795–1798

Rural Magazine
1795–1796

Tablet
1795–1795

Theological Magazine
1795–1799

Experienced Christian's
Magazine
1796–1797

Lady & Gentleman's
Pocket Magazine
1796–1796

Long Island Magazine
1796–1796

Monthly Military Repository
1796–1797

Nightingale
1796–1796

Prospect from the
Congress Gallery, later
Political Censor
1796–1797

American Moral and
Sentimental Magazine
1797–1798

Literary Museum
1797–1797

Connecticut Evangelical
Magazine
1800–1815

New-York Missionary
Magazine
1800–1803

Philadelphia Repository and
Weekly Register
1800–1806

Ladies' Magazine and Musical
Repository
1801–1802

Port Folio
1801–1827

Balance and Columbian
Repository
1802–1808

Boston Weekly Magazine
1802–1806

Wasp
1802–1803

Literary Magazine and
American Register
1803–1807

Massachusetts Baptist
Missionary Magazine, later
Baptist Missionary
1803–1909

Monthly Anthology and
Boston Review
1803–1811

Alethian Critic, or Error
Exposed
1804–1804

Corrector
1804–1804

Evening Fireside, or Literary
Miscellany
1804–1806

Philadelphia Medical Museum
1804–1811

Lady's Weekly Miscellany
1805–1808

Literary Miscellany
1805–1806

Polyanthos
1805–1814

Theatrical Censor
1805–1806

Thespian Mirror
1805–1806

Emerald
1806–1808

Salmagundi
1807–1808

Tickler
1807–1813

American Law Journal
1808–1817

Herald of Gospel Liberty
1808–?

Select Reviews and the Spirit
of the Foreign Magazines
1809–1812

Something
1809–1810

Mirror of Taste and
Dramatic Censor
1810–1811

Niles' Weekly Register
1811–1849

New England Journal of
Medicine and Surgery
1812–1826

Satirist
1812–1812

The Analectic Magazine
1813–1820

Christian Disciple
1813–1823

Boston Spectator
1814–1815

Weekly Recorder, later
Presbyterian Banner
1814–?

Whim
1814–1814

Luncheon
1815–1816

North-American Review and
Miscellaneous Journal
1815–1939

Portico
1816–1818

Recorder, later Boston
Recorder
1816–1867

New-England Galaxy and
Masonic Magazine, later
New England Galaxy and
United States Literary
Advertiser
1817–1834

American Farmer
1819–1897

Ladies' Literary Cabinet
1819–1822

Red Book
1819–1821

Sketch Book
1819–1820

The Saturday Evening Post
1821–1969

The Albion
1822–1876

New York Mirror
1823–1842

New York Observer
1823–1912

Atlantic Magazine
1824–1825

African Repository
1825–1892

The Casket, later Graham's
Magazine
1826–1855

The Friend, later Friend's
Journal
1827–1955

Philadelphia Monthly Magazine
1827–1830

The Youth's Companion
1827–1929

Ladies' Magazine
1828–1836

New York Farmer
1828–1837

Godey's Lady's Book
1830–1898

The Liberator
1831–1865

Emancipator
1833–1842

Knickerbocker Magazine
1833–1865

The Cultivator
1834–1865

1835	1840	1845	1850	1855	1860	1865	1870

Anti-Slavery Record
1835–1837

The New-Yorker
1836–1841

Pennsylvania Freeman
1836–1854

United States Magazine and Democratic Review
1837–1859

The Dial
1840–1844

Ballou's Dollar Monthly Magazine
1841–1893

Dollar Magazine
1841–1842

Ladies' Repository
1841–1876

Peterson's Magazine
1842–1898

Columbian Lady's and Gentleman's Magazine
1844–1849

American Whig Review
1845–1852

National Police Gazette
1845–1932

Scientific American
1845–

DeBow's Review
1846–1880

The Flag of Our Union
1846–1870

Town & Country
1846–

The National Era
1847–1860

Independent
1848–1928

New England Farmer
1848–1871

Moore's Rural New Yorker
1849–?

Harper's New Monthly Magazine, later *Harper's*
1850–

Gleason's Pictorial
1851–1859

Yankee Notions
1852–1875

The Country Gentleman
1853–1955

Frank Leslie's Ladies' Gazette of Fashion and Fancy Needlework
1854–1857

Criterion
1855–1856

Frank Leslie's Illustrated Newspaper
1855–1922

The Moravian
1856–

New York Weekly
1856–1914

The Atlantic Monthly, later *The Atlantic*
1857–

Harper's Weekly
1857–1916

Jolly Joker
1862–1878

Army and Navy Journal, later *Armed Forces Journal International*
1863–

American Journal of Conchology
1865–1872

The Nation
1865–

New England Farmer
1865–1915

Saturday Night
1865–1902

American Freedman
1866–1869

Galaxy
1866–1878

American Naturalist
1867–

Harper's Bazaar
1867–

McGee's Illustrated Weekly
1867–1882

Sporting Times
1867–1872

Lippincott's Magazine
1868–1916

Our Dumb Animals, later *Animals*
1868–

Spectator
1868–?

Zion's Herald
1868–?

Appletons' Journal
1869–1881

Folio
1869–1895

Scribner's Monthly, later *The Century*
1870–1930

American Druggist
1871–

Frank Leslie's Ladies' Journal
1871–1881

Once a Week, later *Frank Leslie's Journal*
1871–1881

Popular Science
1872–

Publishers Weekly
1872–

Saturday Night
1872–1885

The Delineator
1873–1937

St. Nicholas
1873–1943

American Field
1874–

1900

| 1875 | 1880 | 1885 | 1890 | 1895 | | 1905 | 1910 |

Thoroughbred Record
1875–

Frank Leslie's Popular Monthly, later American Magazine
1876–1956

Harvard Lampoon
1876–

The Queen, later McCall's
1876–

Farm Journal
1877–1952

Frank Leslie's Sunday Magazine
1877–1889

Ladies' Home Journal
1877–1887

Puck
1877–1918

Capper's Weekly
1879–1879

The Chautauquan
1880–1914

The Dial
1880–1929

Ladies' World
1880–1918

Judge
1881–1939

Liberty
1881–1908

Archery and Tennis News
1882–1886

Argosy
1882–1979

Grit
1882–

Industry Week
1882–

The Ladies' Home Journal
1883–

American Rifleman
1885–

Good Housekeeping
1885–

B'Nai B'Rith International Jewish Monthly
1886–

Cosmopolitan
1886–

Forum
1886–1930

New-England Magazine
1886–1917

Progressive Farmer
1886–

The Sporting News
1886–

Sports Afield
1887–

Collier's Once a Week, later Collier's
1888–1957

Interiors
1888–

National Geographic
1888–

Pure-Bred Dogs, American Kennel Gazette
1888–

Munsey's Magazine
1889–1979

Judge's Library, later Film Fun
1890–1922

Literary Digest
1890–1938

Review of Reviews
1890–1937

American School Board Journal
1891–

Architectural Record
1891–

Instructor
1891–

Natural History Magazine
1891–

Architectural Forum
1892–1974

Sierra
1892–

Vogue
1892–

Dun's Review, later Dun and Bradstreet's Review
1893–?

McClure's Magazine, later New McClure's Magazine
1893–1929

Field & Stream
1895–

House Beautiful
1896–

New Idea Woman's Magazine, later Woman's Magazine
1896–1920

Ainslee's Magazine
1897–1926

Animal Kingdom Magazine
1897–

Charities, later The Survey
1897–1952

Success
1897–1911

Outdoor Life
1898–

Sunset
1898–

The Woman's Magazine
1898–1910

Audubon
1899–

Capper's Farmer
1899–1960

Everybody's Magazine
1899–1929

Physical Culture
1899–

American Journal of Nursing
1900–

Bostonia, the Magazine of Culture & Ideas
1900–

The Smart Set
1900–1930

World's Work, later Review of Reviews
1900–1932

Connoisseur
1901–

Electrical Construction & Maintenance
1901–

Travel, later Travel-Holiday
1901–

House & Garden, later HG
1901–

ARTnews
1902–

Chemical Engineering
1902–

Countryside Magazine and Suburban Life
1902–1917

Current Events
1902–

Financial World
1902–

Popular Mechanics
1902–

Successful Farming
1902–

Camera Work
1903–1917

Hounds & Hunting
1903–

Independent Agent
1903–

Red Book Magazine, later Redbook
1903–

Commerce
1904–

Leslie's Monthly Magazine
1904–1905

Metropolitan
1905–1925

Agency News
1906–

Motor Boating & Sailing
1907–

Yachting
1907–

Philadelphia Magazine
1908–

Sea Magazine
1908–

The Progressive
1909–

Railfan & Railroad
1909–

Westways
1909–

Boys' Life
1911–

Coal Age
1911–

The Masses
1911–1917

Photoplay
1911–1980

The Rotarian
1911–1917

Nation's Business
1912–

Our Sunday Visitor
1912–

V.F.W. Magazine
1912–

Architecture
1913–

Art in America
1913–

Eagle Magazine
1913–

Scouting Magazine
1913–

Today's Education
1913–

Vanity Fair
1913–1936

Chemical Week
1914–

The Ensign
1914–

Golf Illustrated
1914–

Hadassah Magazine
1914–

The New Republic
1914–

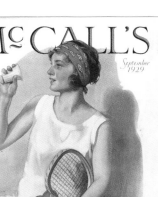

1915　　**1920**　　**1925**　　**1930**　　**1935**　　**1940**　　**1945**　　**1950**

ABA Journal: The Lawyer's Magazine 1915–	Architectural Digest 1920–	Automotive News 1925–	Advertising Age 1930–	Alaska 1935–	Ellery Queen's Mystery Magazine 1941–	The Bulletin of the Atomic Scientists 1945–	Flair 1950–1951
Aviation Week & Space Technology 1916–	Electrical Wholesaling 1920–	The Golden Book Magazine 1925–1935	Analog Science Fiction/Science Fact 1930–1990	Baby Talk 1935–	Gourmet, the Magazine of Good Living 1941–	Commentary 1945–	Golf Digest 1950–
Blood-Horse 1916–	Writer's Digest 1920–	Modern Plastics 1925–	Fortune 1930–	Mademoiselle 1935–	View 1941–1949	Congressional Quarterly Almanac 1945–	In-Plant Reproductions & Electronic Publishing 1950–
Business Marketing 1916–	Athletic Journal 1921–24	The New Yorker 1925–	Hollywood Reporter 1930–	The Workbasket 1935–	Negro Digest 1942–1951	Ebony 1945–	Palm Beach Illustrated, later Illustrated 1950–
Dog World 1916–	Barron's National Business and Financial Weekly 1921–	Vogue Pattern Book 1925–	Apparel Arts, later GQ: Gentleman's Quarterly 1931–	Yankee 1935–	Organic Gardening 1942–	International Management 1945–	Prevention 1950–
Forbes 1917–	Science News Bulletin 1921–	Dance Magazine 1926–	Broadcasting 1931–	American Baby 1936–	Popular Crosswords 1944–	Magazine & Bookseller 1945–	Spur 1950–
The Kiwanis Magazine 1917–	American Horticulturalist 1922–	Parents Magazine 1926–	Scholastic Coach 1931–	American Laundry Digest 1936–	Seventeen 1944–	Highlights for Children 1946–	Family Handyman 1951–
Liberator, later The New Masses 1918–1953	Antiques Magazine 1922–	Current Science 1927–	Family Circle Magazine 1932–	Catholic Digest 1936–		Holiday, later Travel-Holiday 1946–	High Fidelity 1951–
Lion Magazine 1918–	Better Homes and Gardens 1922–	Flying 1927–	Motorcyclist 1932–	Consumer Reports 1936–		Orlando Magazine 1946–	Jet 1951–
Motor 1918–	Dallas Magazine 1922–	American School & University 1928–	Coronet 1936–1961	Coronet 1936–1961		Scholastic Voice 1946–	Read 1951–
American Legion 1919–	Elks Magazine 1922–	Flying Aces, later Flying Models 1928–	Esquire 1933–	Life 1936–1972		Sport 1946–	Skin Diver Magazine 1951–
PGA Magazine 1919–	Foreign Affairs 1922–	Linn's Weekly Stamp News 1928–	Newsweek 1933–	Ski Illustrated, later Ski Magazine 1936–		Audio 1947–	Aperture 1952–
True Story 1919–	Harvard Business Review 1922–	Mechanix Illustrated, later Home Mechanix 1928–	U.S. News & World Report 1933–	What's New In Home Economics 1936–		Changing Times 1947–	Bowhunting World 1952–
	Outdoor America 1922–	Weekly Reader 1928–	American Dry Cleaner 1934–	American Artist 1937–		Golf World 1947–	Cycle 1952–
	Reader's Digest 1922–	Business Week 1929–	Bride's 1934–	Astrology; How It Affects Your Life 1937–1939		Road & Track 1947–	Guidepost 1952–
	Retirement Life 1922–	Model Airplane News 1929–	Down Beat 1934–	Astrology: Your Daily Horoscope 1937–		Skiing 1947–	Mad 1952–
	Ring Magazine 1922–	Radio-Electronics 1929–	Global Trade 1934–	Look 1937–1971		Archaeology Magazine 1948–	Nursing Research 1952–
	4-H Leader 1923–			Popular Photography 1937–		Hot Rod 1948–	Car Craft 1953–
	Frontier Times 1923–1985			Woman's Day 1937–		American Heritage: The Magazine of History 1949–	Nursing Outlook 1953–
	Opportunity Magazine 1923–			Automotive News 1938–		Modern Bride 1949–	Playboy 1953–
	Time 1923–			Ken 1938–1939		Motor Trend 1949–	TV Guide 1953–
	The American Mercury 1924–1980			Muscle & Fitness 1938–			World Tennis 1953–
	Commonweal 1924–			U.S. Camera 1938–			D, later D & B Reports 1954–
	The New Leader 1924–			Glamour 1939–			ID 1954–
	Saturday Review 1924–1986			Kenyon Review 1939–1970			New England Business 1954–
				Salt Water Sportsman 1939–			Sports Illustrated 1954–
							Success Magazine 1954–

ORGANIC GARDENING

MOTOR

THE BULLETIN OF THE ATOMIC SCIENTISTS

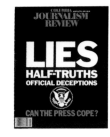

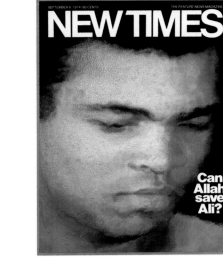

Can Allah save Ali?

1955 **1960** **1965** **1970**

The Drama Review
1955–?

National Review
1955–

Package Printing
1955–

*Young Miss, later YM
Magazine*
1955–

*Alfred Hitchcock's
Mystery Magazine*
1956–

Boating
1956–

Bon Appetit
1956–

Car and Driver
1956–

Co-ed
1956–1985

Income Opportunities
1956–

Photo Business
1956–

Electronic News
1957–

Monocle
1957–1971

Teen
1957–

Workbench Magazine
1957–

AOPA Pilot
1958–

*Dealerscope
Merchandising*
1958–

Florida Trend
1958–

*Flower & Garden
Magazine*
1958–

Guns & Ammo
1958–

Horizon
1958–

Modern Maturity
1958–

Printing Impressions
1958–

Stereo Review
1958–

Consumers Digest
1959–

Adweek
1960–

Back Stage
1960–

Ellery Queen's Anthology
1960–

*50 Plus, later New Choices
for the Best Years*
1960–

*Journal of Advertising
Research*
1960–

Science World
1960–

Shooting Times
1960–

Atlanta Magazine
1961–

Bicycling Magazine
1961–

Columbia Journalism Review
1961–

Cycle World
1961–

Show Magazine
1961–1965

Artforum
1960–

Automobile Quarterly
1962–

Civil War Times Illustrated
1962–

Four Wheeler
1962–

*Hog Extra, later Hogs
Today*
1962–

Ramparts
1962–1975

Sailing World Magazine
1962–

Golf Shop Operations
1963–

33 Metal Producing
1963–

American West
1964–

*Beef Extra, later Beef
Today*
1964–

*Dairy Extra, later Dairy
Today*
1964–

IEEE Spectrum
1964–

Scholastic Scope
1964–

Surfing
1964–

Venture
1964–1971

Signature
1965–1987

Tennis
1965–

American History Illustrated
1966–

American Way
1966–

Circus Magazine
1966–

Crawdaddy
1966–1979

Pacific Northwest Magazine
1966–

Runner's World
1966–

Southern Living
1966–

The Advocate
1967–

Avant Garde
1967–1975

Expecting
1967–

Psychology Today
1967–1990

Rolling Stone
1967–

Theatre Crafts
1967–

New York
1968–

San Francisco Focus Magazine
1968–

Southern Outdoors
1968–

Weight Watchers Magazine
1968–

*Andy Warhol's Interview,
later Interview Magazine*
1969–

Audience
1969–1973

Creem
1969–

Government Executive
1969–

Health
1969–

Metropolitan Home
1969–

National Lampoon
1969–

Penthouse
1969–

The Washington Monthly
1969–

Black Enterprise
1970–

Early American Life
1970–

Essence Magazine
1970–

Intellectual Digest
1970–1974

The Mother Earth News
1970–1990

Pittsburgh Magazine
1970–

Sail
1970–

Scanlan's
1970–1971

Smithsonian Magazine
1970–

Bowhunter
1971–

Chesapeake Bay Magazine
1971–

Connecticut Magazine
1971–

Exploring
1971–

Travel & Leisure
1971–

Adventure Travel
1972–

Data Communications
1972–

*Folio: Magazine for Magazine
Management*
1972–

Gallery
1972–

Lifestyle
1972–1973

Money
1972–

Ms.
1972–

Petersen's Photographic
1972–

Practical Horseman
1972–

W
1972–

Americana
1973–

Backpacker
1973–

*Cricket, Magazine for
Children*
1973–

Ebony Jr.
1973–1985

Entrepreneur Magazine
1973–

New Times
1973–1979

Petersen's Hunting
1973–

Playgirl
1973–

Texas Monthly
1973–

Bassin'
1974–

British Heritage
1974–

Country Journal
1974–

Cruising World
1974–

D Magazine
1974–

*The Electric Company,
later Kid City*
1974–

High Times
1974–

The Homeowner
1974–

*Houston Home & Garden,
later Houston
Metropolitan Magazine*
1974–

Modern Healthcare
1974–

People
1974–

Sacramento Magazine
1974–

Snow Week
1974–

World Press Review
1974–

1975		1980		1985		1990	

American Film Magazine
1975–

American Photographer, later
American Photo
1978–

Cable Guide
1980–

Muppet Magazine
1982–

Elle
1985–

MacWeek
1987–

Countryside
1990–

Biblical Archaeology Review
1975–

Art & Antiques
1978–

Cable Today
1980–1984

PC Magazine
1982–

European Travel & Life
1985–

Parenting
1987–

Egg
1990–1991

Byte
1975–

Cookbook Digest
1978–

Discover
1980–

Satellite Orbit
1982–

L.A. Style
1985–

Premiere Magazine
1987–

Entertainment Weekly
1990–

Crafts 'N Things
1975–

Country Living
1978–

Fine Homebuilding
1980–

Southern Homes
1982–

MacUser
1985–

Buzzworm, The Environmental
Journal
1988–

South Florida Style
1990–

Endless Vacation
1975–

Crafts Magazine
1978–

Milwaukee Magazine
1980–

TV Entertainment Magazine
1982–

Spin
1985–

Allure
1991–

Fine Woodworking
1975–

Food & Wine, The Guide to
Good Taste
1978–

Penny Power
1980–

Digital Review
1983–

Air & Space/Smithsonian
1986–

Fame Magazine
1988–1990

Fortune for Kids
1991–

1,001 Home Ideas
1975–

Phoenix Home & Garden
1980–

Home Office Computing
1983–

Child
1986–

Lear's
1988–

San Diego Home-Garden
1975–

Herb Quarterly
1978–

Practical Homeowner
1980–

M
1983–1990

Harrowsmith
1986–

Long Island Monthly
1988–1990

Inside Hollywood
1991–

Soap Opera Digest
1975–

Monthly Detroit, later Detroit
Monthly
1978–

Previews Magazine, later L.A.
West
1980–

New Connections
1983–1985

Hippocrates, later In Health
1986–

Memories
1988–1990

Sound & Image
1991–

Washington Dossier
1975–1991

North Shore Magazine
1978–

Savvy
1980–1991

Pace Magazine
1983–

Longevity
1986–

Model
1988–

Sports Illustrated Classic
1991–

California Magazine
1976–

Omni
1978–

Snowmobile
1980–

PC Week
1983–

New York Woman
1986–

Sassy
1988–

Mother Jones
1976–

Self
1978–

Video Review
1980–

Vanity Fair
1983–

Private Clubs
1986–

Smart
1988–1990

New Jersey Monthly
1976–

Working Mother
1978–

Woman
1980–1990

The American Woodworker
1984–

Spy
1986–

Snow Country
1988–

Outside
1976–

American Demographics
1979–

American Health
1981–

Artist's Magazine
1984–

Taxi
1986–1990

Special Report
1988–

Working Woman
1976–

Country Home
1979–

Cross Country Skier
1981–

Barbie
1984–

Tikkun
1986–

Victoria
1988–

4-Wheel & Off Road
1977–

Cuisine
1979–1984

Education Week
1981–

Bible Review
1984–

Condé Nast's Traveler
1987–

World Monitor
1988–

Isaac Asimov's Science
Fiction
1977–

Geo
1979–1985

Hands on Electronics, later
Popular Electronics
1981–

City & State
1984–

Country America
1989–

Musician Magazine
1977–

Inc.
1979–

Crain's New York Business
1984–

Elle Decor
1989–

Southern Accents
1977–

Monterey Life
1979–

Hudson Home Guide, later
Home
1981–

Health & You
1984–

Garbage
1989–

US Magazine
1977–

3-2-1 Contact
1979–

Performance Horseman
1981–

Macworld
1984–

Más Magazine
1989–

Washington Journalism
Review
1977–

S. F. Weekly
1981–

Mature Outlook
1984–

Mirabella
1989–

Satellite TV Week
1981–

Mountain Bike
1984–

Sports Illustrated for Kids
1989–

Shape Magazine
1981–

National Geographic Traveler
1984–

Wigwag
1989–1991

Ultra Magazine
1981–

New England Monthly
1984–1990

Details
1982–

Photo/Design
1984–

Dirt Rider
1982–

Teenage Mutant Ninja Turtles
1984–

Fit
1982–1985

Utne Reader
1984–

Acknowledgments

Project Staff

Editorial Steering Committee
Chair: John Mack Carter,
Editor-in-Chief, *Good Housekeeping*

Betsy Carter, Editor-in-Chief,
New York Woman

Elizabeth S. Crow, President,
Editorial Director, Gruner + Jahr
USA Publishing

Byron Dobell, former Editor,
American Heritage

Richard B. Stolley, Editorial Director,
Time Inc. Magazine Company

Ruth Whitney, Editor-in-Chief,
Glamour

Business Steering Committee
Chair: Daniel E. Zucchi, Senior VP,
Director of Consumer Marketing,
Hearst Magazines

James A. Autry, President, Magazine
Group, Meredith Corporation

Gregory G. Coleman, Group
Publisher, Reader's Digest
Association

Elizabeth P. Valk, Publisher,
People Weekly

Project General Manager
P. Robert Farley, Executive VP,
General Manager, Magazine
Publishers of America

Producers of the Book
Jones & Janello

Editors
Amy Janello
Brennon Jones

Designer
Beth A. Crowell

Text Editor
Jon Swan

Copy Editor
Leslie Ware

Editorial Assistants
Joju Cleaver
Jaina Clough
Rhya Fisher
Christine Fitz Gerald
Michelle Lopez

Editorial Consultants
Vicki Gold Levi
Daniel Marcus
Michael Massing
A. Lin Neumann
Elliott S. Rebhun

Researchers
Lori L. Adkins
Donna Lucey
Denise Lynch
Chiara Peacock
Debora Gilbert Ryan
Lisa Shea

Fact Checkers
Nick Jordan
Denise Lynch

Additional Project Support
Donna Bender
Jennifer Escobar
Judith M. Lewenthal
Ellen Mendlow
Kathleen Phelps

Rights and Permissions Coordinator
Aarathi Chander

Counsel
Ellis J. Friedman
Whitman & Ransom

E. Gabriel Perle
Proskauer Rose Goetz & Mendelsohn

Harry N. Abrams Project Staff
Samuel N. Antupit, Art Director
Beverly Fazio, Senior Editor

Historical Consultants
Theodore Peterson
John Tebbel

Writers
Leslie Bennetts
Sean Callahan
Sey Chassler
Owen Edwards
Thomas Forbes
Steven Heller
Rust Hills
Michael Ryan
Betsy Sharkey
Richard Todd

Photographers
Nicole Bengiveno
David Burnett
Misha Erwitt
Jeff Jacobson
Andy Levin
Eli Reed
Eugene Richards
George Steinmetz
Mark S. Wexler

Special thanks to the following for invaluable assistance:
Peter G. Diamandis
John Schenck
A&S Book Company
Tara Abate
David Abrahamson
Peter Agostini
Tim Aiken
Akron Antiquarian Books
Joyce Anil
Avenue Victor Hugo
   Bookshop
Phil Barber
John Barbier
Jeanne Bauer
Margaret Beall
Jack Berkowitz
Susan Biegler
A. L. Blinder
Catherine Bordeman
Brattle Book Shop
Bob Bryson
Virginia Budny
Robert G. Burton
Larry Carter
John Caruso
Tritton Chance
Mark Cheung
Chosen Reflections
William Chrisant
Albert B. Chu
Ellen Cohen
Computertech Design
Margie Cortes
Peter Costiglio
Bonnie Cusack
Custom Applications, Inc.
Peter Cutler
Don Davidson
James A. Dawson
Ray DeMoulin
Karen De Witt
Danielle Di Martino
Waris Dirie
Oscar Dystel
Jeff Edelstein
Susan Edmiston
Eric Etheridge
Steve Ettlinger
Everybody's Magazines
Paul Fargis
Barry Feerst
Kay Fraleigh
James Fraleigh
Gaslight Antiques
George Eastman House
Virginia Gifford
Ben Goldstein
Wade Greene
David Hall
Michelle Hammond
Hawkeye Book and Magazine
   Company
George A. Hirsch
Shay Yandell Hirsch
David Hochman
Kimio Honda
Jay Bee Magazines
Jellybean Photographic
   Services
Robert Johnston
Wilma H. Jordan
Judy S. Jorgensen
Theron Kabrich
Marlene Kahan
Jason Karle
Bethany Karlyn
Chuck Kelton
Kelton Labs
Billie Jean Lebda
Life Picture Collection
Benjamin Lightman
Longfellow's Books &
   Magazines
The Magazine
M. C. Marden
Michael Maren
Marilyn McClean
Robert McClean
Arch McClure III
Timothy J. McIntyre
Michele F. McNally
Memory Shop
Men/Women Model
   Management Co.
Microtek
Toshimasa Mizukami
A. Michael Moloney
George F. Morris
Ann R. Moscicki
Sandra Mullin
Kathie Murtha
Next Management Co.
Jodi Nakatsuka
John O'Toole
Jack Oberhill
Mason Olds
Harvey Osterhoudt
Herbert Oxer
Pageant Book and Print Shop
Honey Ann Peacock
Diana Pearson
Joe Picanello
Jose Picayo
Robert Race
Reborn 14th Street Books
Reedmor Magazine Company
Steve Regina
Sharon Roccaforte
John Roos
Don Ross
Anthony Russo
San Francisco Art Exchange
Mitzi Sandman
Chris Schwer
Toshiyuki Sekiguchi
Nancy G. Shapiro
Leslie Sheryll
Kirk Shorte
Skyline Books
Ted Slate
Rick Smolan
David Sokosh
John Suhler
Sylvia Surdoval
Hiroshi Takanashi
Stephen Lee Taller M.D.
Time Warner Inc. Library and
   Research Services
Judd Tully
Deborah Turner
Marie Vachon
Michael Vachon
Jerry Valente
John Veronis
Thomas K. Walker
Edna McClean Wallen
Leon G. Williams
Nancy Williamson
Carey Winfrey
Henry Wolf
Elsa Zion
Sidney Zion

Finally, thanks to all the editors, publishers, art directors, and magazine staff who assisted the project making available their magazines and artwork and sharing their experience and knowledge of the magazine business.

The American Magazine was produced using Macintosh IIci's with eight megabytes of RAM, Apple High Resolution 13" RGB Monitors, Apple 80SC hard disks and a Laserwriter IInt printer. A Microtek 300SZ color scanner was used to input flat art for preliminary layouts. The computers were linked to a MCS/Canon Color Laser 500 copier with an image processing unit. Magazine covers and speads, photographs, and transparencies of all sizes were scanned into the CLC 500. Spreads were output, tabloid size, in color (for presentation comps) and in black-and-white (for proofing) using the CLC 500. Custom Application's Freedom of Press software was used to interpret type in PostScript.

Index

Credits